Dunhuang

敦煌

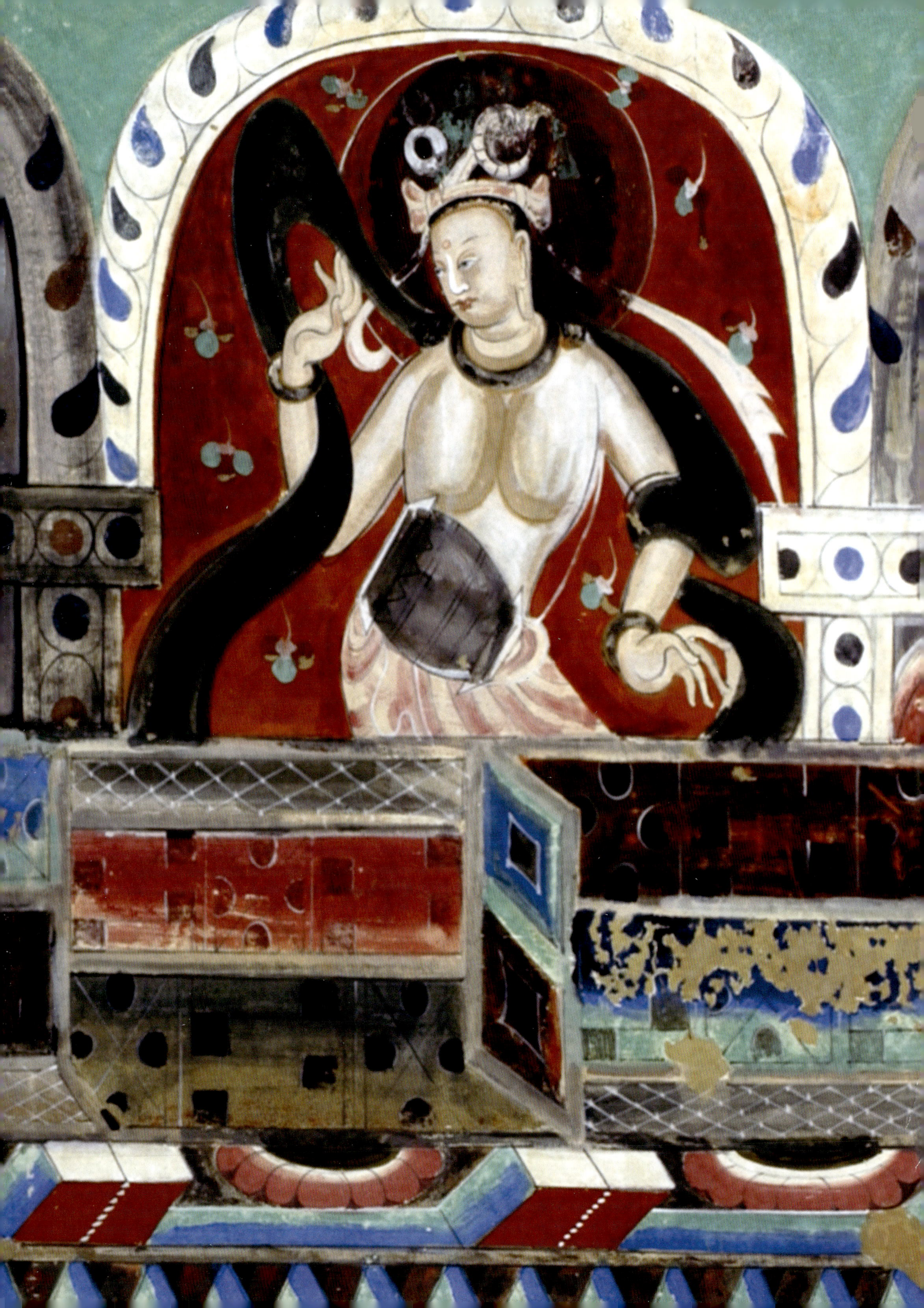

Dunhuang

Buddhist Art at the Gateway of the Silk Road

敦煌

丝路佛光

Edited by Fan Jinshi and Willow Weilan Hai
樊锦诗　海蔚蓝　主编

Essays by Fan Jinshi and Annette L. Juliano
樊锦诗，朱安耐 /论文

and contributions from Lou Jie, Liang Xushu,
Huang Yuanwei, J. May Lee Barrett, and Clarissa von Spee
娄婕，梁旭澍，黄苑薇，鐘美梨，史明理 / 圖錄附錄介紹

Dunhuang Academy and China Institute Gallery
敦煌研究院　华美协进社中国美术馆

2013

Distributed by Art Media Resources, Ltd.

The catalogue was published to accompany the exhibition
Dunhuang: Buddhist Art at the Gateway of the Silk Road
敦煌：丝路佛光
Organized by Dunhuang Academy and China Institute Gallery

April 19–July 21, 2013
China Institute Gallery
125 East 65th Street
New York, NY 10065
212.744.8181

Library of Congress Control Number: 2013933262
ISBN-10: 0977405494
ISBN-13: 978-0-9774054-9-7

Curator 策展人 / Fan Jinshi 樊锦诗
Project Director 艺术总监 / Willow Weilan Hai 海蔚蓝
Editors 编辑 / Lou Jie 娄婕, Liang Xushu 梁旭澍
Consulting Editor 编辑顾问 / J. May Lee Barrett 钟美梨
English Translator 翻译 / Huang Yuanwei 黄苑薇, Wang Pingxian 王平先
Catalogue Designer 图录设计 / Peter Lukic 鲁克彼得
Exhibition Designer 展览设计 / Perry Hu 胡维智
Photos by Li Tao, Shen Yanhai, and Liu Fei courtesy of Dunhuang Academy unless otherwise noted
照片提供者，敦煌研究院　李涛、盛龑海、刘斐

Printed in the United States of America

Note to the Reader
This publication uses Sanskrit names and terms rather than the Chinese equivalent because they are more familiar to Western students of Buddhist art. A comparative table of Sanskrit and Chinese terms has been provided in Appendix 5. For the convenience of the non-specialist reader, the Sanskrit used in this publication has been transliterated without diacritical marks, and the specialist is referred to the same appendix for terms in the standard IAST system. Chinese names and terms are romanized in the *pinyin* system throughout the text and bibliography except for the names of Chinese authors writing in Western languages. Chinese terms cited in Western-language titles remain in their original form and have not been converted.

FRONT COVER
Detail of painted clay stucco bodhisattva from the main niche
Mogao Cave 45
High Tang period (705–781)

INSIDE FRONT/BACK COVER
Panoramic view of Mogao Grottoes

BACK COVER
View of the Northern Area of the Mogao Grottoes in snow
Photo by Perry Hu, 2012.

FRONTISPIECE
Detail, *Celestial Music*
Mogao Cave 288
Western Wei dynasty (535–556)
[cat. no. 31]

CONTENTS
目录

Sponsors of the Exhibition

This exhibition, related programming, and catalogue
*have been made possible in part through the generous support of the following **

Benefactors

Blakemore Foundation
E. Rhodes & Leona B. Carpenter Foundation
Henry Luce Foundation

Patrons

New York City Department of Cultural Affairs
in partnership with the City Council

Contributors

Anla Cheng and Mark Kingdon / Mark and Anla Cheng Kingdon Foundation
Susan and Jay Goffman
Virginia A. Kamsky
Lianjun Ma
Sophia and Abel Sheng
Oscar L. Tang
Mary and James G. Wallach Foundation
Wan-go H. C. Weng

Supporters

Hart and Nancy B. Fessenden
Carolyn Hsu-Balcer and René Balcer
Marie-Hélène Weill
The J. and H. Weldon Foundation, Inc.

Individuals

Lawrence Benjamin
Lois M. Collier
Jay Collins
John R. and Julia B. Curtis
Richard A. and Ruth Dickes
Charlotte Ford
Henry Johnson
William W. Karatz
Susan and Chip Kessler
Sanjeev Khemlani
Angela H. King
Kevin J. and Laura Lavin
T. K. Lee
Robert W. and Virginia Riggs Lyons
Gerard M. Meistrell
Gayle Ong and James J. Chin
William N. Raiford
Diane H. Schafer and Jeffrey A. Stein
George Sing and Nellie Chi
Dana Tang and Andrew Darrell
Barbara and Donald Tober
Denis C. and Kathleen Yang

* At time of printing

MESSAGE FROM THE DUNHUANG ACADEMY

Dunhuang was not only a transportation hub and trade center on the ancient Silk Road, but also a melting pot in which four great world civilizations, six religions, and the cultures of a variety of ethnic groups met and interacted. Beginning in the fourth century, the Mogao Grottoes, the Western Caves of a Thousand Buddhas, the Yulin Grottoes, and the Eastern Caves of a Thousand Buddhas were created one after another; they are generally called "the Dunhuang caves" because they are all within the boundaries of the ancient Dunhuang commandery and are similar in their contents and styles. Among them, the Mogao Grottoes site is the most significant; it includes 735 caves housing 45,000 square meters of wall paintings, more than 2,000 painted sculptures, and five wooden eaves, as well as the more than 50,000 historical documents and artworks discovered in the Library Cave. It is the largest and best-preserved Buddhist cave temple site in China, representing the excellent achievements of Buddhist art in China, and even the world, from the fourth to the fourteenth centuries and enjoying a significant position in the history of the world's fine arts.

With their long history, rich contents, and exquisite artwork, both the Dunhuang caves and the cultural relics from the Library Cave are manifestations of the growth and evolution of cave architecture, mural paintings, and the art of painted sculpture. They reflect the Sinicization of the thoughts, beliefs, and arts of medieval Buddhist sects; exhibit scenes with historical features and scenes of life in medieval Dunhuang society, as well as in China and even wide-flung regions; and indicate the cultural exchanges between Chinese and Eurasian civilizations as well as among the ethnic groups of China. The great value of these caves and the cultural relics from the Library Cave lies in their diverse and global character. They possess a timeless fascination.

Both China and the United States are compatible multi-cultural countries. Exchanges between the peoples of the two countries, although they are located far from each other, have had more than a hundred years of history. "All living creatures grow together without harming each other, and all ways run parallel without interfering with one another." Exchanges between different cultures are likely to make each culture more creative. The exhibition to be held now by China Institute in America, New York, is the first time Dunhuang's art will be displayed in the United States; the exhibits mainly highlight masterpieces of wall paintings, painted sculpture, and historical documents. Most historical documents from the Library Cave are national treasures. We hope this exhibition will help American visitors to appreciate the splendor and beauty of the wide-ranging and profound art from the Dunhuang caves as if "they were there" and that it will strengthen Sino-U.S. cultural exchanges, enhance mutual understanding and friendship, and promote the harmonious co-prosperity of the world's diverse cultures.

Fan Jinshi
Director of the Dunhuang Academy

致辞

敦煌，是古丝绸之路上的交通枢纽、商业贸易集散之处，也是世界四大文明、六种宗教、多种民族文化交汇之地。从公元4 世纪开始，在古老的敦煌土地上，莫高窟、西千佛洞、榆林窟、东千佛洞等佛教石窟群先后应运而生。因为这些石窟地域相近、内容相同、风格相近，统称为敦煌石窟。莫高窟是其中的杰出代表，迄今保存了735 个洞窟、45000 平方米壁画、2000 多身彩塑、5 座木构窟檐，以及藏经洞出土的5 万多件文献和艺术品等珍贵文物，它是中国现存规模最大、保存最好的佛教石窟寺，代表了公元4－14 世纪中国乃至世界佛教艺术的高度成就，在世界美术史上占有重要的地位。

敦煌石窟藏经洞文物历史绵延久长、内容丰富、艺术精湛，表现了石窟建筑、壁画和彩塑艺术演变发展的历程；反映了中古时期佛教思想信仰、佛教思想和佛教艺术的中国化过程；展示了中古时期敦煌甚至中国和更广大区域的历史风貌和社会生活场景；展现了中国各民族之间以及中国与欧亚文明间的文化交流。敦煌石窟及藏经洞文物蕴含的珍贵价值是多元的、世界的，具有超越时空、经久不衰的魅力。

中国和美国都是兼容多种文化的国家，中美两国虽然远隔千山万水，但两国人民之间开始交往已有一百多年的历史。“万物并育而不相害，道并行而不相悖”，不同文化的交流会使各自文化更具创造性。这次美国纽约华美协进社举办的展览是敦煌艺术第一次在美国展出。展品主要包括壁画、彩塑、文献等敦煌艺术的精品，其中在敦煌藏经洞发现的文献典籍，多为国宝级文物。我们希望通过纽约华美协进社举办的敦煌艺术展，使美国广大观众能身临其境地领略敦煌石窟艺术的博大精深、富丽辉煌，并加强中美两国文化交流，增进相互了解和友谊，促进世界多元文化的和谐共荣。

敦煌研究院　院长　樊锦诗

Foreword

Dunhuang—its name is mysterious and alluring. Remotely situated far in China's west at the gateway to the Silk Road, it provided access for over a thousand years of trade and commerce. Amidst the tinkling sounds of camel bells, the material and spiritual world of the east and west collided, fused, and rose to a higher realm in its magnificent Buddhist art. Despite the transience of the lives of those who came here, Dunhuang's art endures as a testament to the eternal fascination held by the feelings and spirit of humankind.

Although a native Chinese, I never had chance to visit Dunhuang when I was in China. It seemed so distant, like murmurings in a dream. However, since 2007, it became for me not only a frequently repeated word, but also a frequently visited sacred site. Thus, for more than its mystery and seductive charm, Dunhuang became very dear to me.

In the late fall of 2007, the international organization Friends of Dunhuang held an event at the Lotus Club in Manhattan to celebrate its establishment. On that occasion, I met for the first time Ms. Fan Jinshi, Director of the Dunhuang Academy. A renowned scholar who devoted her entire life to Dunhuang, she showed her deep love of this place in her speech, her voice, and her gestures. She made a passionate appeal for the world to learn about the site and support its conservation and protection. After that event, Director Fan and Deputy Director Wang Xudong very warmly invited me to visit Dunhuang.

A year later, in the fall of 2008, I finally made the trip. When I met Director Fan in Beijing, she held my arm and said with concern, "You need to wear more clothing. On the mountain (by which she meant the Mogao Grottoes) and in the caves, it is so cold." I therefore went to the cloth market near the Beijing Zoo to especially get a down jacket. On the second day after my arrival, Dunhuang had a rare snowfall for such a dry place; the surrounding Gobi Desert was covered with white. What a purified world! I fell in love with it instantly.

During the five years that passed since that time, I went to Dunhuang again and again, at least once a year—to discuss the possible exhibition, to negotiate a contract, to select artwork, and to work out our installation. For their great support in a long process, I am very grateful to Director Fan and her colleagues, especially to Deputy Director Luo Huaqing, Ms. Lou Jie, and Mr. Li Tao. Their collaboration, diligence, and hard work made it possible for this first exhibition on Dunhuang in the United States to finally be opened to the public.

I take this opportunity to also sincerely thank the sponsors of the exhibition, China Institute's Board of Trustees, and the Gallery Committee for their part in making this exhibition possible. In addition to the scholars and staff members of the Dunhuang Academy who contributed to this project, I am grateful to Annette L. Juliano, Professor of Asian Art History at Rutgers University-Newark Campus, for her essay in this catalogue and to Clarissa von Spee, a curator in the Asia department of the British Museum, for her contribution to the appendices. A debt of gratitude is owed to my teammates: Jennifer Lima, Yue Ma, and Eva Wen in the Gallery; J. May Lee Barrett, consulting editor; Peter Lukic, catalogue designer; Perry Hu, exhibition designer; and Nicole Straus, marketing consultant. Finally, I would especially like to thank Sara Judge McCalpin, President of China Institute, and the Development team for their support.

Willow Weilan Hai
Director
China Institute Gallery
12 March 2013

前言

敦煌，是一个神秘而诱人的名字。在遥远的西边，丝绸之路的门户，千年商贸往来的必经之路，驼铃叮当中，是东西方物质和精神的融汇冲撞和升华。在那戈壁滩的沙砾峭壁上，一代又一代虔诚礼佛的痕迹，化为瑰丽的佛教艺术。敦煌，见证了生命的易逝和经久，见证了艺术再现人类精神和情怀的永恒魅力。

我虽然是土生土长的中国人，在中国时，可从没去过敦煌，那是多么遥远的地方，也许只有在梦中呓语过。但是，自从2007年以来，敦煌不仅常挂在嘴边，而且成为我最常造访的圣地。敦煌，除了神秘和诱人以外，对我来说，她又是如此的亲切。

那是2007年的深秋，曼哈顿东64街的莲俱乐部里，举行了美国的“敦煌之友”成立招待会，会上我第一次见到敦煌研究院鼎鼎大名的樊锦诗院长，这个把一辈子给予敦煌的学者，言谈举止和对敦煌了如指掌的介绍，都透露着她对敦煌的深情厚爱，她呼吁着世界对敦煌的关注和爱护。会后，樊院长和同行的王旭东副院长热情地邀请我去敦煌。

一年后，2008年深秋，我终于可以成行。在北京碰到樊院长，她捏着我的胳膊，细心地嘱咐我千万多穿衣服，山上（敦煌研究院的人称莫高窟为“山上”）洞里可冷了。于是我还特意去北京的动物园服装市场买了一件羽绒服御寒。到达敦煌的第二天，常年缺水少雨的敦煌就下了一场雪，戈壁沙丘一片银白，真是个干净的世界，我一见衷情。

从那起到现在，近五年的时间了，我最少一年去一趟敦煌，洽谈展览，协商合同，选择展品，商量布展，反来复去，感谢樊院长和她领导下的同仁们的大力支持，特别是罗华庆副院长，娄婕和李涛老师的积极配合和努 力，这个在美国的第一个敦煌展终于即将开幕了。

借此机会我衷心感谢所有展览的赞助者，感谢华美协进社的董事和艺术委员会，感谢美国新泽西州罗格斯大学纽瓦克分校的朱安耐教授为展览图录撰写论文及为展览提供建议，感谢大英博物馆亚洲部的史明理博士介绍其馆藏敦煌佛画。我衷心感谢我的梯队每个成员的奉献，李轶青，马玥，温玺，以及顾问编辑鐘美梨，展览设计师胡维智，图录设计师彼得鲁克，公共关系尼可尔。斯乍丝等以各自的特长，保证了这一展览和图录的最终完成。最后我特别感谢华美协进社社长江芷若和发展部各位同仁的支持。

海蔚蓝
华美协进社中国美术馆馆长
2013年3月12日

Timeline of Key Events in Dunhuang and Chinese History

Dynasties and Historical Periods in China		Significant Events in China	Events in Dunhuang
Han Dynasty (206 BCE–220 CE)	Western Han (206 BCE–9 CE) Xin Dynasty (9–23) Eastern Han (25–220)	Dominance of Confucianism **139 BCE & 119 BCE** • Diplomatic expeditions to Central Asia by Zhang Qian, opening the Silk Road Transmission of Buddhism to China **73 CE** • Diplomatic expedition to Central Asia by Ban Chao **105** • Significant improvement of papermaking by Cai Lun	**111 BCE** • One of the four frontier garrison towns
Three Kingdoms (220–280)	Wei (220–266) Shu (221–263) Wu (229–280)	Development of Buddhism and Daoism	
Jin Dynasty (265–420)	Western Jin (266–316) Eastern Jin (317–420) 16 Kingdoms (304–439)		**366** • Construction of the first cave of Mogao Grottoes by a Buddhist monk Lezun (or Yuezun) **400–405** • Capital of Western Liang
Southern and Northern Dynasties (420–589)	Liu Song (420–479) Southern Qi (479–502) Northern Wei (386–534) Liang (502–557) Western Wei (535–556) Eastern Wei (534–550) Chen (557–589) Northern Zhou (557–581) Northern Qi (550–577)	Large scale migrations, and hence diversity of cultures Localization of Buddhism Flourishing of Buddhism and Daoism	
Sui Dynasty (581–618)		Establishment of the imperial examination system Construction of the Grand Canal	94 caves were constructed at Mogao in the short-lived Sui dynasty
Tang Dynasty (618–907) **[Second Zhou (690–705)]**		**627** • Xuanzang's pilgrimage to India to collect Buddhist texts **641** • State marriage of Princess Wencheng to Songtsän Gampo, the king in Tibet	**695** • Construction of the Northern Giant Buddha (Cave 96) **721** • Construction of the Southern Giant Buddha (Cave 130)

<table>
<tr><th colspan="4">Dynasties and Historical Periods in China</th><th>Significant Events in China</th><th>Events in Dunhuang</th></tr>
<tr><td colspan="4"></td><td>Woodblock printing of books</td><td>781 · Occupation by the Tibetan Kingdom

851 · Assignment of Zhang Yichao as the military governor of Guiyi Circuit

851 · Assignment of Hongbian as the leader of Buddhists in Hexi area

868 · The oldest known dated printed Buddhist scripture found in Dunhuang</td></tr>
<tr><td colspan="3">5 Dynasties and 10 Kingdoms (907–979)</td><td rowspan="2">Liao
(916–1125)</td><td rowspan="3">Use of gunpowder in warfare

1040 · Development of movable type printing

Use of compass in maritime navigation

Start of seaborne trade</td><td rowspan="3">914 · Assignment of Cao Yijin as the military governor of Cao's Guiyi Circuit

1036 · Occupation by Tangut Western Xia (Xixia) empire

1036–1227 · Restoration of 60 caves in Mogao</td></tr>
<tr><td rowspan="2">Song Dynasty (960–1279)</td><td>Northern Song (960–1127)</td><td rowspan="2">Western Xia (1038–1227)</td></tr>
<tr><td>Southern Song (1127–1279)</td><td>Jin
(1115–1234)</td></tr>
<tr><td colspan="4">Yuan Dynasty (1271–1368) [Mongol Empire (1206–1271)]</td><td>Dadu (modern Beijing) serves as the capital city of the Yuan dynasty</td><td>1227 · Occupation by Mongol Empire</td></tr>
<tr><td colspan="4">Ming Dynasty (1368–1644)</td><td>Construction of the Ming dynasty Great Wall

1405–1433 · Voyages of Zheng He, flourishing of sea trade, abandonment of the Silk Road

1406–1420 · Construction of the Forbidden City</td><td>1372 · Construction of Jiayuguan and withdrawal of military forces to the east of Jiayuguan

1404 · Chinese garrison re-established in Dunhuang

1516 · Occupation by the Tibetan kingdom

1524 · Closure of Jiayuguan, abandonment of Dunhuang</td></tr>
<tr><td colspan="4">Qing Dynasty (1644–1911)
[rose to power as the Later Jin (1616–1636) and known as the Qing from 1639]</td><td>1683 · Taiwan annexed

1840 · First Opium War

Introduction of Western culture, science, and technology</td><td>1715 · Occupation by the Qing dynasty

1900 · Discovery of Dunhuang manuscripts in the Library Cave by a Daoist cleric, Wang Yuanlu</td></tr>
<tr><td colspan="4">Republic of China (1912–1949)</td><td>1937–1945 · Second Sino-Japanese War</td><td>1944 · Establishment of the Dunhuang Research Institute</td></tr>
<tr><td colspan="2">People's Republic of China (1949–present)</td><td colspan="2">Republic of China (Taiwan) (1949–present)</td><td></td><td>1984 · Establishment of the Dunhuang Academy</td></tr>
</table>

中國 敦煌年表

中国历史		事件	敦煌大事记
汉朝 **(前206 - 220)**	西汉（前206 - 9） 新朝（9 - 23） 东汉（25 - 220）	儒学独尊 前139、前119年 • 张骞出使西域，开通丝绸之路 传入佛教 73年 • 班超出使西域 105年 • 蔡伦改进造纸术	前111年 • 设立敦煌郡
三国 **(220 - 280)**	曹魏（220 - 266） 蜀汉（221 - 263） 东吴（229 - 280）	佛教、道教逐渐发展	
晋朝 **(266 - 420)**	西晋（266 - 316） 东晋（317 - 420） 十六国（304 - 439）		366年 • 僧人乐僔修建莫高窟第一个洞窟 400 - 405年 • 为西凉国都
南北朝 **(420 - 589)**	宋（420 - 479） 齐（479 - 502） 北魏（386 - 534） 梁（502 - 557） 西魏（535 - 556） 东魏（534 - 550） 陈（557-589） 北周（557 - 581） 北齐（550 - 577）	族群大迁徙及文化交融造成南北文化分野 佛教中土化，与道教逐渐成为宗教主流	
隋朝（581 - 618）		创建科举制度 兴修大运河	隋代年间，莫高窟开凿94个洞窟
唐朝（618 - 907） {**武周**（690 - 705）}		627年 • 玄奘远赴天竺取经 641年 • 文成公主远嫁吐蕃 雕版印刷	695年 • 修建北大像 721年 • 修建南大像 781年 • 为吐蕃占领 851年 • 张议潮被册封为归义军节度使 851年 • 洪䛒被册封为河西都僧统 868年 • 敦煌发现的最早的雕版印刷佛经

<table>
<tr><th colspan="4">中国历史</th><th>事件</th><th>敦煌大事记</th></tr>
<tr><td colspan="3">五代十国（907 - 979）</td><td rowspan="2">辽
（916 - 1125）</td><td rowspan="4">火药应用于军事上

1040年 • 发明活字印刷

指南针应用于航海技术上

开通海上丝绸之路</td><td rowspan="4">914年 • 曹议金被册封为曹氏归义军节度使

1036年 • 为西夏占领

1036 - 1227年 • 西夏重修60窟</td></tr>
<tr><td rowspan="3">宋朝
（960 - 1279）</td><td rowspan="2">北宋
（960 - 1127）</td><td rowspan="3">西夏
（1038 - 1227）</td></tr>
<tr><td rowspan="2">金
（1115 - 1234）</td></tr>
<tr><td>南宋
（1127 - 1279）</td></tr>
<tr><td colspan="4">{大蒙古国（1206 - 1271）}
元朝（1271 - 1368）</td><td>定都元大都（现今北京）</td><td>1227年 • 为蒙古占领</td></tr>
<tr><td colspan="4">明朝（1368 - 1644）</td><td>修建明长城

1405 - 1433年 • 郑和下西洋，海上贸易繁荣，路上丝绸之路渐被废弃

1406 - 1420年 • 修建紫禁城</td><td>1372年 • 修建嘉裕关，敦煌被置之关外

1404年 • 明朝设沙州卫

1516年 • 为吐鲁番占领

1524年 • 闭锁嘉裕关，敦煌被废弃</td></tr>
<tr><td colspan="4">{后金（1616 - 1636）}

清朝（1636 - 1911）</td><td>1683年 • 统一台湾

1840年 • 第一次鸦片战争</td><td>1715年 • 复设敦煌县

1900年 • 王圆箓道士发现藏经洞</td></tr>
<tr><td colspan="4">中华民国（1912 - 1949）</td><td>西方科学与文化引入中国</td><td>1944年 • 设立国立敦煌研究所</td></tr>
<tr><td colspan="2">中华人民共和国
（1949至今）</td><td colspan="2">中华民国（台湾）
（1949至今）</td><td>1937 - 1945年 • 抗日战争</td><td>1984年 • 成立敦煌研究院</td></tr>
</table>

Map of The Silk Road
丝绸之路地图

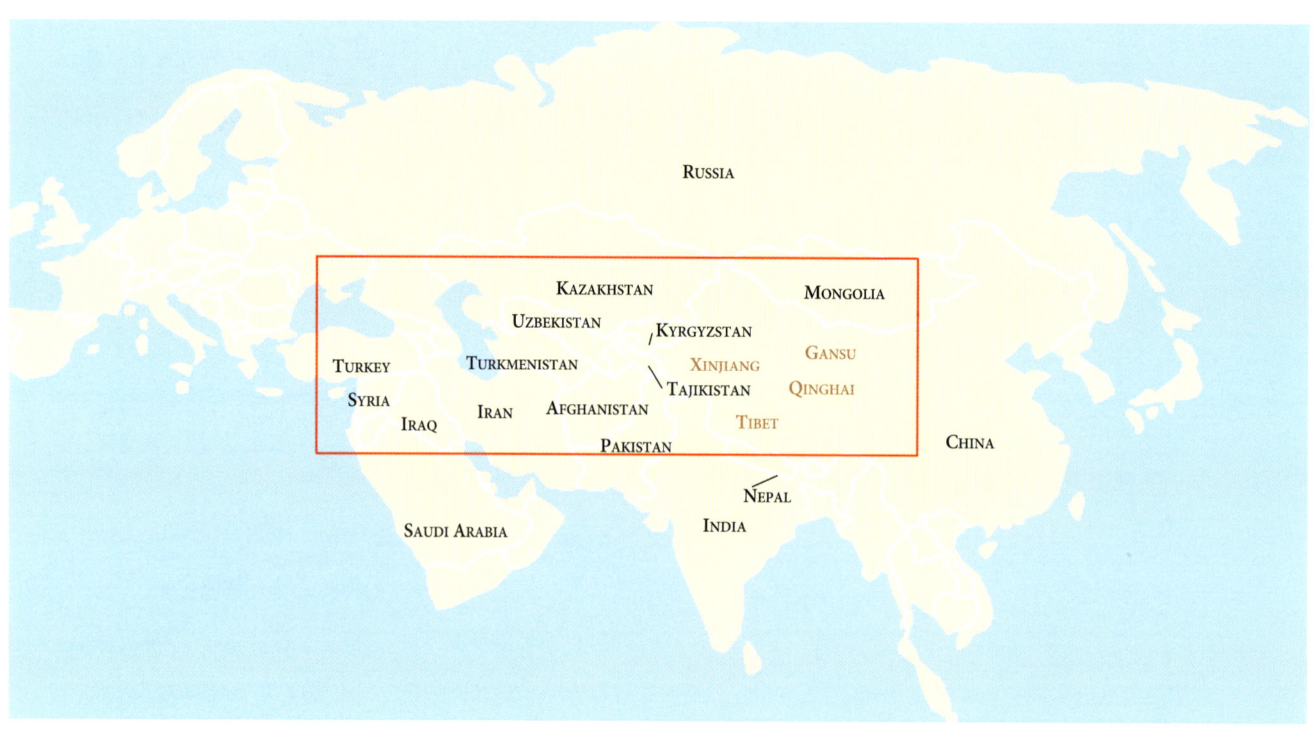

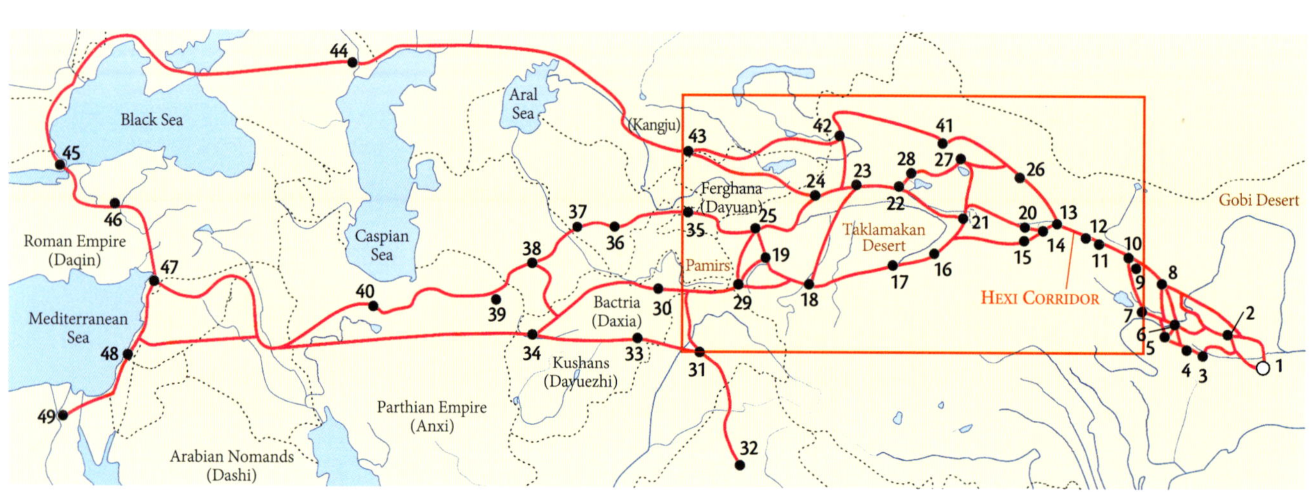

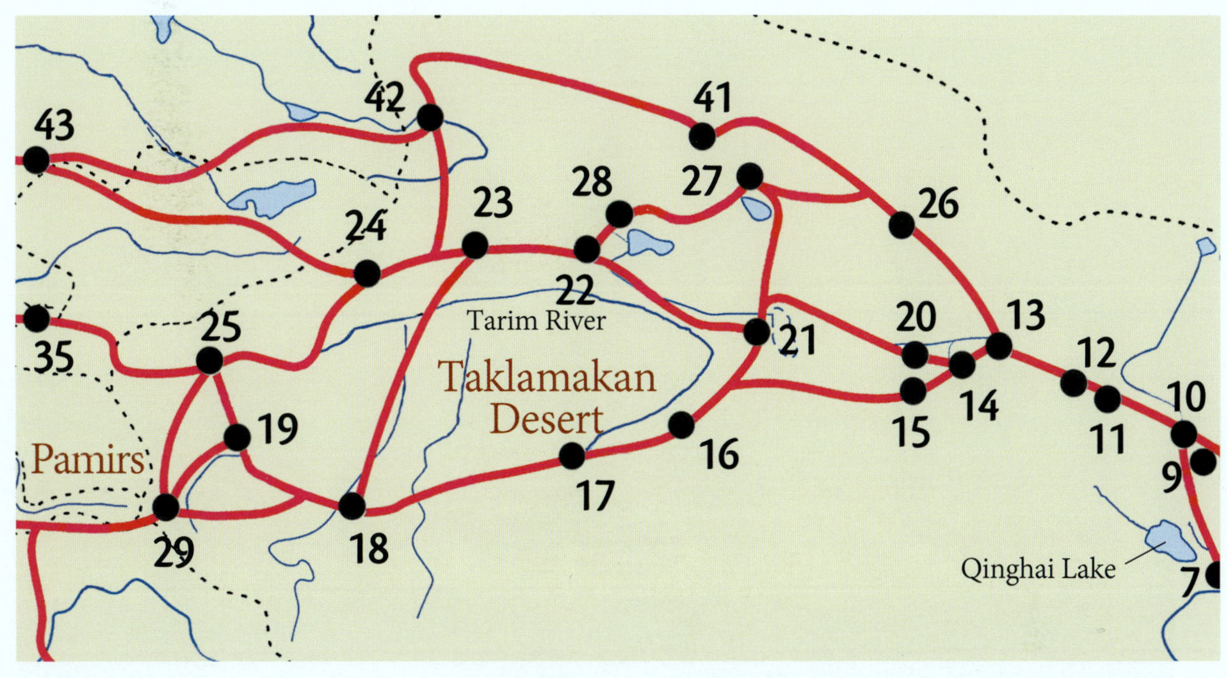

Sites Along the Silk Road
丝路驿站

1 Chang'an 长安
2 Anding (commandery) 安定
3 Tianshui 天水
4 Longxi (commandery) 陇西
5 Baohan 枹罕
6 Jincheng (Lanzhou) 金城（兰州）
7 Xining 西宁
8 Wuwei (commandery) 武威
9 Lijian (near Yongchang) 骊靬（永昌）
10 Zhangye (commandery) 张掖
11 Jiuquan (commandery) 酒泉
12 Jiayuguan Pass 嘉峪关
13 Guazhou 瓜州
14 Dunhuang (commandery) 敦煌
15 Yangguan Pass 阳关
16 Qarkilik (Ruoqiang) 若羌
17 Qarqan (Qiemo) 且末
18 Khotan (Yutian) 于阗
19 Yarkand (Shache) 莎车
20 Yumen Pass 玉门关
21 Loulan 楼兰
22 Korla 库尔勒
23 Kucha (Kuche or Guizi) 库车（龟兹）
24 Aksu (Gumo) 姑墨
25 Kashgar (Kashi) 喀什
26 Kumul (Hami) 哈密
27 Turfan / Gaochang (Kocho, Turpan) 吐鲁番 / 高昌
28 Karashahr (Yanqi) 焉耆
29 Tashkurgan 塔什库尔干
30 Fayzabad 法扎巴德
31 Islamabad 伊斯兰堡
32 New Delhi 新德里
33 Kabul 喀布尔
34 Herat 赫拉特
35 Ferghana (Dayuan) 大宛
36 Samarkand 散马尔罕
37 Bukhara 布哈拉
38 Merv 木鹿城
39 Mashhad 马什哈德
40 Tehran 德黑兰
41 Urumqi 乌鲁木齐
42 Amaliq (Huocheng) 霍城
43 Taraz 怛罗斯
44 Sarai 萨莱
45 Constantinople 君士坦丁堡
46 Ankara 安卡拉
47 Antioch 安塔基亚
48 Tyre 推罗
49 Cairo 开罗

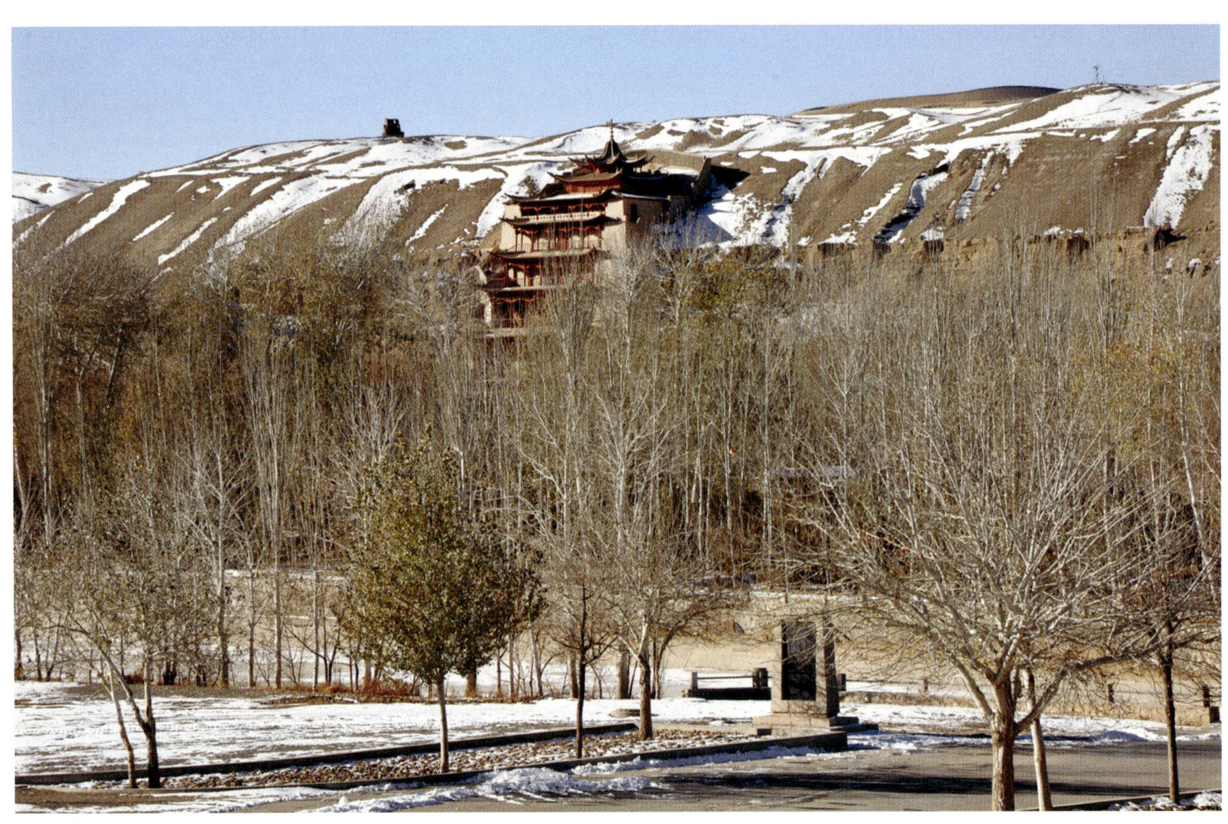

Front view of the Mogao Grottoes. Photo by Perry Hu, 2012. 莫高窟前景，胡维智摄

Art of Dunhuang Cave Shrines– A Splendid Achievement

By Fan Jinshi

Geography and History

Dunhuang is located at the western end of the Hexi Corridor in Gansu province, China. Sandwiched by Mazong (Horse Mane) Mountain (also known as North Mountain) to its north and Qilian Mountain (also called South Mountain) to its south, Dunhuang is an oasis fed by the constant flooding of the ancient Dizhi River (present-day Dang River), which flows from South Mountain. Surrounding this oasis are mostly the Gobi Desert and sand dunes. In the Han dynasty (206 BCE–220 CE), when the famous Silk Road first opened, it held a strategic position on the trade route. It came to be known as the "throat" of the Silk Road. Going east from Dunhuang through the Hexi Corridor, the Silk Road led to the ancient capitals of Chang'an and Luoyang. In the other direction, going west, the Road split into two routes—one to the south and one to the north. The southern route went through the Yangguan Pass; stretched southward along the northern foot of the Kunlun Mountains through Ruoqiang, Qiemo, Yutian, and Shache;[1] and, climbing over the Cong Ridge (the Pamirs), entered the empires of the Dayuezhi,[2] Anxi,[3] and others (see map on p. xvi). The northern route of the Silk Road extended from Dunhuang through the Yumenguan Pass and along the southern foot of the Tian Mountains, passing through Turfan, Yanqi,[4] Kucha, and Kashi[5] before climbing over the Cong Ridge and finally entering Dayuan,[6] Kangju,[7] and Daxia.[8] With the two passes Dunhuang controlled the flow of traffic between east and west and served as a hub for east-west trade. The trade goods that came through here included silk and porcelain from central China, precious stones from the West, camels and horses from the north, and local grain products. In addition to being a business center, it would also become a cultural melting pot. During the Han dynasty, the culture of central China started to take root in Dunhuang. Meanwhile, because of its proximity to the Western Regions, Dunhuang's growth was greatly influenced by the Buddhist culture of India as well. Furthermore, the eastward movement of Buddhism also brought the cultures of Western Asia and Central Asia. Here in Dunhuang the traditions of China and countries to its west met, collided, and merged. As Ji Xianlin, a renowned Dunhuang scholar, rightly states, "In the world there are only four . . . complete cultural systems which have exerted a far reaching influence: that of China, India, Greece, and Islam. And there is only one place in the whole world where these four cultural systems meet: that is the Dunhuang and Xinjiang region in China."[9] Mr. Ji's statement summarizes well the historic importance of Dunhuang's geographic location (fig. 1).

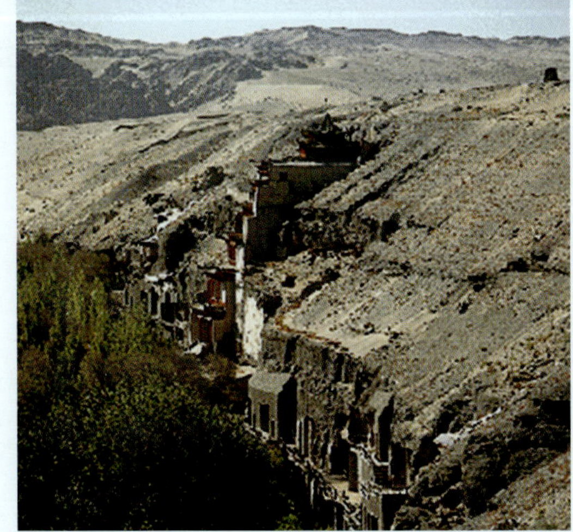

Fig. 1. General view of the Mogao Grottoes. 敦煌莫高窟远外景

Dunhuang has a history of more than 2,000 years. Before the Qin (221–206 BCE) and Han dynasties, the area was inhabited by the Yuezhi and Wusun tribes. At the beginning of the Western Han dynasty (206 BCE–24 CE), the Xiongnu of the northern deserts drove out the Yuezhi and occupied Dunhuang. In the second year of the Yuanshou era (121 BCE), armies of the Western Han defeated the Xiongnu and annexed Dunhuang and the Hexi Corridor. In the sixth year of the Yuanding era (111 BCE), the Western Han

---

This essay was previously published in *Dunhuang: A Centennial Commemoration of the Discovery of the Cave Library*, ed. Zhang Wenbin (Beijing: Morning Glory Publishers, 2000), pp. 5–17. It has been revised and annotated for the current publication.

designated Dunhuang a prefecture along with Jiuquan, Zhangye, and Wuwei. These four prefectures came to be known in history as the Four Prefectures of the Hexi Corridor. As part of Dunhuang's defense scheme, a long wall (which later became part of the Great Wall) was erected to its north, and two fortresses, the Yangguan Pass and the Yumenguan Pass, were built to its west. From then on, Dunhuang became a doorway to the Hexi Corridor and central China and served as a vital military outpost.

To further strengthen Dunhuang's strategic position, the Western Han court resettled people from the Central Plains to Dunhuang and also stationed troops to farm and guard the frontier. Thus, during the Western Han dynasty Dunhuang was established in Chinese history as a place of importance. During the subsequent Eastern Han dynasty and Northern and Southern Dynasties, Dunhuang developed further and enjoyed a relatively long period of stability. It grew into an important commodity trading center as well as a grain production base on the Silk Road. Here the culture of central China took root and continued to develop while Buddhist scriptures and India's Buddhist culture were introduced into the area. The famous great translator of Buddhist scriptures and Dunhuang native Dharmaraksa, also known as the Dunhuang Bodhisattva, and his disciples were active at Dunhuang, studying the scriptures and propagating Buddhism, during the Western Jin dynasty (265–316).

During the period of the Sixteen Kingdoms, central China was in turmoil and war was frequent. Only Dunhuang escaped the ravage of war; it continued to enjoy peace and prosperity. Many people of the Hexi Corridor and central China fled to Dunhuang, thus dramatically increasing Dunhuang's population and helping to preserve the Han-Jin-period Central Plains culture of Dunhuang and the Hexi Corridor. At that time a group of eminent Confucian scholars opened schools, wrote books, and developed their ideas in Dunhuang. In the meantime, Buddhists who came from the West to teach the Dharma (Buddhist Law) to the Chinese and those from China who traveled west in quest of the Dharma had to pass through Dunhuang on their respective journeys. These traveling Buddhists established a growing Buddhist community in Dunhuang. As indicated in "A History of Buddhism and Daoism," in the *Weishu* (The Book of Wei), "Dunhuang is on the border with the Western Regions, where clergy and the lay population intersect. Although their traditional villages are quite similar to ours, there are numerous stupas and temples."[10]

While the development of Buddhist culture in Dunhuang was inevitable, cave construction at Mogao in Dunhuang started quite accidentally. According to the "Stele for a Mogao Cave Buddhist Niche" erected by Li Kerang in 698, "The Mogao Caves were started at the beginning of the second year of the Jianyuan era of the Qin (366 CE), when a traveling monk named Shamen Lezun, arriving one day at Mount Mogao, suddenly saw golden lights appearing from the spot as if they were the Thousand Buddhas. He then dug a cave in the Mogao cliff and built a shrine. After him came Chan (Zen) Master Faliang from the east, who hollowed a second cave next to it."[11] Thus began the trend of cave building in Dunhuang that was to last for more than a thousand years. After these humble beginnings, more serious endeavors supported by local authorities ensued. Two early magistrates of Guazhou prefecture (Dunhuang) need special mention here: Yuan Tairong, a Northern Wei royal clansmen enfeoffed as Prince Dongyang, and Yuyi, a Northern Zhou nobleman titled Duke of Jianping. Both of them were Buddhist devotees who had greatly encouraged cave excavation and shrine building at Mogao.

In the Sui dynasty, Emperors Wen and Yang both initiated a national movement to spread Buddhism and ordered stupas to be built in every region of the nation. Accordingly, Guazhou prefecture (Dunhuang) built its stupas in Chongjiao Temple (now the Mogao Grottoes or Mogao Caves). Buddhist scriptures hand-copied at the central court also reached Dunhuang. During the relatively short Sui dynasty, cave carving became a fad which continued into the Tang dynasty. The Tang court strengthened Dunhuang's security by establishing the Anxi (Pacified Western Region) garrison and four towns. It raised ten armies and stationed them in Dunhuang and the Hexi Corridor. The strong military presence in the area guaranteed unimpeded traffic along the Silk Road and thereby a continued and steady development of Dunhuang's economy and culture. It is said that, "from the west of Dunhuang to the east of Persia, [the Silk Road] saw no end of merchants and travelers as well."[12] The peaceful environment and continued cultural and economic exchange between east and west were conducive to cave building at Dunhuang. Unfortunately, in the fourteenth year of the Tianbao era (755), a large uprising (the An Lushan Rebellion) broke out in China, leading to the decline of the Tang.

Tibetan powers (Tubo regime) took advantage of the weakening Tang and annexed Longyou and Hexi. In the second year of the Jianzhong era (781), the Tibetans occupied Shazhou (present-day Dunhuang) and imposed its administrative, economic, and cultural system. Since the Tibetans were for the most part Buddhist supporters, the development of Buddhist culture and art in Dunhuang was unimpeded under Tibetan rule. Cave building at Mogao even increased. In the second year of the Huichang era (842), an internal rivalry broke out in Tibet, weakening its political clout in the Western Regions. Seizing this opportunity, Zhang Yichao of Shazhou Prefecture staged an insurrection and successively recaptured eleven prefectures successively, including Yizhou, Xizhou, Guazhou, Suzhou, Ganzhou, and Liangzhou from Tibetan hands. Zhang sent an envoy to the Tang court to pledge his allegiance to the Tang; it was accepted, and Zhang was conferred with the rank of general of the Insurrection Army. Thus began more than two hundred years of administration of Dunhuang by the Insurrection Army Government (Guiyijun). Zhang's administration reintroduced the Tang system and enforced Han culture. Dunhuang again regained its political stability. Under the protective rule of the Zhang family, Buddhist devotees continued to build temples and cave shrines on a large scale. In the Five Dynasties period, Cao Yijin took over Zhang Chengfeng's government. Cao maintained a close relationship with the courts of central China and received their support. He made good use of the strength, reputation, and prestige that the old Tang court had enjoyed among the people of the northwest to strengthen his position among powers to the west in Inner Asia. Through strategic marriage alliances, he struck good relationships with the Muslims of Ganzhou, Muslims of Xizhou, and Yutian (Khotan). Cao's efforts to build good relations with the central courts and surrounding minority nationalities were effective; they contributed not only to peace in the Central Plains, but also to the safety of the Silk Road and growing exchange between Dunhuang and the Buddhist culture of the West. Moreover, they created favorable political conditions for the development of Dunhuang's Buddhist art.

In the third year of Jingyou in the Song dynasty (1036) and the third year of Baoqing in the Southern Song dynasty (1227), Dunhuang was occupied by the Dangxianqiang and the Mongols respectively.[13] Since both of these peoples were devout believers of Buddhism they regarded the Mogao Grottoes in Dunhuang as an important Buddhist sanctuary to be protected and improved. Therefore, there were still a few new cave additions to the Mogao Grottoes during these periods. Then the development tapered off. With the rise of an "Ocean Silk Road" and expansion of the Mongol empire, Dunhuang started to lose its strategic position as a hub of east-west transportation and the gateway of the Chinese West. Along with it, Mogao Grottoes fell into decline.

After the Yuan dynasty, no new caves were excavated and Dunhuang was gradually forgotten. In the seventh year of Jiajing in the Ming dynasty (1528), the Ming court closed the Jiayuguan Pass, turning Dunhuang into a frontier herding ground. Dunhuang did not see its revival until the first year of Yongzheng in the Qing dynasty (1723), when an outpost was set up there again. Three years later (1725) the outpost was upgraded to a garrison, and many immigrants were brought in from every prefecture in Gansu to farm and rebuild the city of Shazhou. In the twenty-fifth year of Qianlong in the Qing dynasty (1760), the Shazhou garrison became Dunhuang county. Dunhuang became alive again, and the Mogao Grottoes also began to attract people's attention. In the twenty-sixth year of Guangxu (1900) in the Qing dynasty, the world-famous Dunhuang Library Cave was discovered. Unfortunately, the Qing government was so corrupt and incompetent that Western powers availed themselves of Chinese treasures at their will. Not long after the discovery of the Library Cave by Sir Marc Aurel Stein (fig. 2), a Hungarian-British archaeologist, he was followed in turn by Paul Pelliot of France, Zuicho Tachibana of Japan, and Sergei Oldenberg of Russia, and other Western adventurers who came to the site. Using unfair means, they spirited away a large number of the Library Cave deposits from the Daoist priest Wang Yuanlu. Most of these materials were then scattered around the world and are now in the collections of private individuals and national museums in England, France, Russia, Japan, and other countries. Only a small part remains in China. This misfortune is a tremendous loss for China, unprecedented in the history of Chinese culture.

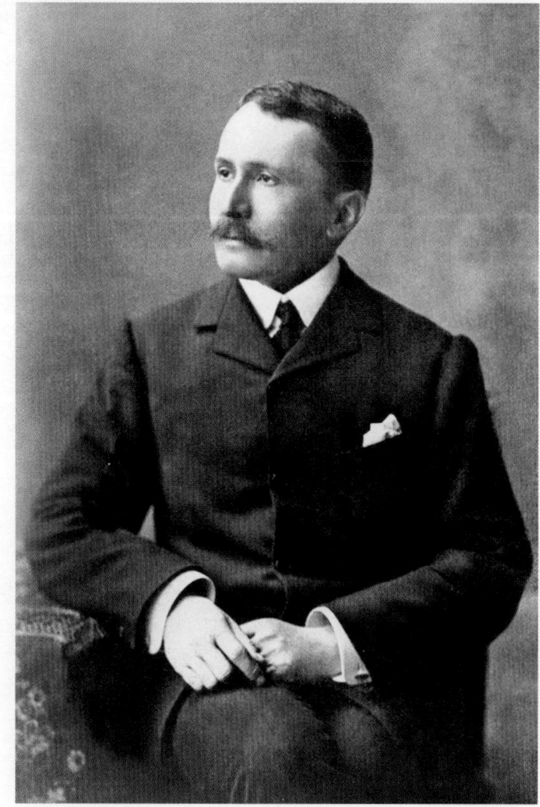

Fig. 2. Sir Marc Aurel Stein (1862–1943).
英国考古学家斯坦因 (1862–1943)

Art of Dunhuang Cave Shrines

"Dunhuang Cave Shrines" is a general term referring to the five groups of cave shrines in the greater Dunhuang area. These five groups are the Mogao Grottoes outside the town of Dunhuang, the Western Caves of a Thousand Buddhas, the Yulin Grottoes in Anxi county, the Eastern Caves of a Thousand Buddhas, and the Five-Temple Grottoes in Subei county. Although different in scale, these cave shrines are all located within the boundary of the old Dunhuang prefecture and are similar in content, style, and artistic expression. This is why they are generally grouped together and called the Dunhuang Cave Shrines. There are 812 caves in all. The Mogao Grottoes has 735, the Western Caves of a Thousand Buddhas has twenty-two, the Yulin Grottoes has forty-two, the Eastern Caves of a Thousand Buddhas has seven, and the Five-Temple Grottoes has six.

Among these cave shrines, the most magnificent are those of the Mogao Grottoes, which have been recognized as one of the world's most important cultural heritage sites. The Mogao Grottoes lie at the eastern edge of the Mingsha Dunes (Dunes of the Singing Sands), 25 kilometers southeast of Dunhuang town. It faces east toward Sanwei Mountain, a range of the Qilian Mountains, and in front of it runs Shiquan River. From the fourth to the fourteenth century, cave construction and Buddhist image production were continuous, and the result is the spectacular cluster of caves stretching 1,680 meters from south to north. Altogether, 735 caves distributed on four different levels have been dug out of a cliff which ranges in height from fifteen to thirty meters. The Mogao Grottoes can be divided into two areas: southern and northern. The southern area has 492 caves with more than 2,000 painted sculptures, more than 45,000 square meters of wall painting, and five wooden porticos. The northern caves has 243 caves which served as religious practice spaces and living quarters for monks. These caves have earthen beds, hearth pits, smoke ducts, wall shrines, lamp stands, and other practical features. There are no painted images or wall paintings in these caves.

Since the cave temples were dug out of a sandstone cliff, fine sculpturing was impossible at the entire site. Therefore, painted clay stucco sculpture and murals became the major artistic media. Artists conveyed skin tone, facial expression, fluffy hair and beards, and costume texture through painted additions rather than carving. To make a painted clay stucco sculpture, the artist first built an armature of bound straw and then stuccoed it with a mixture of dried reed and clay. A mural was executed on a treated wall on which two or three layers of a reed and clay mixture were first applied as a base. Then the process of composition selection, layout, sketching, and coloring ensued. The art of the Dunhuang Cave Shrines is a comprehensive one, unifying architecture, painted sculpture, and wall painting. A cave's architectural shape is determined by its content and function. Placed in a wall niche, in a central stupa-pillar, or in a prominent position on an altar, the painted sculpture in a cave is the major focus of worship. It is coordinated with the surrounding wall paintings in theme and color scheme. The colorful wall paintings would depict a complex narrative or make a detailed decorative visual statement. They occupy the whole cave, covering niches, the four walls, and ceiling and complementing the sculpture that sits at the focal point. Together, they set off each other and form a complete ensemble of Dunhuang cave art.

Fig. 3. Interior view of a meditation cave, Mogao Cave 285. Western Wei dynasty (535–556). 莫高窟西魏第285窟（禅窟内景）

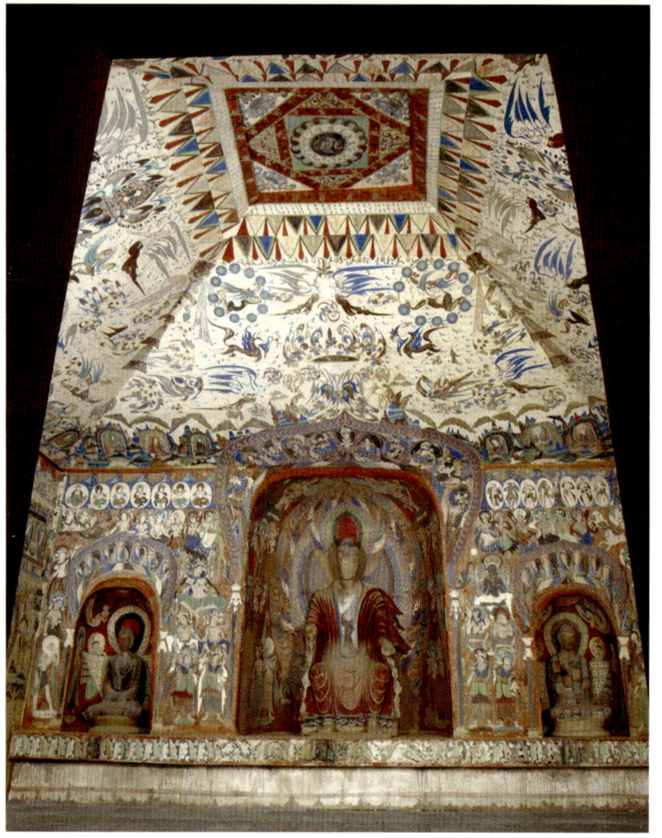

The art of the Dunhuang Cave Shrines is Buddhist with Chinese national and folk art characteristics. It is based on the artistic tradition of the Han and Jin dynasties and has drawn rich inspiration from the art of other lands. With its long history, large scale, profound content, splendid art, good condition, and domestic and international fame, the Dunhuang Cave Shrines are a treasure trove of Chinese as well as world Buddhist art.

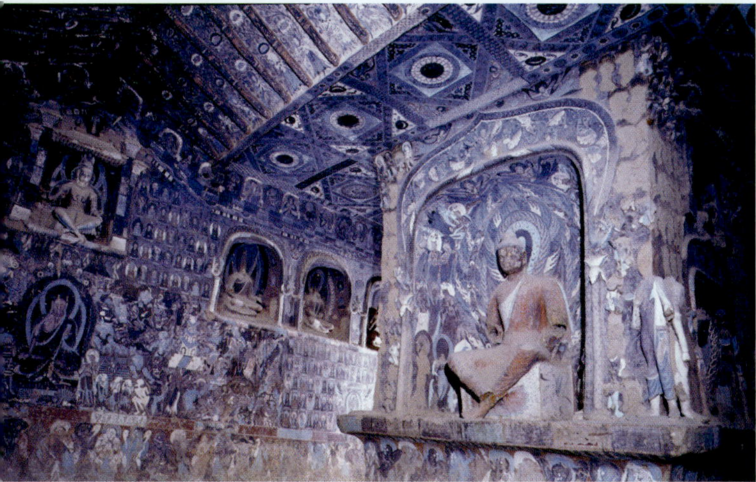

Fig. 4. Central pillar of Mogao Cave 254. Northern Wei dynasty (386–534). 莫高窟北魏第254窟中心塔柱

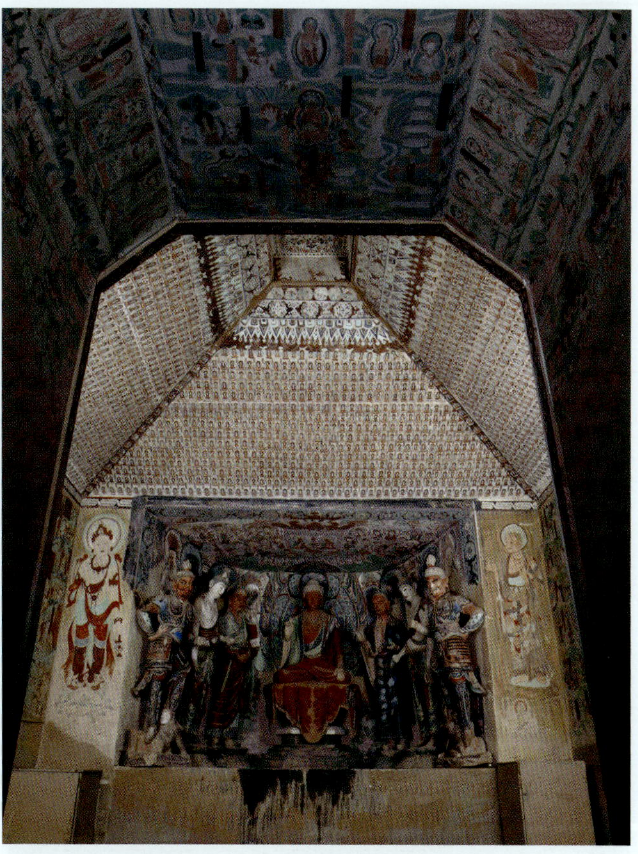

Fig. 5. Interior view of Mogao Cave 45. High Tang period (705–781). 莫高窟盛唐第45窟内景

I. Cave Art of the Northern Dynasties

During this period, Dunhuang's cave art was in its early stage of development. Its theme and style show a strong presence of the Buddhist art of the West as well as deep roots in the culture of the Central Plains (central China). Dunhuang's Buddhist art, from its very beginning, bore strong characteristics of local Jin and Wei period art. However, a dominantly Chinese Dunhuang Buddhist art did not take shape until the late Northern Dynasties.

A. Architectural Forms of the Caves

1. *Chan (Zen) meditation caves.* Chan caves were built for monks to practice meditation. They developed out of the vihara halls of India. The main chamber of the cave is oblong or square. In its rear wall a niche (or niches) is dug for sculptural images, which were used by Chan monks while meditating. Two or four small rooms with only enough space for one person to practice meditation were cut into the right and left side walls. The ceilings of these caves were either flat or recessed. The early models were plain, but the later ones had paintings on the walls and ceilings (Caves 267, 268, 269, 270, 271, and 285 [fig. 3]).

2. *Caves with a central stupa-pillar.* These caves were also called central pillar caves or stupa caves. Originating from the chaitya halls of India, they were the most popular caves of this period. A stupa is built as the cave's focus for worship. The main chamber is oblong. Just behind the cave's center a square stupa column is connected to the ground and the ceiling. A niche on each side of the column houses a painted sculptural image for worship by devotees. The ceiling in front of the stupa is gabled in the Han architectural style, and the ceilings surrounding the stupa are flat (Caves 254 [fig. 4], 288, and 428).

3. *Assembly caves.* These are places of worship. The form of this kind of cave was influenced by traditional Chinese assembly-hall architecture. The main hall is square. At its rear wall, a painted sculpture would be set in a niche or erected without a niche. The other three walls are filled with paintings (murals). There are several assembly caves that have niches for images on the side walls. The ceilings are either recessed or gabled (Caves 45 [fig. 5], 249, and 275).

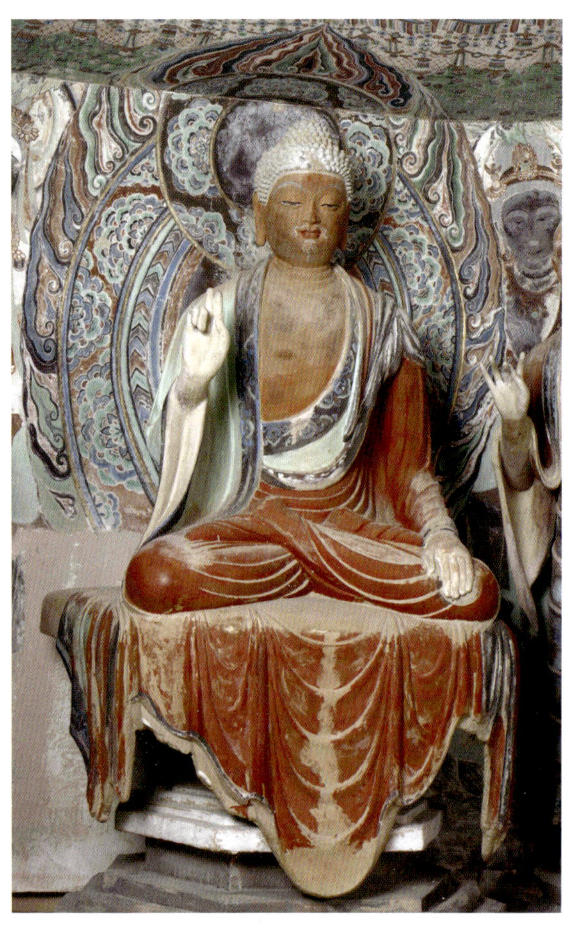

B. Painted Sculpture

Painted sculpture in the Northern Dynasties can be classified into two groups: full-bodied images and attached, low-relief images. The full-bodied images are high-relief figures connected to the walls. They are images of Buddhas, bodhisattvas, and disciples. The Buddha images include those of Maitreya, Shakyamuni, and the paired Shakyamuni and Prabhutaratna. The Shakyamuni images are further divided into those of a meditating Buddha, a practicing Buddha, a preaching Buddha, an enlightened Buddha, and a pensive Buddha. Early images of Shakyamuni have two attendant bodhisattvas, but in later ones his disciples Kashyapa and Ananda are added.

The attached, low-relief images include attendant bodhisattvas, *apsaras*,[14] and the Thousand Buddhas. They are modeled from clay and then affixed to the central stupa or walls of the cave. Low-relief images on the walls appear to be used to set off the full-bodied images. Buddha images of the early Northern Dynasties generally wear robes leaving the right arms bare or round-necked robes covering both shoulders. Images of bodhisattvas have high topknots and crowns of precious stones. Their hair is shoulder length; their upper bodies are bare or covered with silk robes, and their lower bodies are attired in skirts

Fig. 6. Painted clay figure of Buddha in Mogao Cave 45. High Tang period (705–781). 莫高窟盛唐第45窟西壁龛内主尊佛像

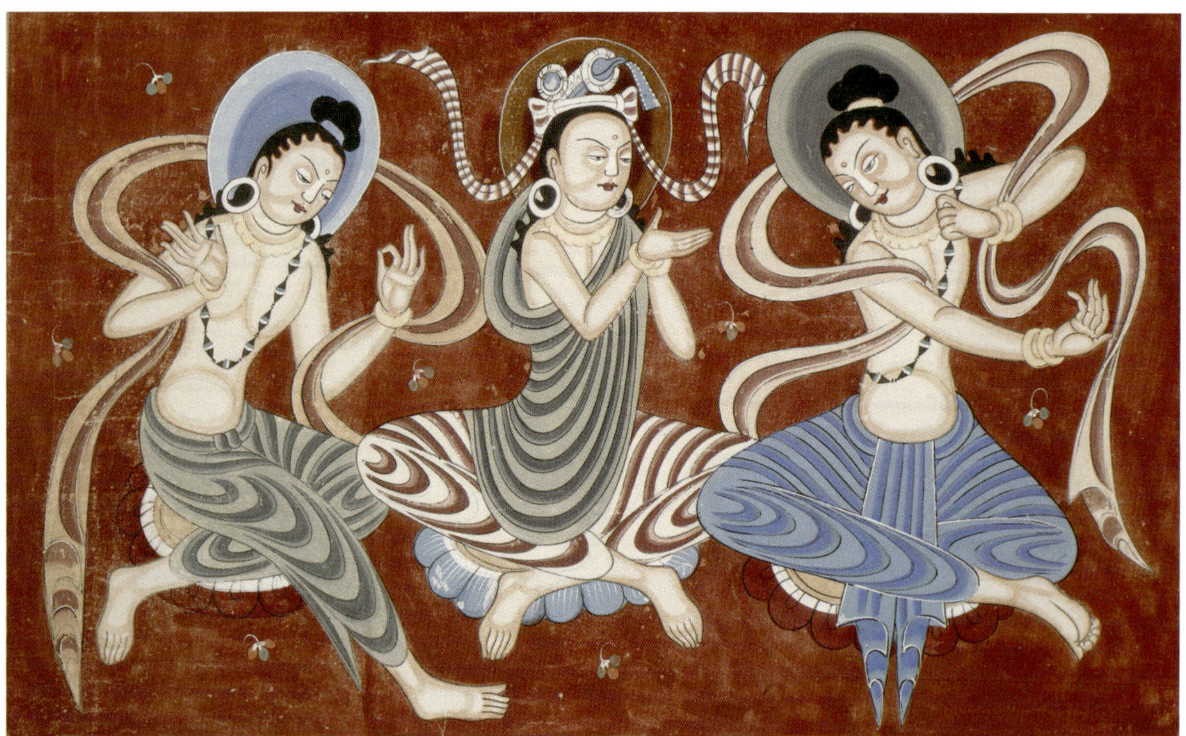

Fig. 7. Mural painting of deities from Mogao Cave 263. Northern Wei (386–534). 莫高窟北魏第263窟壁画伎乐菩萨

with fine folds. Round- or full-faced, wide-shouldered, and flat-chested, they sit looking robust, dignified, natural, peaceful, calm, and thoughtful. In this period, the art of painted sculptural images had its foundation in the art of the Han and Jin of the Central Plains. But at the same time it greatly absorbed influences from the artistic tradition of western Buddhism. During the late Northern Dynasties' Western Wei period, the Chinese artistic style of "delicacy and elegance" became fashionable with the introduction of Chinese-style costumes to Dunhuang from the Central Plains. The painted clay figures in this period wore a high-collared and large-sleeved robe with a sash tied in a small knot on the chest and topped with a *kasaya* vestment in the style of a Chinese *duijin* (style of clothing fastened in the middle front rather than at the side) jacket. These figures, with their square and thin faces and narrow, flat bodies, appear more Chinese (fig. 6).

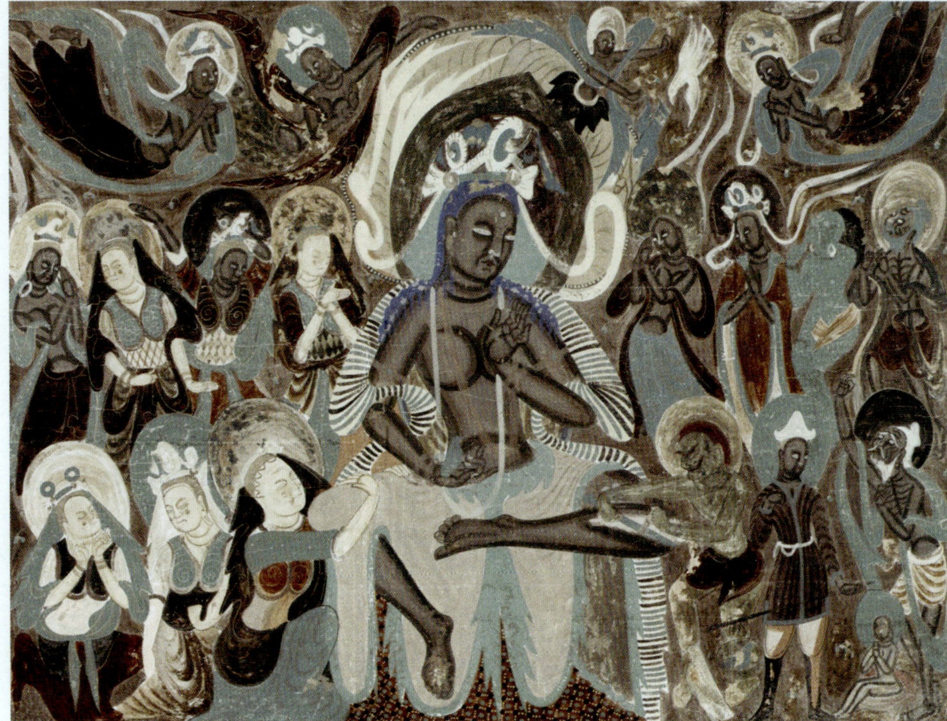

Fig. 8. Detail of *Sivi Jataka* from mural in Mogao Cave 254. Northern Wei dynasty (386–534).
莫高窟北魏第254窟壁画尸毗王本生故事

C. Wall Paintings

The wall paintings of the Northern Dynasties follow a fixed layout. Encircling the cave on the upper borders of the four walls are heavenly dancers and musicians. The middle part of the walls are filled with pictures of Buddhas in different postures and settings, such as the Thousand Buddhas; the preaching Buddha with the Thousand Buddhas; and a preaching Buddha with a Thousand Buddhas, jataka tales,[15] and other Buddhist legends. Lining the lower borders of the walls are *vajrapani* guardian figures or decorative patterns. Ceilings of the early Northern Dynasties are painted with decorative designs while the gabled or recessed ceilings of the late Northern Dynasties are painted with jataka tales, Buddhist legends, and the Thousand Buddhas. According to their content, these wall paintings can be classified into five types.

1. ***Paintings of deities.*** This includes all categories of Buddhist deities. Depictions of preaching Buddhas are composed strictly according to canonical rules. An example is the repetitive but colorful painting of the Thousand Buddhas. Painted images of worshipping bodhisattvas dance in an orderly and graceful fashion (fig. 7); compositions of joyous heavenly dancers and musicians are also common. Strong, fierce-looking *vajrapani*, defenders of the Law (Dharma, the Buddhist doctrine) and destroyers of evil spirits, populate other works.

2. ***Paintings of jataka tales, cause-and-effect (*avadana*) tales, and other Buddhist legends.*** Jataka tales record Shakyamuni's various meritorious deeds from his former lives as a bodhisattva (fig. 8). Cause-and-effect tales relate how Shakyamuni, after becoming a Buddha, preached the Dharma to enlighten transient beings. Other Buddhist legends include episodes from the life of Shakyamuni, the historical Buddha. The main themes of these legendary stories feature tenets of Buddhist doctrine, such as renouncing the householder's life to enter monkhood; practicing charity, forbearance, and self-discipline; doing good and punishing evil; cause and effect of actions; and the power of the Dharma. The narrative paintings of the late Northern Dynasties gradually incorporated more Chinese themes, including Confucian ideas of loyalty, piety, humanity, gentility, and familial harmony. These narratives are presented in a variety of layouts. Monoscenic or synoptic paintings illustrate one particular scene in the story. There are also multiple-theme murals; these encompass several scenes from the same story in one picture; further, continuous narratives are composed of a series of pictures illustrating a complete story.

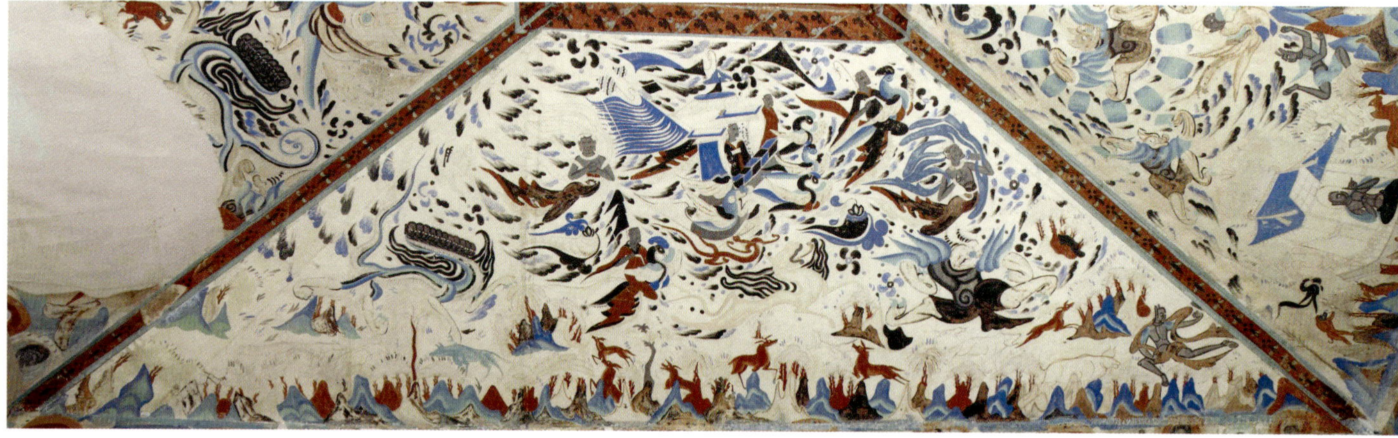

Fig. 9-a. Painting with Queen Mother of the West from Mogao Cave 249. Western Wei dynasty (535–556). 莫高窟西魏第249窟壁画西王母

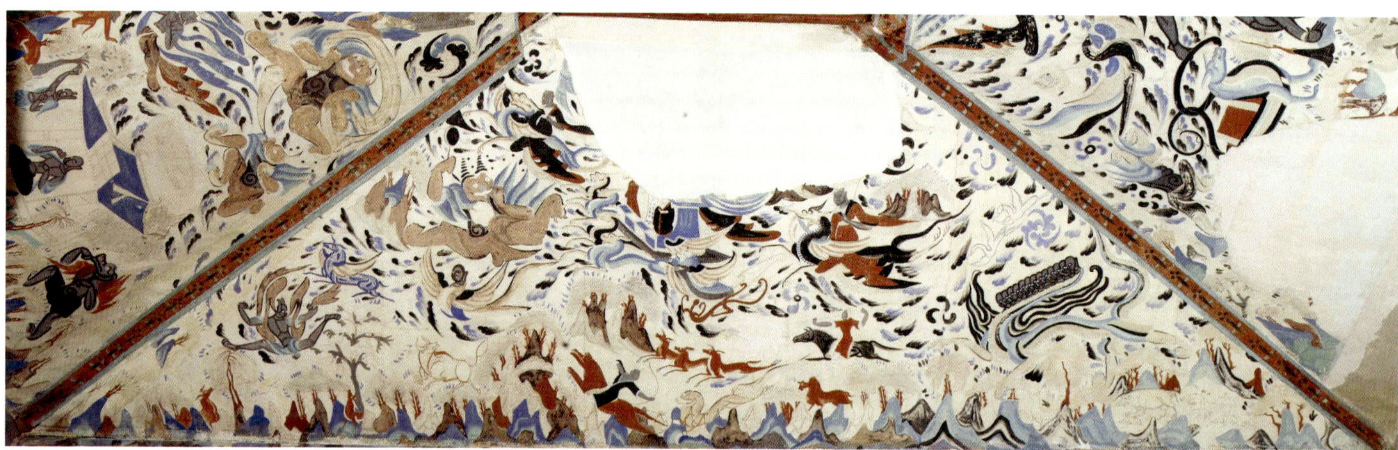

Fig. 9-b. Painting with the Lord of the East from Mogao Cave 249. Western Wei dynasty (535–556). 莫高窟西魏第249窟壁画东王公

3. *Paintings of mythical figures*. These murals did not appear until the late Northern Dynasties. They originated with depictions of Daoist mythical figures such as Xi Wangmu (Queen Mother of the West) and the Lord of the East (Dong Wanggong), who ride on a dragon or phoenix and in carriages (fig. 9-a); the snake-bodied and human-faced Fuxi and Nuwa; the flying Green Dragon (eastern deity); the winged, galloping White Tiger (western deity); the soaring Red Sparrow (southern deity); and Xuanwu (northern deity). There are also monsters such as the immortal winged man with two raised, pointed ears and long feathers growing on his arms; the god of thunder with an animal head and a human body; and the god of lightning, who also has an animal head and human body (fig. 9-b).

4. *Paintings of donors*. Many donors and their family members wished to be depicted in procession on the walls they dedicated. They were usually painted at the bottom of the main murals in small scale, no higher than a foot.[16] The donors are positioned according to gender, with monks and nuns leading and laymen and laywomen following. They include kings, nobles, and their attendants (fig. 10).

5. *Decorative patterns*. In the period of the Northern Dynasties, decorative patterns are used to embellish the architectural features of the caves. They are painted on the gabled ceilings, rafters, lintels, and bracket sets; on the flat ceilings of caves with central stupas and the sunken ceilings of the assembly caves; and on niche frames, painted nimbuses, and wall borders of various cave types. Flat ceilings are covered with triple-layered coffered-ceiling patterns; large lotuses are painted in the center; and the corners are decorated with flames, *apsaras*, and acanthus designs. Recessed ceilings are decorated with a canopy design; in the center of the design is a large lotus, and its borders are embellished with acanthus, cloud, and flame patterns. Around the recessed panel are depicted hanging banners and painted bells. The rafters of a gabled ceiling, the borders of the walls, and the frames of niches are covered with designs of lotus, acanthus, auspicious animals, clouds, and geometrical forms.

In the early wall paintings, artists used red ochre as the ground color; the figures in these paintings assume strong, well-proportioned, masculine features and are dressed in western-style costumes. Their faces and bodies are painted with shading (typically found in Inner Asian and Indian painting) to increase the effect of three-dimensionality and roundness of the body. The colors are plain and heavy, and the lines are thin but forceful. Two different styles are employed. One is a continuation of the style of the early wall paintings, improving them with the shading technique. In the second style, white is used as the ground color and the figures are thin, delicate, and elegant, with well-defined brows and eyes and a natural and unrestrained expression; they are dressed in the Chinese style with square-collared, dark-colored robes. Faces are shaded with red according to the Chinese tradition. The colors are fresh and bright, and the lines appear quick, rhythmic, unrestrained, and elegant. This latter style is greatly influenced by the new Chinese trend (fig. 11).

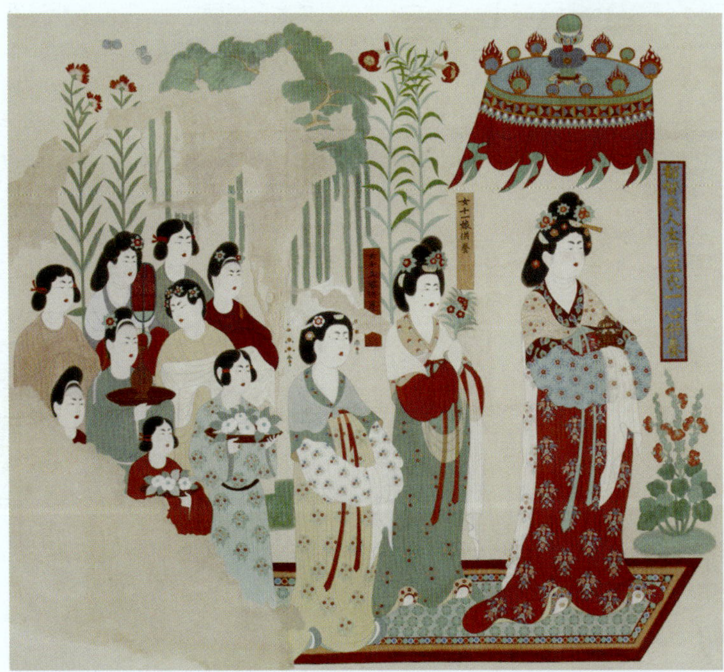

Fig. 10. Painting (replica) of governor's wife leading donors from Mogao Cave 130. High Tang period (705–781). 莫高窟盛唐第130窟都督夫人礼佛图 （复原）

Fig. 11. Decorative pattern with peacock designs painted on southern wall of Mogao Cave 285. Northern Wei dynasty (386–534). 莫高窟北魏第285窟南壁孔雀窟楣

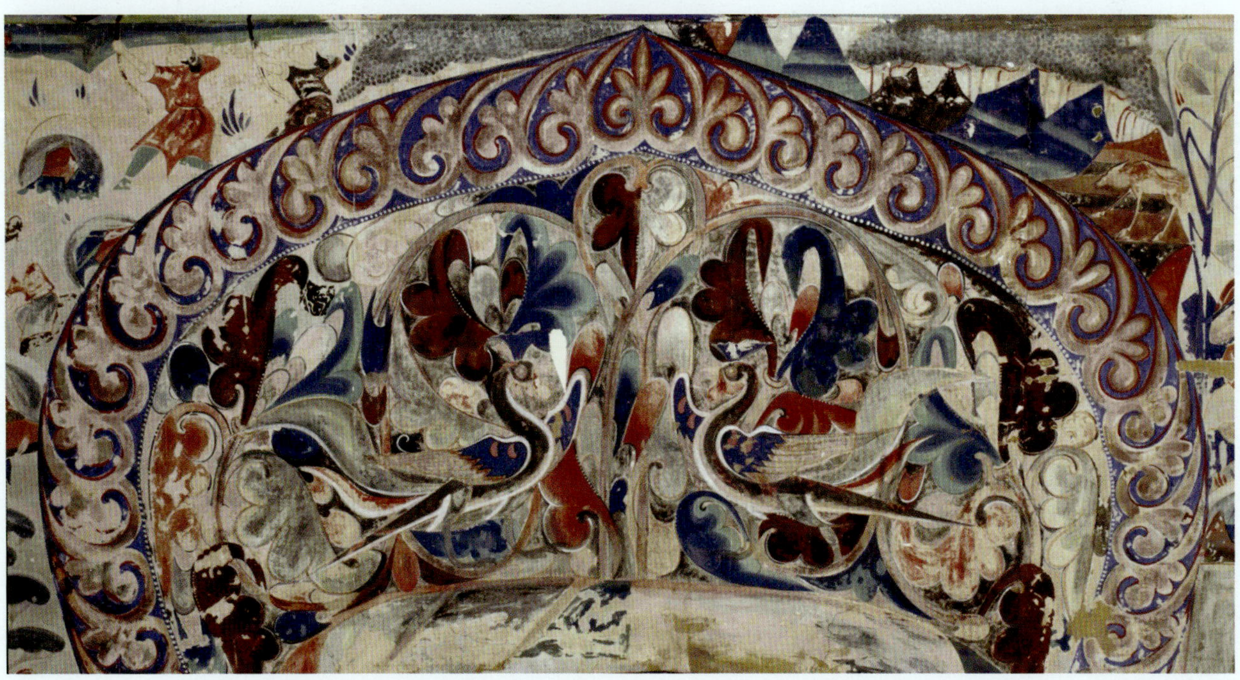

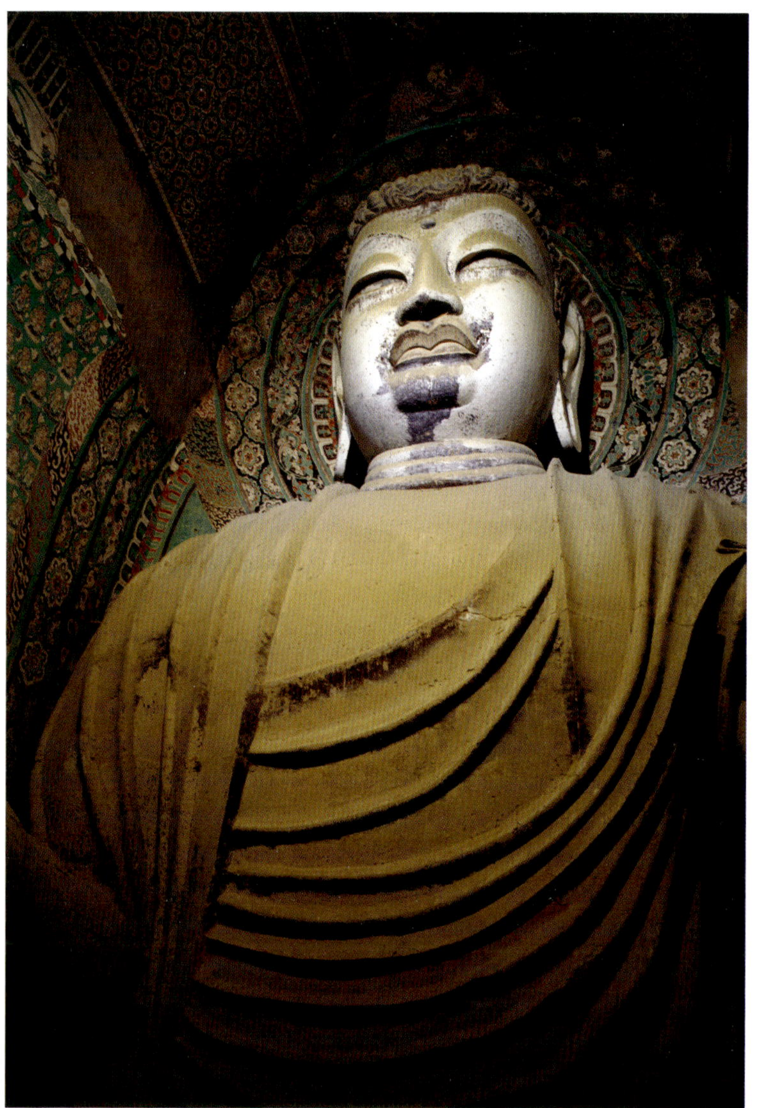

Fig. 12. Colossal figure of seated Maitreya from Mogao Cave 130. High Tang period (705–781). Painted clay. 莫高窟盛唐第130窟彩塑倚坐弥勒像

II. Cave Art of the Sui and Tang Dynasties

Buddhism and Buddhist art developed greatly in China during the Sui and Tang dynasties and formed a unique tradition with Chinese characteristics. In this favorable environment, Dunhuang cave art reached its peak of artistic achievement. The secularization, popularization, and diversification of cave architecture, painted sculpture, and wall paintings during this period demonstrate a successful Chinese acculturation of Buddhist art.

A. Architectural Forms of the Caves

In this period, cave designs moved toward diversification, localization, and secularization. The majority of the new caves were assembly caves. Niches in the caves became wider and deeper and had three different forms. A typical niche of the Sui dynasty had two layers, an inner layer and an outer layer. In the early Tang period, the niche had a smaller interior, but a wider opening. The niche in the late Tang was modeled on the style of a secular canopied bed. In this kind of niche was set a horse-hoof-shaped (U-shaped) altar on which was placed a painted clay figure (for example, in Caves 329 and 384). Although small in number, some assembly caves built in both the Sui and Tang dynasties had niches cut into the back walls and side walls of the main rooms for painted sculptures of the Trikala Buddhas (for example, Cave 420).[17] Caves with altars were new additions in this period. In the Sui and early Tang periods, an oblong or horse-shoe-shaped altar was carved out of the back wall of the main room, while in the late Tang period a square pedestal was carved out in the center of the main room of large caves. A screen, connected to the top of the recessed ceiling, stands at the back of the altar. There are stairs at the front of the altar on which a group of painted clay figures are set high. Believers could circumambulate the altar, turning to the right, while observing the image in worship of the Buddha. This kind of cave was an assembly cave and resembled the main hall of a temple or a royal palace (for example, Cave 196).

Parinirvana caves and seven-Buddhas caves. These caves are so named because they contain sculptures of the Buddha entering *parinirvana* or of the seven Buddhas sitting together; both types typically have pedestals. The main room of this kind of cave is oblong, and out of its back wall a cave-length bed is carved, on which rests the figure of a reclining Buddha (for example, Cave 148 of the high Tang and Cave 158 of the mid-Tang) or, in the other case, seven Buddhas (Cave 365 of the mid-Tang) are seated. The ceiling is either sunken or arched.

Caves of large images. These caves are thus named because they contain colossal, seated images of Maitreya (Mogao Cave 96 of the early Tang, Mogao Cave 130 of the late Tang [fig.12], and Yulin Cave 6 of the Tang). These caves are large and tall, and their main rooms are square with a smaller top and a larger bottom. A large, stone-bodied and clay-stuccoed sculpture is erected against the back wall. A U-shaped passage is carved out from behind the statue for circumambulation. In the middle and upper part of the front wall a large window lets in light. The ceiling is either recessed or vaulted. On the exterior, multi-storied wooden verandas are built.

During this period, caves with central stupas greatly decreased and fell into a decline because of the simplification of liturgical procedures and the expansion of lay worship of Buddhism. Central stupas lost their favor as the focus of worship, and in their place arose the sculptural altars of the assembly caves.

B. Painted Sculpture

In the Sui and Tang period, the painted sculpture placed in niches or on pedestals were full-bodied, three-dimensional figures, completely detached from the walls. Along with the development of Buddhist ideas, painted images of deities also changed and developed in number and content. The number of images placed in a niche or pedestal ranged from three to eleven with seven and nine being the most common. In the Sui dynasty, the main deities were expanded to include the Buddha of the past; Shakyamuni, Buddha of the present; and Maitreya, Buddha of the future; Dharmakaya, embodiment of truth and the law; Nirmanakaya, incarnation of *bhutata-thata*[18] and the metamorphized body;[19] and Samboghakaya, the beatific body. Shakyamuni, Amitabha, and Maitreya were the most popular images worshiped in the Sui and Tang. During this period, images of the four deva-kings (*devaraja*) and *vajrapani*, all defenders of the Buddhist law (Dharma), were added to the antechambers; in the late Tang they were moved into the main rooms to be grouped with images of Buddhas, bodhisattvas, and disciples. A typical layout is the Buddha positioned in the center and flanked by the disciples Kashyapa and Ananda; the bodhisattvas Avalokiteshvara and Mahasthamaprapta, standing or sitting; Deva-kings of the South and North; and *vajrapani*. Added to some of the groups were also small images of worshipping bodhisattvas in kneeling positions with palms together in reverence.

The *parinirvana* scenes were the largest image groups. In Cave 148 of the high Tang, a 15.8-meter long image of Shakyamuni lying on his right side was constructed in the main room. Surrounding it stood seventy-two images—bodhisattvas, disciples, *vajrapani*, earthly kings, and high court officials—each a meter high. Cave 158 (fig. 13) of the mid-Tang is similar to Cave 148 in scale.

Tang dynasty Cave 96, built in the second year of the Yanzai era (695), and Cave 130, built between the ninth year of the Kaiyuan era (721) and the Tianbao era (742–56), are noteworthy. Both contain colossal sculptures. The figure in Cave 96 is 35.5 meters tall while the one in Cave 130 is 27.3 meters tall. Their bodies are constructed of rock at their core, followed by layers of clay stucco and pigments.

A transitional period, the Sui dynasty was comparatively short. Though the art of painted sculpture had seen important achievements, there remained many areas for improvement. The figures' heads were large, shoulders wide, and legs short, and the sculpture lacked dynamic rhythm and uniformity. These inconsistencies all disappeared from Tang sculpture. Tang figures are better proportioned, more elegantly and colorfully dressed, more individualistic, and truer to life.

C. Wall Paintings

The wall paintings of the early Sui dynasty adhere to the three-register (top, middle, and bottom) layout of the Northern Dynasties. In the late Sui and early Tang periods, the layout changed to a two-register format. The upper register typically depicts a preaching Buddha, the Thousand Buddhas, or an illustration of a Buddhist sutra; the lower register contains donors. Some cave walls in the early Tang are fully occupied by huge illustrations of Buddhist sutras. When Buddhist art became more secularized in the late Tang period, the layout of the caves changed dramatically. Traditional screen painting was introduced. The walls of a cave contain illustrations of two to four different Buddhist sutras. Each illustration is divided into two portions: the upper portion, which represents a

Fig. 13. Figure of Shakyamuni lying on his right side in *parinirvana* from Mogao Cave 158. Mid-Tang period (781–848). Painted clay.
莫高窟中唐第158窟彩塑涅槃卧佛

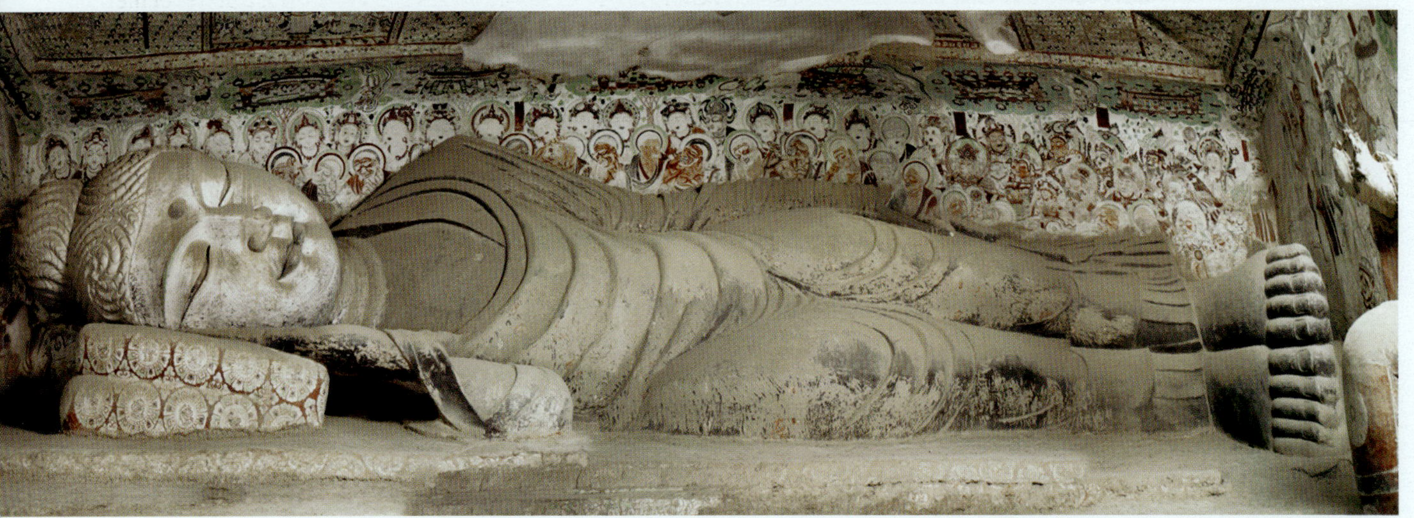

scene of a Dharma sermon, and a lower portion, which narrates stories from a Buddhist sutra in the style of a screen painting. Portraits of donors fill the walls of the corridor connecting the anteroom and the main room; they are also found at the lower portion of the front wall of the main room.

The wall paintings of this period are very rich in content and can be classified into the following categories:

1. ***Images of Buddhas and bodhisattvas.*** Besides depictions of preaching Buddhas, there emerged numerous portrayals of other deities, such as Bhaisajyaguru (the Medicine Buddha), Vairochana, Avalokiteshvara (Bodhisattva of Compassion), Mahasthamaprapta, Ksitigarbha, and Tantric bodhisattvas (in esoteric Buddhism), due to the growing diversification of Buddhist beliefs.

2. ***Sutra illustrations.*** These depict the contents of a specific Buddhist sutra in narrative form. There are more than thirty themes in Dunhuang caves, including the *Amitabha Sutra* (Sutra of the Buddha of Boundless Light), the *Amitayuh Sutra* (Sutra of Infinite Life), *Amitayurdhyana Sutra* (Sutra of Meditation on Amitabha), *Maitreya Sutra*, *Medicine Buddha Sutra*, etc. The center is occupied by a Dharma sermon Buddha flanked by bodhisattvas and other divine beings: lively *apsaras* depicted as heavenly musicians and dancers.

3. ***Paintings of Buddhist legends.*** These paintings, which depict historical Buddhist stories, began in the Sui dynasty and reached their zenith in the late Tang. The stories or legends came from India, Nepal, Pakistan, and central China. There are more than ten kinds of stories, including those of miracles, eminent monks, divine appearances, the Pure Land, and other sacred settings.

4. ***Donors portraits.*** Donors include monks, nuns, local lords and nobles, civil and military officials, craftsmen, herders, travelers, attendants, servants, maids, and other devotees. During the Sui and Tang period, portraits of donors grew gradually larger and reached life-size proportions in some caves built in the late Tang. These portraits were painted with close attention to details.

5. ***Decorative patterns.*** Decorative patterns during this transitional period in the history of Dunhuang decorative art developed from the "architectural style" of the Northern Dynasties to the "ceiling panel style" of the Sui and to the "fabric style" of the Tang. They grew in variety and in complexity and reached the peak of their development in the Tang dynasty, when decorations were modeled on the complicated patterns used on fabrics such as brocade, satin, and silk.

III. Cave Art of the Five Dynasties, Song, Western Xia, and Yuan

A. Architectural Forms of the Caves

The cave architecture of this period continued in the style of the late Tang assembly cave with a niche in the back wall of the main room or a square altar set up to the middle of the room. The caves with central altars built in the Five Dynasties and the Song are larger than those of the previous period (Caves 427, 431, 444, and 437). In the Western Xia (Xixia) and Yuan dynasty, the altar in an assembly cave became round and multi-layered (Mogao Cave 465 and Yulin Cave 3).

B. Painted Sculpture

Most of the sculptural images made in this period have been severely damaged. What remain are only those in Cave 261 of the Five Dynasties, Cave 55 of the Song dynasty, and Cave 246 of the Western Xia. The sculpture of this period carried on the themes and style of the Tang tradition, but lacked the Tang spirit. There are some new images, such as the principal group in Cave 55, consisting of three forms of Maitreya, and a heavenly donor girl in the Western Xia Cave 491.

C. Wall Paintings

The majority of Five Dynasties and Song wall paintings are large compositions. Although their contents remained the same as those of the previous period, their size increased due to larger dedications. Some of the new subjects include the depiction of a Manjushri in Cave 220 and the illustrations of the *Avalokiteshvara Sutra* and the *Eight Stupa Sutra* in Cave 76. Although declining in number, type, and variety, a new feature was added to the wall paintings in this period. Almost every painting has cartouches that describe the content of each anecdote. In the Western Xia and the Yuan period, most illustrations of traditional themes fell into decline and some ceased to be depicted. The composition of the painting became more schematic. Some paintings show the strong impact of the Song dynasty painting style of central China (Yulin Caves 2, 3, and 29) and the arts of Tibetan esoteric Buddhism.

1. ***Paintings of Buddhist legends.*** These kinds of paintings continued to develop in this period and are found in more than forty caves. Depictions of auspicious signs and omens are painted on the cave ceiling (Mogao Caves 98 and 454). In some caves, multiple narratives share the same wall (Mogao Cave 72). Paintings of Buddhist sacred places reflect the strong influence of landscape painting from central China

2. ***Deities.*** Large images of the Four Heavenly Guardians, Eight Divine Beings, Eight Dragon Kings—all defenders of the Law—were executed during the Five Dynasties and Song periods. In the Song and Western Xia periods, large paintings of arrayed attendant bodhisattvas and the Sixteen Arhats were new additions.

3. ***Paintings of jataka tales,* avadana *tales, and historical anecdotes.*** Although small in number, these paintings are gigantic compositions; they are painted in the lower portion of the walls in some large caves built in the Five Dynasties and Song periods.

4. ***Portraits of donors.*** Donor portraits increased in number during the Five Dynasties and Song periods, and they appear much larger than those of the previous period. For example, the king of Khotan (Yutian) in Cave 98 is 2.9 meters tall. In the donor paintings of the Western Xia and Yuan, personages of other nationalities appear in costumes indigenous to their respective kingdoms.

5. ***Decorative patterns.*** Five Dynasties decorative patterns used for ceiling panels were inherited from the Tang. At the apex of the ceiling, a lotus flower is encircled by writhing dragons; borders are decorated with scroll designs and fret patterns. In the Song and Western Xia, some of the dragons are raised in relief and gilded. Some ceilings are decorated with medallions at the apex. Among the medallion designs are intersecting *vajras*[20] and Dharma wheels; on the edges of the medallion are fret, scroll, or pearl patterns. Decorative motifs of the Yuan dynasty, in addition to employing Western Xia features, show influences from secular culture and Tibetan esoteric Buddhism.

In short, from the Five Dynasties to the early Song, wall painting carried on the Tang artistic tradition, producing many worthy works of landscape, narrative, and portraiture with individual characteristics. The paintings of this period are characterized by full figures, warm colors, and unrestrained, dynamic lines. During the Song dynasty, wall painting fell into a decline. The figures look stereotypical and less than animated; the colors are monotonous and lines weak. The figure paintings of the Western Xia combined the styles of central China and the Dangxiang nationality.[21]

The art of the Yuan dynasty consists of two different styles. One is represented by the image of the thousand-armed and thousand-eyed Avalokiteshvara (Bodhisattva of Compassion) in Mogao Cave 3. The figure is drawn with tremulous strokes, bent-reed strokes, and unfluctuating, continuous line; colored lightly and elegantly with wash, it reveals the standard high skills of Chinese painting. The other style appears in the murals of Mogao Cave 465. These show a strong presence of the art of Sakyapa, a Tibetan Buddhist order. The figures bear some characteristics of Indian and Nepalese painting. They are painted with straight, clean iron-wire line and colored with black, white, green, and other rich, heavy colors. They evoke a feeling of mystery and awe. This style originated in the artistic tradition of Tibetan esoteric Buddhism.

IV. The Significance of the Art of Dunhuang Cave Shrines

Although the art of Dunhuang Cave Shrines is largely based on Buddhist literature in its content, it cannot be severed from its historical and social circumstances. From this perspective, the art from a thousand years of creativity at Dunhuang reveals some idea of life in its ancient society and manifests a thousand years of a rich cultural tradition. The Dunhuang Cave Shrines are not only a treasure house of art, but are in themselves a cultural treasure with historic, artistic, scientific, and technological value.

A. Historical Significance

Although little has been written about Dunhuang's long history, its influential local families have left accurate information about themselves, their relationship with neighboring nationalities, and western religions in thousands of donor images, paintings, and donor inscriptions. From these images and records we learn of the deep involvement of eminent local families—Yin, Suo, Li, Ju, Zhang, and Cao—in cave construction, their complex interrelationships, and their connections with neighboring nationalities. These are invaluable materials for the study of Dunhuang under the reign of Zhang and Cao's Insurrection Army Government. We can also learn about the extent of involvement neighboring powers had in the life of Dunhuang. These images and paintings also provide

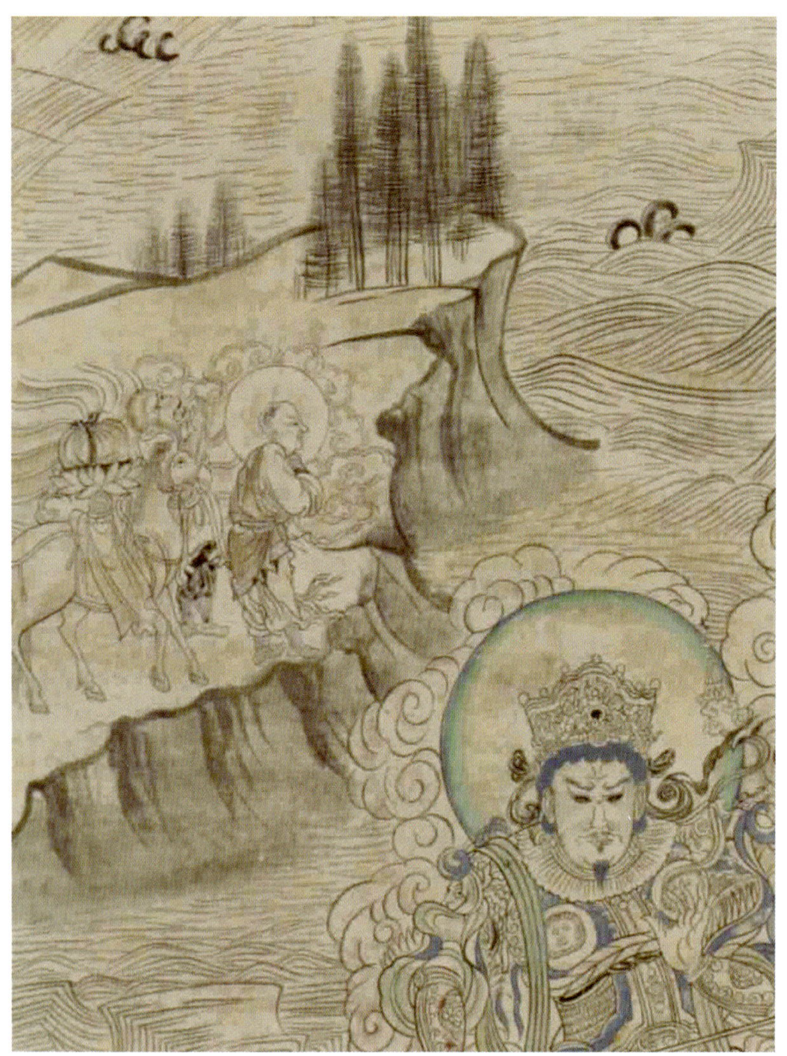

Fig. 14. Xuanzang on his journey to the west, detail of the Samantabhadra mural from Yulin Cave 3. Western Xia dynasty (1038–1227). 榆林西夏第3窟普贤变壁画中玄奘西行图

information about the *yiwei* honor guard and *nubi* servant systems of the Tang dynasty, the Tibetan official system, and the Insurrection Army's administrative style.

The ancient economic life of Dunhuang—including farming, harvesting, fishing, domestic animal breeding, and hunting—is evident in motifs found in illustrations of jataka tales, Buddhist legends, Maitreya's paradise, *Futian jing*,[22] and the *Lankavatara Sutra*,[23] as well as donor portraits and inscriptions. Indications of the arts industries can be found, including casting, wine brewing, pottery, weaving, knitting, leather processing, shoe making, painting, sculpting, carpentry, masonry, cave excavating, jewelry making, and bow making. Commercial enterprises evident in visual and written records include slaughterhouses, meat markets, wine houses, inns, gold and silver trade, lumber mills, and archery bow-making workshops. According to the manuscripts found in the Library Cave more than twenty kinds of crafts were practiced. The cave-temple murals and the Library Cave manuscripts together give us a clear picture of the handicraft industry and commerce in medieval Dunhuang.

Illustrations of the *Lotus Sutra* and *Parinirvana Sutra* present information on ancient military training, expeditions, conquering, defense and offence, and weaponry. The wall paintings also provide details on ancient sports, including mounted archery, target shooting, equestrian techniques, galloping, wrestling, weight lifting, chess, martial arts, swimming, feather-ball kicking, etc.

Dunhuang was once a hub of east-west trade on the Silk Road. Some paintings record this historical role. For example, a painting in Cave 296 of the Northern Zhou depicts a foreign merchant with a prominent nose and deep-set eyes leading a loaded camel on one side of a bridge while a Chinese merchant on a horse, escorting a team of loaded donkeys, rides on the other side of the bridge. The Silk Road was not always safe. A *Lotus Sutra* illustration in Sui period Cave 420 tells a story of highway robbery: merchants with teams of camels and donkeys loaded with silk being robbed by armed bandits.

The Silk Road was not only a trade route, but also a channel of diplomatic and cultural exchange. Some murals depict these activities. Cave 323, dated to the Tang dynasty, has a painting of Zhang Qian, a famous Western Han diplomat who was dispatched to the Western Regions. Wall paintings portraying Wang Xuance, Tang ambassador to India, are found in Cave 98 of the Five Dynasties and Cave 454 of the Song. The deeds of Liu Sahe, an eminent monk who ventured west in search of the Buddhist Dharma, are found in Caves 231, 237, 98, 61, and 72. The famous story of Xuanzang, a high monk of the Tang, is told in Mogao Cave 126 and Yulin Caves 2, 3 (fig. 14), and 29. There are also wall paintings depicting the activities of abbots from western China, such as An Shigao, Kang Senghui, and Fu Tudeng, in Caves 323, 9, 108, and 454 of the Tang and Song dynasties.

Scenes of daily life in ancient society can be seen in various murals. These include activities such as births, weddings, and funerals. Illustrations of the *Maitreya Sutra* generally include scenes of weddings. There were two marriage customs widely practiced at Dunhuang in the Tang and Song period: one is rooted in the Han Chinese tradition, in which the man would send betrothal gifts to the bride's family and bring the bride home to marry into his family; the other is influenced by the custom of the Western Regions in which the groom would marry into the bride's family. The mural scenes of weddings and marriage usually include the whole wedding process.

From the narratives of Buddhist legends and illustrations of the *Parinirvana Sutra* of the Northern Zhou through the Song, one can find scenes of funerals and burials: body visitation, memorial service, funeral procession, burial, and mourning after the burial.

Most of the painted sculptural images and wall paintings in the Dunhuang caves are Buddhist in content. The sculpture and wall paintings of Buddhist deities, jataka tales, Buddhist historical anecdotes, illustrations of various sutras, and numerous paintings of mythical figures provide us with a large body of material for the systematic and comprehensive study of Buddhism, including its ideas, orders and sects, beliefs, propagation, and especially its influence on Chinese life and its assimilation into greater Chinese culture. They also provide valuable information about India, Western Asia, Central Asia, and Xinjiang.

B. Artistic Value

The art of the Dunhuang Cave Shrines, with more than a thousand years of history and development, is rich in content and style. It is a combination of the local artistic tradition of the Han and Jin periods, the imported styles of the Southern and Northern Dynasties, Tang and Song styles from central China, and the foreign artistic traditions of India, Central Asia, and Western Asia. It is a product of cultural and artistic exchanges between Dunhuang, central China, and the West.

Wall paintings in the Dunhuang caves fall under the following genres: figures, landscapes, animals, and decorative patterns. Each genre can be studied on its own, because each has had a history of more than a thousand years of development. The most valuable works are the paintings done before the Song dynasty. They are extremely rare. No museum in the world has any collection of these paintings.

More than two hundred caves have murals containing musical themes. There are more than five hundred musical ensembles of various kinds, thousands of musicians, and more than forty kinds of musical instruments totaling 4,500 pieces depicted in the wall paintings of Dunhuang's caves. In addition, many music manuscripts have been discovered in the Library Cave. These documents provide invaluable material for the study of the history of Chinese music and of the musical exchange between China and regions to the west.

Dance is another art form abundantly portrayed in the murals; most of the wall paintings contain scenes of various kinds of dance. There are dancing scenes from secular events, such as wedding banquets and other festivals, and scenes from court life as well as supernatural scenes, such as dancing *apsaras* and other heavenly musicians and dancers. From the Library Cave, we have also found manuscripts of dance compositions. The art of dance is an ephemeral art, difficult to preserve. So we know little of the dance movements of the past. But in these caves, a large number of beautiful dancing images have been preserved. These caves can be rightly called a museum of ancient dance.

Dunhuang also offers rich material for the study of ancient architecture. There are thousands of buildings of various kinds painted in the murals dating from the Sixteen Kingdoms to the Western Xia. There are monasteries, city walls, palaces, watchtowers, huts, domes, tents, inns and restaurants, slaughterhouses, beacon towers, bridges, prisons, and tombs. They have also left rich information about building components and decorative details, such as recessed beams, pillars, windows, and basic framework. There is little recorded about Chinese architecture from the Southern Dynasties to the high Tang elsewhere; Dunhuang wall paintings have captured many architectural forms of this period and helped fill gaps in our knowledge. In addition, more than 800 caves are extant, built in different periods and forms; five of their wooden verandahs, built in the Tang and Song, and their stupas are all precious original material for the study of ancient architecture.

C. Scientific and Technological Significance

There are many farming scenes in the paintings of jataka tales, episodes from the life of the historical Shakyamuni Buddha, Maitreya, and the *Lotus Sutra*. These scenes offer a glimpse into the agricultural life of Dunhuang from the Northern Zhou to the Western Xia, a span of 600 years. The farming activities portrayed in these paintings include plowing, seed broadcasting and planting, harvesting, thrashing, and winnowing. The tools consist of straight shaft plows, curved shaft plows, iron plowshares, grinders, forks, hoes, spades, shoulder posts, steelyards, jars, and measures—*dou* (a unit of dry measure for grain, equivalent of one deciliter), *sheng* (a unit of dry measure for grain, equivalent of one liter), and *hu* (a dry measure, originally equal to 10 *dou*, later 5 *dou*). The most valuable image is that of a curved shaft plow from an illustration of the *Maitreya Sutra* in the high Tang Cave 445; the depth of the plow can be adjusted in this tool. It is the only picture that records the most advanced farming tool used in that period.

Dunhuang cave murals also record transportation methods used in medieval times, including oxen, horses, camels, mules, donkeys, elephants, boats, ships, carriages, sedan chairs, and imperial carriages. The most significant ancient Chinese contributions to the field of transportation are the invention of one-wheeled vehicles, horse harnesses (chest harness and shoulder harness), spurs, and horseshoes. Their images have been well preserved in the wall paintings at Dunhuang.

Murals in both the Western Wei Cave 285 and the Northern Zhou Cave 296 tell the story of five hundred robbers regaining their eyesight and converting to Buddhism. There are battle scenes of horsemen fighting foot-soldiers (bandits). The horses in the pictures all wear armor and other protective gear for battle. The horse armor is ancient China's unique contribution to world military gear.

In the figures of deities from the Sui to the Western Xia and in illustrations of the *Medicine Buddha Sutra*, glassware is seen held in the hands of Buddhas, bodhisattvas, and disciples or placed on offering tables. There are glass bowls, alms bowls, cups, bottles, and trays. They are transparent, featuring different pale tones of blue, green, and brown. Their shapes, colors, and decorative patterns represent the styles of Rome and the Sassanians of Western Asia. These paintings not only reflect the technical characteristics of early glass, but also tell the story of glass trade between China and the West.

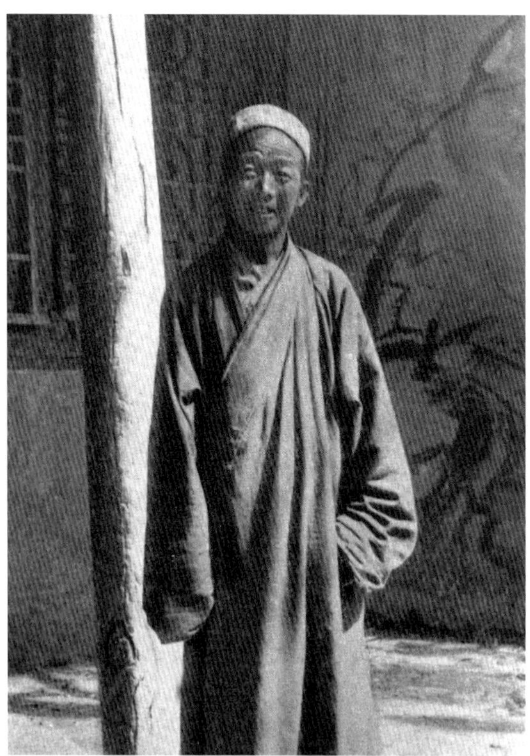

Fig. 15. Daoist priest Wang Yuanlu (1849–1931).
王圆箓道士

Dunhuang Library Cave

On June 22, 1900 (26th year of the Guangxu reign in the Qing dynasty, 26th day, 5th month), Wang Yuanlu (fig. 15), a Daoist priest practicing in the Lower Monastery of Mogao Grottoes, stumbled upon the Library Cave (Cave 17) while cleaning Cave 16. He discovered a cultural treasure trove of more than fifty thousand objects, including Buddhist sutras, assorted manuscripts, embroidery, paintings on silk, and other religious objects. His path-breaking discovery provided the world with a large number of study materials for the history, geography, religion, economics, politics, language, literature, art, and science of China and Western Asia (fig. 16). These documents have been affectionately called the "Encyclopedia of the Middle Ages" and the "ocean of ancient knowledge."

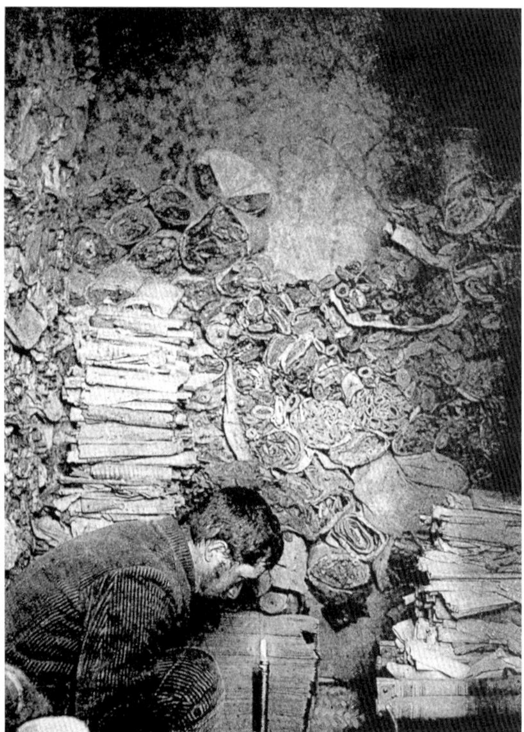

Fig. 16. Early 20th-century French sinologist and explorer Paul Pelliot (1878–1945) in the Library Cave (Cave 17).
二十世纪初，法国学者伯希和在藏经洞

Ninety percent of the materials are Buddhist manuscripts. The earliest handwritten sutra found in the Library Cave is an *avadana* (parable). At the end of the book, there is an inscription indicating, "Completed on the seventeenth day of the third month of the first year of Ganlu." The first year of Ganlu refers to the Ganlu reign of the Former Qin (359 CE). This is also the oldest document among all the manuscripts. The Library held all kinds of Buddhist classics, including the *Sutrapitaka*, *Vinayapitaka*, and *Abhidharmapitaka*.[24] But the most valuable documents are the classics of Chan (Zen) Buddhism and the manuscripts of the Three Stages Sect (a Buddhist sect in the Sui and Tang China, 6th to 10th centuries). The jewel among the Chan documents is the earliest version of the *Analects of the Sixth Chan Patriarch Huineng*, which differs in many ways from the version circulated after the Song dynasty. The works of the Three Stages Sect include *Three Stages Dharma*, *Secrets of Three Stages Dharma*, and *Dharma of the*

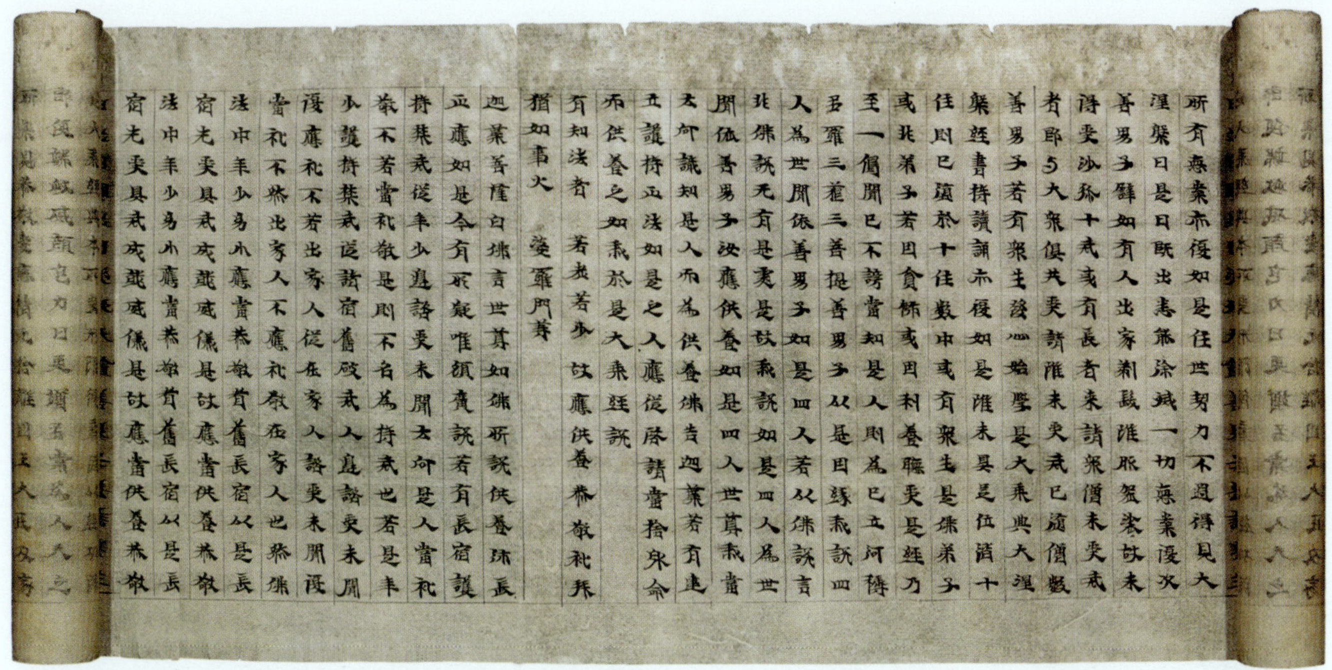

Fig. 17. Apocryphal sutra from the Library Cave. Northern Dynasties (420–589). Ink on paper. Collection of the Dunhuang Academy.
敦煌研究院收藏，藏经洞出土的北朝的大般涅槃如来性品写经

Three Realms. Their discovery adds new material to the study of the history of Chinese Buddhism.

The Library also held many lost Buddhist works (documents that are not collected in the *Tripitaka*). The discovery of these missing documents helps complete gaps in the *Tripitaka* after the Song dynasty.[25]

Some of the manuscripts are apocryphal sutras written first in Chinese but given a Central Asian and Indian pedigree to lend an air of authenticity (fig. 17). This phenomenon reflects a unique feature of Chinese Buddhism. These documents are invaluable for the study of the development of Buddhism in China.

Among the manuscripts are many written in languages other than Chinese, such as Sanskrit, early Tibetan, Huihu,[26] Yutian, and Turfan. There are also some bilingual scriptures. These bilingual documents are extremely valuable for research on the sources of Chinese translations of Buddhist classics and as a check on the accuracy of translations. Moreover, the Buddhist scriptures found in Dunhuang's Library Cave, especially the calligraphic examples produced in the Sui and Tang period, were well proofread and, thus, contain few errors. They may serve as standard texts for checking on the accuracy of the scriptures printed after the Tang.

Included in the library holdings are documents of the local monasteries. They consist of asset records, lists of monks' and nuns' names, official papers, reports on religious activities, and speeches for different occasions. They are rare materials for research on monastic life in Dunhuang.

Although Daoism was not as popular as Buddhism in Dunhuang, it flourished for a short period of time in the early Tang dynasty because the early Tang monarchs worshiped Laozi, the founder of Daoism. Therefore, a large number of Daoist classics were also found in the Library Cave. There are approximately five hundred scrolls, mostly handwritten. In addition to Buddhist and Daoist documents, there are Manichean and Nestorian papers, which help us to understand the cultural exchanges between China and Persia.

The works of history and geography and private and official documents in the Library are first-hand material for the study of medieval society. Some ancient books of history, long believed to have been lost, were found in the Library collection. There are books of local history that are valuable for the study of ancient Dunhuang, such as *Shazhou Yizhou dizhi canjuan* (An Incomplete History of Shazhou and Yizhou), *Shouchang xiandi jing* (Territory of the Shouchang county seat), and the *Shazhou dizhi* (Shazhou Chronicles). Some works of geography have also attracted a great deal of attention, such as *Shazhou dudu fu tujing* (Maps of Shazhou).

Little has been written about the history of Dunhuang under the rule of the Insurrection Army, and what has been recorded in existing literature contains many errors. Preserved in the Library Cave are some one hundred documents that are a rich source of material about this part of Dunhuang's history.

A great number of Chinese literary classics have also been well preserved. They include Confucian classics and collections of poems, lyrics, prose poems, novels, and folk drama. Most of the literary holdings in the Library are

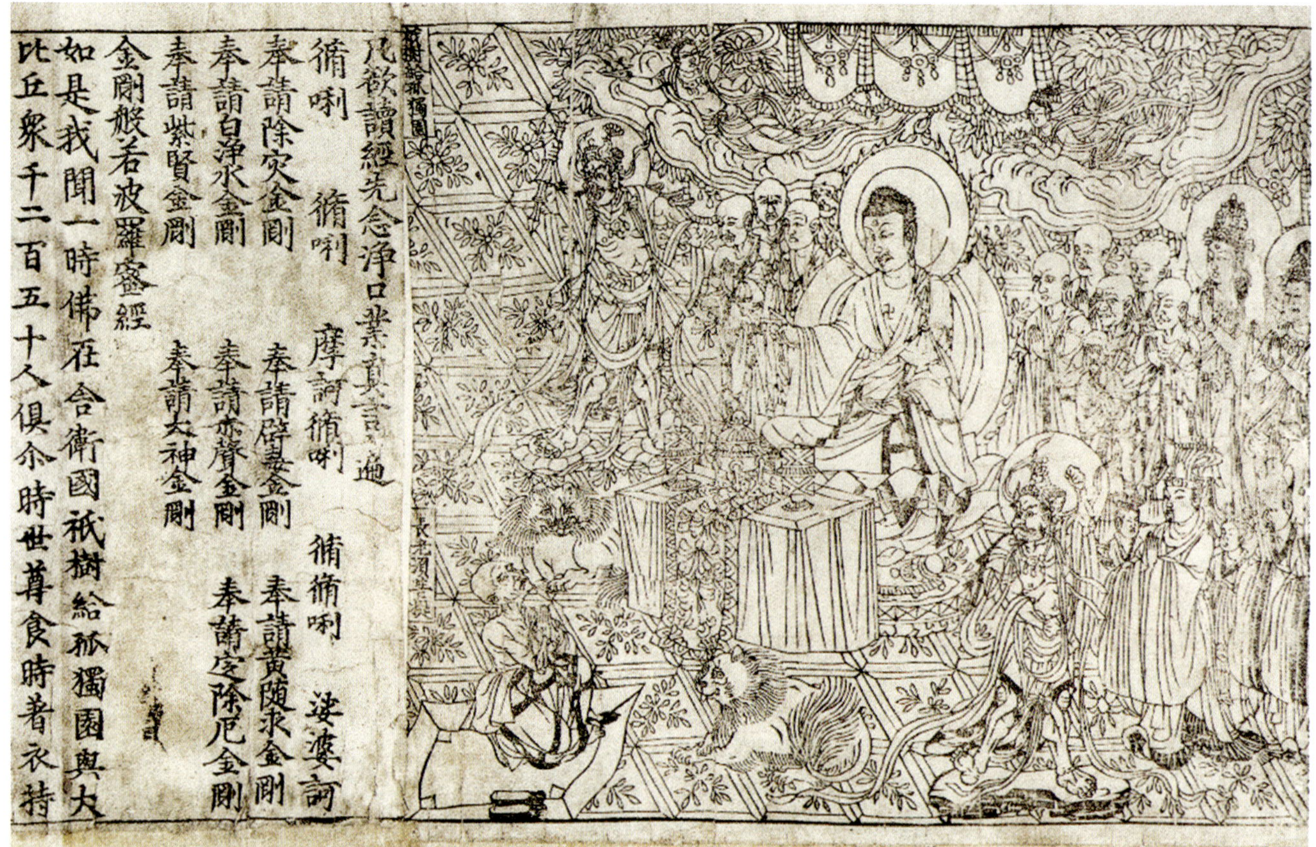

Fig. 18. ***Diamond Sutra*** **from the Library Cave. Tang dynasty, ninth year of Xiantong [868]. Woodblock printed scroll, ink on paper. The British Library Or.8210/P.2. © The British Library Board.** 英国图书馆收藏，藏经洞出土的唐代咸通九年（868年）雕版印刷的《金刚经》

works of folk literature, and most of the numerous poems found belong to the Tang and Five Dynasties. The importance of the Confucian classics found in the Library is their role as standard texts for editing modern versions.

The most significant finding of the literary material is *bianwen*, a unique literary genre that combines verse and a prose component that would be spoken and sung. As a genre, it was unknown before the discovery of the Library Cave. Its discovery fills a gap in the study of Chinese literature. There are also some important linguistic treatises found in the Library collection. They include texts on rhymes, phonology and semantics, and lexicology.[27]

The Library has many works of science and technology ranging from mathematics to astronomy, medicine, paper-making, and printing. Works on math include the *Jiujiu chengfa ge* (Nine times nine multiplication song), *Suanjing* (Classic of mathematical calculations), and *Licheng suanjing* (Classic of quick calculations). They are all the earliest handwritten documents on math in China.

There are many star maps in the Library collection. These maps are evidence of ancient China's advanced knowledge of astronomy. In ancient times, astronomy and the calendar were closely related. Dunhuang's calendars are made by local astrologers. One calendar that is worth a special note here is the one made in the third year of Yongxi during the Song (986); it used the week system of the Christian West. At least sixty volumes of medical works have been found in the Library Cave as well. There are four kinds of medical works: principles of medicine, acupuncture, dictionary of medicinal herbs, and prescriptions. They offer many new materials regarding medical diagnosis and treatment.

Since the manuscripts cover the period from the fourth to the twelfth century, they can serve as a witness to the history of Chinese papermaking and printing. *The Diamond Sutra* found in the Library is dated to the ninth year of the Xiantong era during the Tang (868) and is the earliest woodblock print, evidence of the Chinese invention of this technology (fig. 18).

The Dunhuang Cave Shrines, with its large number of caves, sculptures, murals, manuscripts, and other religious and artistic objects, have attracted the interest of scholars all over the world. The interest persists to this day, and the study of these art and cultural treasures has become a unique and independent discipline by itself. Dunhuang studies will occupy an important place in the fields of humanities and social science and will have a splendid future.

NOTES

1. Also known as Qarkilik, Cherchen or Qarqan, Khotan, and Yarkand, respectively.
2. This refers to the empire of the Yuezhi, a powerful nomadic people who lived west of the Gansu area during the Han dynasty. They eventually moved west and founded the Kushan empire.
3. Mentioned in historical records, this is Parthia. The Parthians, an ancient Iranian tribe, founded an extensive empire in the late third to second century BCE.
4. This ancient kingdom is better known in the West by its Uighur name, Karashahr (meaning "Black City").
5. This is the modern Chinese name for Kashgar, located in Xinjiang.
6. Described in Han dynasty records, this is a country located in the Ferghana Basin, modern Kirgizstan.
7. This is the name of a federation of nomadic tribes centered in the region of Tashkent in Uzbekistan and Shymkent in Kazakhstan, northwest of Dayuan.
8. This was the name given by the Han Chinese to Bactria, a region south of the Amu Darya and west of Gandhara. After 135 BCE, it was invaded and occupied by the Kushans (Dayuezhi).
9. Ji Xianlin 季羡林, "Dunhuang xue, Tulufan xue zai Zhongguo wenhuashi shang de diwei he yong" 敦煌学、吐鲁番学在中国文化史上的地位和作用 [Status and role of Dunhuang studies and Turfan studies in Chinese cultural history], *Hongqi* 红旗 [Red Flag] 1986.3: 138.
10. 《魏书·释老志》:"敦煌地接西域，道俗交得，其旧式村坞相属，多有塔寺"。
11. Li Yi (style name Kerang) was a Tang dynasty native of Dunhuang, a noteworthy military officer, and patron of the Li family temple, near Cave 332. He purportedly wrote the text for the now-fragmentary stele (dated 698) from Cave 332. The text is preserved in the form of rubbings and in manuscript form. For a transcription, see Sonya S. Lee, *Surviving Nirvana: Death of the Buddha in Chinese Visual Culture* (Hong Kong: Hong University Press, 2010), Appendix 3, pp. 278–81.
12. 伊吾之西，波斯以东，朝贡不绝，商旅相继。
13. *Dangxiangqiang* refers to the Tangut people, founders of the Western Xia dynasty in northwestern China.
14. In Indian mythology, *apsaras* are ethereal female beings associated with entertainment, often depicted flying.
15. Tales of the previous lives of the Buddha.
16. A Chinese foot is by modern standards exactly 1/3 meter (approx. 1.094 ft.).
17. These are the three Buddhas of the past, present, and future.
18. That is, absolute reality.
19. That is, the body of the Buddha.
20. A ritual object, originally a short metal weapon, with prongs at either end. Its name means "thunderbolt" or "diamond" in Sanskrit.
21. That is, Tangut people.
22. That is, the *Foshuo zhude futian jing* 佛說諸德福田經 (Scripture of the Field of Blessings and Merit).
23. *Scripture of the Descent into Lanka* (capital city of Ravana).
24. These are the three categories of texts that make up the Buddhist canon known as the *Tripitaka*, or the "three baskets": the *Sutrapitaka* (Buddha's sermons); *Vinayapitaka* (code of monastic conduct); and *Abhidharmapitaka*, (philosophy, metaphysics, psychology).
25. The *Tripitaka* is the earliest collection of Buddhist writings in the Pali language, recorded by the third century BCE.
26. This is the Tang name for the Uighur ethnic group.
27. Among the titles are the *Qieyun* 切韵 (a rhyme dictionary), *Maoshi yin* 毛诗音 (phonetic annotations to the Mao version of the Book of Songs), *Chuci yin* 楚辞音 (phonetic glossary of the Chuci), *Zhengming yaolu* 正名要录 (Essential record of rectified names [a dictionary]), *Yupian* 玉篇 (a dictionary compiled ca. 543), and so on.

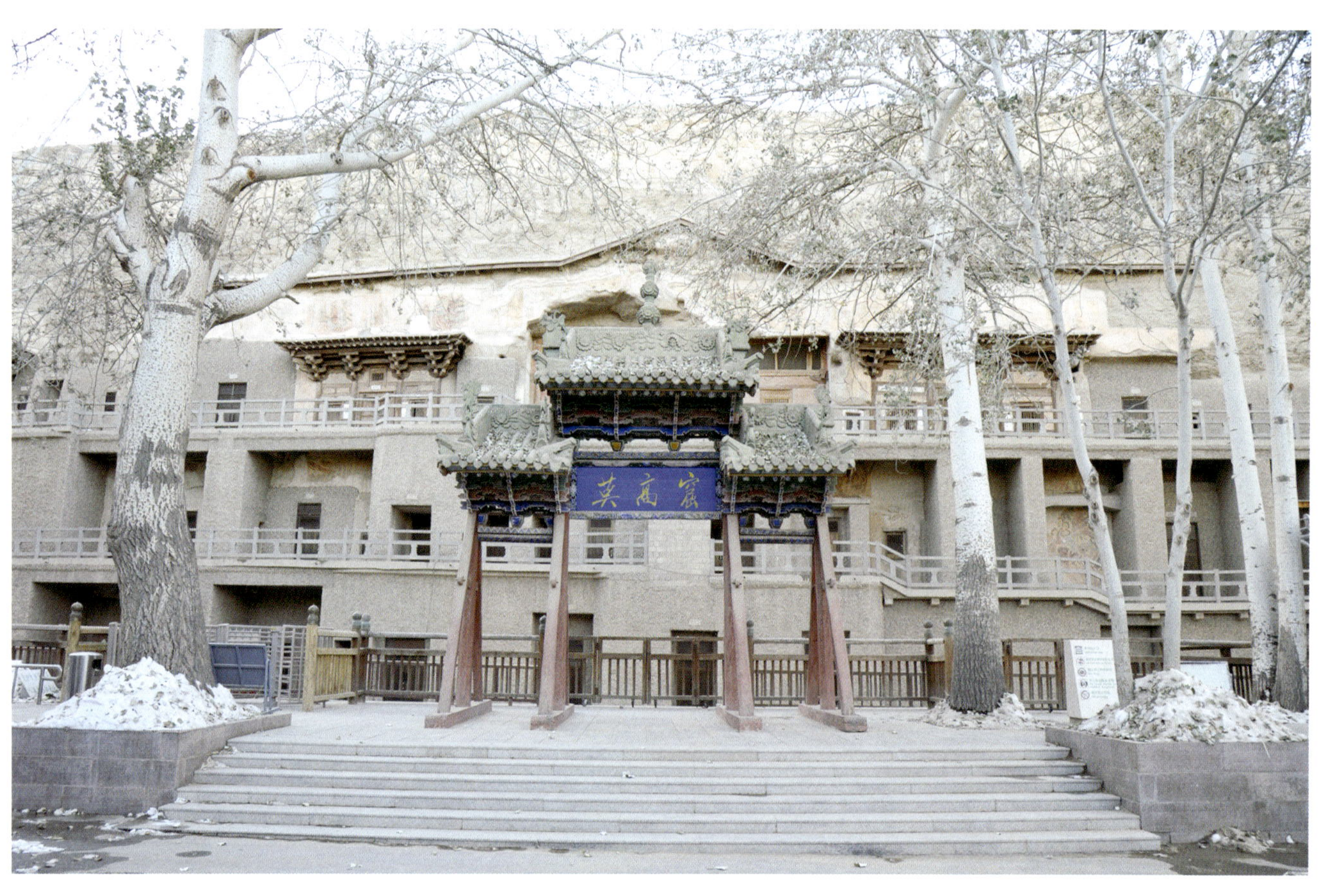

Gate to the Mogao Grottoes. Photo by Perry Hu, 2012. 莫高窟牌楼，胡维智摄

辉煌灿烂的敦煌石窟艺术

樊锦诗

敦煌的地理和历史

敦煌，是位于甘肃省河西走廊最西端的城市，北有北山（马鬃山），南有南山（祁连山），是一个冲积而成的绿洲，由南山流来的古氐置水（今党河）泛滥所造成，绿洲周围多戈壁和沙丘。它的地理位置十分重要，东接中原，西邻新疆，自汉代以来，一直是中原通西域交通要道的"咽喉之地"，是著名的丝绸之路上的重镇。由敦煌出发，向东通过河西走廊去古都长安、洛阳。敦煌西去阳关，沿昆仑山北麓。经鄯善（若羌）、且末、于阗（和田）至莎车，逾葱岭（帕米尔）进入大月氏、安息等国，是为丝路南道；由敦煌出玉门关北行，沿天山南麓，经车师前工庭（吐鲁番）、焉耆、龟兹（库车）、到疏勒（喀什）、越葱岭，进入大宛、康居、大夏，是为丝路北道。敦煌总扼两关，控制着东来西往的商旅。位于丝绸之路上的敦煌，成为东西方贸易的中心和中转站。史书称敦煌是"华戎所交一大都会"，西域商胡与中原汉族商客在这里从事中原的丝绸和瓷器，西域的珍宝，北方的驼马，与当地粮食的交易。与此同时，自汉代中西交通畅通以来，中原文化不断传播到敦煌，在这里深深扎了根。地接西域的敦煌，较早地就接受了发源于印度的佛教文化。西亚、中亚文化随着印度佛教文化的东传，也不断传到了敦煌。中西不同的文化都在这里汇聚、碰撞、交融。著名的敦煌学者季羡林先生指出："世界上历史悠久、地域广阔、自成体系、影响深远的文化体系只有四个：中国、印度、希腊、伊斯兰，再没有第五个；而这四个文化体系汇流的地方只有一个，就是中国的敦煌和新疆地区，再没有第二个。"季先生的论说充分说明敦煌所处的地理位置在历史上的重要性。

敦煌距今已有2000多年的历史。秦汉之前，居住着月支、乌孙等少数民族。西汉初，漠北的匈奴赶走月支，占领敦煌。元狩二年（前121）西汉军队打败河西匈奴，敦煌与河西走廊归入西汉王朝版图。元鼎六年（前111）在敦煌设郡，与酒泉、张掖、武威并称河西四郡。在敦煌之北修筑了长城，在西部设立了阳关、玉门关，敦煌成为西域进入河西走廊与中原的门户和军事重镇。为了巩固敦煌的战略要地，从内地移民来此定居，调遣士兵屯田戎守，西汉王朝对敦煌的经营与开发，确立了敦煌在历史上的重要地位。经过东汉王朝与曹魏政权的继续经营与开发，敦煌在较长时期内保持相对稳定，成为丝绸之路上一处重要的商品交易中心和粮食生产基地。中原文化在这里生根和发展，儒家经典得到传播。产生于印度的佛教文化也传到了敦煌，西晋时号称"敦煌菩萨"的译经大师竺法护及其弟子在此译经传教。

十六国时期，先后由前凉、前秦、后凉、西凉、北凉五个政权统治敦煌。此时中原大乱，战乱频繁。唯敦煌相对平安，人口增加，中原与河西走廊的百姓避乱在此，中原汉晋文化在敦煌与河西走廊得以保存和延续。敦煌产生一批著名儒家学者，他们设馆讲学，著书立说。中原传统文化在敦煌已十分成熟。与此同时，西行求法与东来传教的佛教僧人都经过敦煌，促进了敦煌佛教的发展。《魏书·释老志》说："敦煌地接西域，道俗交得，其旧式村坞相属，多有塔寺"。敦煌莫高窟应运而生。据唐代圣历元年（698）李克让修《莫高窟佛龛碑》记载："莫高窟者，厥初，秦建元二年（366）有沙门乐僔，戒行清虚，执心恬静，尝仗锡林野，行至此山，忽见金光，状有千佛……造窟一龛。次有法良禅师，从东届此，又于僔师窟侧更即营建，伽蓝之起，滥觞二僧。"此后，北魏宗室东阳王元太荣、北周贵族建平公于义先后出任瓜州（敦煌）刺史，信奉佛教，莫高窟的开窟造像活动逐渐发展兴盛起来。

隋代统一南北，击败西北的突厥和吐谷浑侵扰，保持丝路畅通，商贸繁盛。文帝和炀帝倡导佛教，令天下各州建造舍利塔，瓜州也在崇教寺（莫高窟）起塔，宫廷写经也传至敦煌。短暂的隋代，在敦煌大兴开窟之风。唐王朝前期扼制了西域最大的威胁西突厥的进犯，在西域设立安西都护和安西四镇。为加强军事防卫，在敦煌和河西走廊设立豆卢军、墨离军、玉门军、赤水军、建康军等河西十军，使敦煌经济得到稳步发展，丝绸之路全线畅通，"伊吾之西，波斯以东，朝贡不绝，商旅相继”。中西经济文化交流频繁。敦煌石窟的营造达到了极盛，敦煌文化进一步凝聚了来自中原的汉文化，以及来自印度、西亚、中亚的文化。

天宝十四载（755）发生安史之乱，唐王朝由盛而衰，吐蕃乘机攻占陇右、河西。建中二年（781）吐蕃占领沙州，推行吐蕃行政、经济制度和习俗，同时，大力扶植佛教，佛教势力迅速膨胀，推动了莫高窟继续兴建。

会昌二年（842），吐蕃内乱，势力大衰。大中二年（848）沙州张议潮乘机率兵起义，陆续收复伊、西、瓜、肃、甘、凉等十一州，并遣使奉表归唐，被唐王朝册封为归义军节度使，从此开始了归义军长达200多年的统治时期。张氏归义军政权恢复唐制，推行汉化，使敦煌的政局得到了稳定，佛教在张氏归义军政权的保护下，继续兴建寺院和石窟。宋干化四年（914），曹议金接替张承奉政权在瓜沙二州六镇地区重建归义军政权，一直保持与中原王朝的密切来往，接受中原王朝封号，奉中原为正朔，利用旧日唐朝在各族人民中的声威，以求在西北各民族中树立自己的地位，又以和亲的方式，东与甘州回鹘，西与西州回鹘、于阗政权结好。曹氏政权与中原王朝及周围少数民族政权建立的良好关系，不仅保持境内相对稳定的局面，且共保丝路畅通，促进了敦煌与中原和西域佛教文化的交流，为敦煌佛教艺术继续发展创造了条件。

宋景佑三年（1036）和南宋宝庆三年（1227），敦煌先后为党项羌和蒙古族占领。西夏和元蒙统治者笃信佛教，敦煌莫高窟作为佛教要地，依然受到重视，仍有建造。但随着海上丝绸之路的发展、陆上丝绸之路的衰落、元蒙疆域的扩大，敦煌失去了中西交通中转站与西域门户的重要地位。莫高窟也告衰落。

元代以后敦煌停止开窟，逐渐冷落荒废。明嘉靖七年（1528年）封闭嘉峪关，使敦煌成为边塞游牧之地。清康熙五十七年（1718）平定新疆，雍正元年（1723）在敦煌设沙州所，三年（1725）改沙州卫，并从甘肃各州移民敦煌屯田，重修沙州城。干隆二十五年（1760）改沙州卫为敦煌县，敦煌经济开始恢复。莫高窟开始被人们注意。清光绪二十六年（1900）发现了震惊世界的藏经洞。不幸的是，在晚清政府腐败无能、西方列强侵略中国的特定历史背景下，藏经洞文物发现后不久，英人斯坦因、法人伯希和、日人橘瑞超、俄人鄂登堡等西方探险家接踵而至敦煌，以不公正的手段，从王道士手中骗取大量藏经洞文物，致使藏经洞文物惨遭劫掠，绝大部分不幸流散，分藏于英、法、俄、日等国的众多公私收藏机构，仅有少部分保存于国内，造成中国文化史上的空前浩劫。

灿烂的敦煌石窟艺术

敦煌石窟，是敦煌地区石窟之总称，包括敦煌市的莫高窟、西千佛洞、安西县的榆林窟、东千佛洞、肃北县的五个庙石窟。这些石窟虽规模悬殊，但同在古敦煌郡境内，它们地域相近，内容相同，风格相似，同属敦煌石窟艺术范畴，人们通常将它们统称为敦煌石窟。现共有洞窟812个，分别为莫高窟735个、西千佛洞22个，榆林窟42个、东千佛洞7个、五个庙石窟6个。

敦煌石窟中首推世界历史文化遗产——莫高窟。它位于敦煌市东南25公里的鸣沙山东麓，前临宕泉，东向祁连山支脉三危山。自4至14世纪，连续开窟造像不止，形成南北长1680米的石窟群。现存历代营建的洞窟共735个，鳞次栉比分布于高15—30多米高的断崖上，上下分布1—4层不等。分为南北两区，其中南区的492个洞窟乃礼佛活动的场所，拥有彩塑2000多身，壁画45000多平方米，木构窟檐5座；北区的243个洞窟（另有5个洞窟已编号），乃僧侣修行、居住、瘗埋的场所，内有修行和生活设施土炕、灶坑、烟道、壁龛、灯台等，但多无彩塑和壁画。

敦煌石窟开凿于石质疏松的砾岩之上，无法精雕细刻，便采用泥塑彩绘和壁画的艺术形式。彩塑以人工制作的木架为骨，束以苇草、外敷草泥，通过塑造和描绘的结合，表现人体的肌肤，面部的表情，须发的蓬松，服饰的质地。壁画在整治过的石壁上，涂抹二至三层草泥，通过布局定位，起稿、涂色、定形，完成壁画形象的绘画。敦煌石窟艺术是集建筑、彩塑、壁画于一体的综合艺术。石窟建筑形制根据内容、功能之不同而定。彩塑是石窟艺术的主体，崇拜的主要偶像，置于石窟佛龛，或中心塔柱龛，或佛坛的显著位置，并与周围的壁画内容相连，色彩和谐。壁画是敦煌石窟艺术的重要组成部分，适于表现复杂的场面和丰富的内容。石窟的佛龛，四壁和窟顶，布满了色彩缤纷的壁画。与居于主体位置的彩塑，互相辉映，相得益彰，共同构成完整的石窟艺术。

敦煌石窟艺术，是在传统的汉晋艺术基础上，吸收融合外来艺术的营养，创造的具有中国风格的民族民间佛教艺术。因其历史悠久、规模宏大、内涵深邃，艺术精美、保存完好，享誉国内外，是我国乃至世界佛教艺术的瑰宝，在中国文化史以至世界文化史上，具有重要的地位。

一、十六国、北朝时期石窟艺术

包括北凉、北魏、西魏、北周四个时代。是敦煌早期石窟艺术。无论石窟建筑形制、彩塑艺术或壁画艺术的思想内容和形式风格，都明显地受到西域佛教艺术的深刻影响。但在中原文化扎根很深的敦煌，这种西域佛教艺术，自开始就具有浓厚的本土魏晋艺术的特点。至北朝后期随着中原艺术影响的西来，出现了中国式的佛教艺术。

（一）石窟建筑形制

共有三种：1、禅窟　供僧人禅行的洞窟。此类洞窟由印度毗诃罗窟发展变化而成，禅窟主室为长方形或方形，正壁开龛塑像，供（坐禅者）修行者（坐禅者）观像之用，左右两侧壁各开两个或四个仅能容身的斗室，修行者在内坐禅修行。窟顶有平顶，或覆斗顶（其形如同倒置的量米之斗）。最初禅窟内素壁无画，后来窟内壁面与窟顶均绘壁画，如第268（包括第267、269、270、271窟）、285窟。

2、中心塔柱窟　又叫中心柱窟、塔庙窟。是这个时期流行的主要洞窟形式。来源于印度支提窟，即在石窟中供奉佛塔。其形式主室平面长方形，中央偏后凿出连接窟顶与地面的方形塔柱，柱的四面开龛塑像，以供修行者绕塔观像与礼佛。中心塔柱之前的窟顶为仿汉式建筑的中间起脊两面斜坡的人字披顶。塔柱周围窟顶为平顶。如第254、288、428窟。

3、殿堂窟　为修行者礼佛的场所。其形式受到中国传统殿堂建筑的影响，主室平面方形，正壁开龛塑像，或仅塑像而无龛，洞窟的其余三壁大都绘壁画，也有个别洞窟在两侧壁上部开列龛塑像，窟顶为覆斗顶或人字披形顶。如第275、249窟。

（二）彩塑

北朝时期彩塑有主体性圆雕和附属性影塑。主体性造像都是身体紧贴墙面的高浮雕，有佛、菩萨、弟子像。佛像有弥勒佛像、释迦佛像、释迦与多宝并坐佛像。释迦佛像按其事态之不同，又可分为禅定像、苦修像、说法像、成道像、思惟像。前期佛像两侧仅有侍从菩萨像，后期佛像两侧又增加了迦叶、阿难侍从弟子像。

附属性影塑，有供养菩萨、飞天、千佛等。以泥制模具翻制的影塑，粘贴于中心塔柱或四壁上部，相当于凸于壁面的浮雕，用以陪衬主体性造像。北朝前期佛像的服饰或袒裸右臂的偏袒袈裟，或圆领通肩袈裟。菩萨高髻宝冠，辫发垂肩，上身袒裸或斜披络腋，下身羊肠裙，衣裙上装饰着密集的衣纹。人物面相丰圆，造型雄健厚重，肩宽胸平，姿态端庄，动态朴拙，神情宁静沉稳、含蓄。此时彩塑艺术和风格以中原汉晋艺术为基础，较充分地融合了来自于西域佛教艺术的营养。北朝后期的西魏时期，中原汉式衣冠传到敦煌，南朝“秀骨清像”艺术风格盛行。此时彩塑身着高领大袖襦服，胸前系小结，外罩对襟式袈裟。人物面相方瘦，身躯扁平。北朝后期的北周时期彩塑进一步民族化。

（三）壁画

北朝时期壁画，在石窟内大致有固定布局：四壁上部为绕窟一周的天宫伎乐；中部为壁画的主要部分，或满壁千佛，或佛说法图和千佛，或佛说法图和千佛及释迦本生、因缘、佛传故事画；下部为绕窟一周金刚力士，或装饰图案。北朝前期的窟顶均绘装饰图案，后期的窟顶在覆斗顶与人字披顶增绘本生、佛传故事画、千佛等。按壁画内容可分为五类：

1、尊像画　表现佛教诸神，有构图严谨的佛说法图；有既千篇一律，又色彩缤纷的十方诸佛，即千佛；有排列有序，舞姿婀娜、作群舞的供养菩萨；有高居天宫楼阁欢畅地奏乐歌舞的伎乐天；有健壮有力，浓眉怒目，驱逐魔鬼的护法神——金刚力士。

2、本生、因缘、佛传故事画　本生故事画表现释迦牟尼佛在过去世中为菩萨时行种种善行，救度众生事迹，此类题材有毗楞竭梨王身钉千钉、虔阇尼婆梨王身燃千灯、尸毗王割肉贸鸽、月光王施头、快目王施眼、九色鹿王（行忍辱）拯救溺人、摩诃萨埵太子舍身饲虎、雪山大士施身闻偈、须达拿太子以子妻施婆罗门、独角仙人为淫女所骑、须阇提太子割肉事亲复国、善事太子入海求珠、睒子孝养盲亲等；因缘故事画表现释迦牟尼成佛后说法教化众生、度化外道的各种事迹，有须摩提女请佛、沙弥守戒自杀、五百盲贼得眼皈依、微妙比丘尼现身说法；佛传故事画描绘释迦牟尼一生或某些主要事迹的故事。故事画的主题思想大多为坚持出家修行，强调布施、忍辱、持戒的修行方法，宣传惩恶扬善、因果报应、佛法威力的佛教思想。至北朝晚期的故事画逐渐地民族化，则渗透进中国传统的忠君、孝悌、仁爱、和顺、父子恩等的儒家思想。故事画的结构形式多样：主要有主体式单幅画，以一个画面表现故事的一个典型情节；异时同图单幅画，一个画面上表现故事不同时间，不同地点的若干个情节；多幅连环画，多个画面表现有时间、有地点、有完整情节的故事。

3、神话人物画　为佛教传入之前，中原汉地流行的道教神话人物形象，此类画出现于北朝后期，传自于中原，有乘坐龙车、风辇的东王公、西王母，蛇身人面的伏羲氏、女娲氏，昂首飞腾的东方之神青龙，振翼奔腾的西方之神——白虎，展翅欲飞的南方之神——朱雀，龟蛇相交的北方之神——玄武，两耳竖过头顶，臂生羽毛，长生不死的羽人，兽头人身振臂运转连鼓的雷神、兽头人身手执铁钻敲击的霹电等等。

4、供养人画像　出资开窟造像的功德主及其眷属为祈福求愿，在窟内绘画的礼佛画像。多绘于主要壁画的下方，形象较小，高不及尺，男女分列成行，僧尼为首，世俗人物随后，有王公贵族和侍从像，有少数民族人物形象。服饰有中原汉装，西域胡装，汉胡混合装。

5、装饰图案　装饰石窟建筑、彩塑和壁画的纹样。北朝时期是以表现石窟建筑形式为特征的建筑装饰图案。图案分布于中心塔柱窟人字披顶两披的望板、椽、枋、斗拱及平顶，殿堂窟的覆斗顶，以及不同类型洞窟的佛龛龛楣、彩塑背光、四壁壁带等处。平顶饰平棋图案，均为三层方井叠套，井心绘大莲花，错叠的井角绘火焰纹、飞天、忍冬等纹样。覆斗顶正中饰华盖式藻井，井心垂大莲花，四边饰忍冬、云气、火焰纹，井外饰垂幔、彩铃。人字披顶的椽间望板、壁带边饰、龛楣的主要纹样有莲荷纹、忍冬纹、祥禽瑞兽纹、云气纹、几何纹等等。

前期壁画以土红为底色，人物造型健壮，比例适度，穿西域式衣冠服饰，面部与肢体晕染采用西域表现明暗的凹凸法，以表现人物面部和肢体的立体感，此时色彩质朴厚重，线描细劲有力。这是中原传统艺术和西域艺术的结合。后期壁画为两种风格，一种风格大体继承前期特征，传自西域的晕染法又有新的发展；另一种风格的壁画，以白色为地色，人物身材修长，相貌清瘦，眉目疏朗，神情潇洒，风骨飘逸，穿汉式方领深衣大袍，面部以民族传统晕染法在面颊涂红色，此时色彩清新明快，线条秀劲洒脱，运笔疾速，富于韵律感。这种风格是传自于中原的新风。

二、隋、唐时期石窟艺术

佛教与佛教艺术传入后，在其漫长、曲折的传播进程中，经过与中国汉晋文化艺术的不断碰撞、融合，至隋唐时期佛教和佛教艺术得到了极大的发展，形成了中国式的佛教宗派、佛教思想、佛教信仰、佛教艺术。隋唐时期的敦煌石窟艺术发展到了最辉煌的巅峰。石窟建筑、彩塑、壁画所表现的世俗化、大众化、多样化，都是佛教艺术中国化的体现。

（一）石窟建筑形制

1、殿堂窟　呈现多样化、民族化、世俗化趋势。殿堂窟数量最多，长盛不衰，且不断变化发展。窟内佛龛加深加大，形式早晚不同，隋代为内外二层龛；唐前期为内小外大之敞口龛；唐后期为仿照世俗床帐形式的盝顶帐形龛，龛内设马蹄形佛坛，坛上置彩塑像，如第329、384窟。殿堂窟还出现一种主室正壁和两侧壁均开佛龛，龛内造像的形式，用以表现三世佛或三身佛，此类洞窟数量虽不多，但隋唐两代均有之，如第420窟。佛坛窟是新出现的窟形。隋至唐前期主室正壁凿长方形或马蹄形佛坛，唐后期大型洞窟主室中央凿出方形佛坛，坛后部有一道连接覆斗顶的背屏。坛前有阶陛，彩塑群像高踞于佛坛之上，信徒可围绕佛坛右旋环通、礼佛观像，此类洞窟应是殿堂窟之一种。其形式与寺庙佛殿，乃至世俗宫室殿堂格局相类似，如第196窟。

2、涅盘窟、七佛窟　因涅盘像和七佛像而得名，其实亦为佛坛之一种。主室横长方形，正壁有横贯全窟的佛床，上塑佛涅盘像，如晚盛唐148窟，中唐第158窟，或塑七佛并坐像，如中唐第365窟，窟顶为盝顶或券顶。

3、大像窟　因窟中巨大的弥勒佛坐像而得名，如莫高窟初唐第96窟、盛唐第130窟、榆林窟唐代第6窟。大像窟洞 窟高耸，主室平面方形，上小下大，贴正壁造石胎泥塑大像，佛座后凿出供信徒巡礼用的马蹄形信道。前壁上、中部各开一大型明窗，以供采光之用。窟顶为覆斗形或圆穹形，窟外建多层木构窟檐。

中心塔柱窟数量极少，趋于衰落，由于修行简化和佛教世俗化，中心塔柱作为塔的功能逐渐减弱，而与殿堂窟佛龛形式靠近。

崖面留存遗迹与文字记载说明，隋唐时代各窟前室外，均有木构窟檐。这些窟檐“上下云矗，构以飞阁，南北霞连”。各窟又有木构栈道相通，蔚为壮观。

（二）彩塑

置于佛龛和佛坛上之彩塑像，均为圆雕，已完全离开墙壁，充分发挥彩塑的主体性，独立性的特长。随着佛教思想的发展，塑造最精的群像，数量与内容有较大变化发展，少则三身，多则十一身，大多七身一组或九身一组。主像隋代出现了过去、现在、未来三世佛，法身、应身、报身三身佛。隋唐两代主像流行释迦牟尼佛、阿弥陀佛、弥勒佛。隋至初唐，在前室增加了天王和力士的护法像，由盛唐始，护法像进入主室，与佛、菩萨、弟子像组合在一起。佛像居中，佛的两侧依次侍立迦叶、阿难两弟子，观音、势至两大菩萨或立或坐，南、北两大天王和金刚力士。有的群像中还有胡跪，合十礼佛的小供养菩萨加入其内。佛国世界不同职守的代表人物按等级差别有序地汇聚于一堂，展示了立体的佛界说法会之场景。

数量最多，规模最大的群像当为佛涅盘像和举哀者组成的群像。如盛唐第148窟主室的主像为释迦牟尼佛，长15.8米，右胁而卧，绕佛塑有高约1米的菩萨、弟子、护法、国王、大臣举哀的群像72身。中唐第158窟规模与第148窟相当，以绘塑结合的手法表现群像。围绕释迦牟尼涅盘像的众举哀者绘于三面壁面，通过细腻地表现群像举哀，更好地衬托出释迦牟尼恬静自然，涅盘为乐的神情。

莫高窟最引人注目的乃是建于唐代武则天延载二年（695）的第96窟的北大像和唐玄宗开元九年（721）至天宝（742—756）的第130窟的南大像，前者高35.5米，后者高27.3米，均是石胎泥塑，先凿出身体的轮廓大 形，然后敷泥，最后塑造彩绘而成。其题材是两腿下垂的善跏坐弥勒说法像。造大像与武则天登位称帝有关，武氏欲取代李唐，命僧人造《大云经疏》，称武则天是弥勒下世。南大像保存完好，造型雄伟高大，神情庄严慈祥。

有隋一代，历时短暂，上承北朝，下启唐代，彩塑艺术取得了重要成就，但其形象尚存在头大、肩宽、腿短、动态单调、人物留有类型化痕迹等不足。在隋代艺术基础上，经过继续探索和创造，吸收西域佛教艺术的营养，唐代彩塑艺术臻于成熟与完美。唐代艺术匠师以高超的写实技巧，卓越的创造才能，绘塑技法的巧妙结合，通过对人物形象、衣冠服饰、体态动作、外部特征、面部表情、细致入微的刻画，成功地塑造了许多比例准确、衣饰华丽、造型健美、色彩灿烂、神态逼真、个性鲜明的完美艺术形象，成为具有永恒艺术魅力，经久传世的典范性不朽之作。

（三）壁画

隋代前期壁画布局大致继承北朝上、中、下三段式特点。隋后期开始至唐前期，改为壁面上部安排说法图或千佛、或经变，下部为供养人。作为盛世的唐代前期也往往通壁安排一幅大型经变。随着佛教艺术世俗化，唐后期洞窟格局发生了变化，传统的屏风画进入洞窟与佛龛。洞窟内通壁安排2至4幅经变不等，各种经变的说法会在上部，经变的情节性故事内容安排于下部的屏风画。供养人像列分布在由前室通向主室的甬道，或主室正壁与前壁下部。壁画内容十分丰富

1、佛教尊像画　除说法图外，随着佛教信仰的多样化，出现了较多的单身尊像，如药师佛、卢舍那佛、观音、势至、地藏以及密教题材的菩萨像。

2、经变画　广义而言，凡依据佛经变成绘制之图画，均可称为“变”。狭义而言，指将某部佛经的内容变成一幅首尾完整有情节铺陈的大画。据统计敦煌石窟有经变三十余种，有表现不同净土思想的阿弥陀经变、无量寿经变、观无量寿经变、弥勒经变、东方药师变、十方净土变；有表现天台最高圆满的大乘佛法，一切众生都能成佛思想的法华经变；有宣扬人人都有佛性的涅槃经变；表现大乘般若性空思想，众生成佛的《维摩诘经变》；有反映禅宗思想的天请问经变、思益梵天请问经变、金刚经变、楞伽经变等；有宣传密教持咒诵经，祈福禳灾的千手千眼观音经变、不空羂索观音经变、如意轮观音经变等等。通常经变画总是以说法会为中心，佛在中央，两侧分列大菩萨、天龙八部，还刻划生动活泼的飞天，载歌载舞的乐舞伎形象。不同的经变画有各自不同的佛经内容。阿弥陀经变，在凭台上以坐于莲花座上说法的阿弥陀佛与两侧的观世音、大势至菩萨，即所谓的西方三圣为主体，周围围有众多的听法菩萨，凭台后与两侧矗立着宫殿楼阁，凭台前有舞伎起舞和乐队伴奏，凭台下面绿色的七宝池，八功德水，池水莲花盛开，化生童子嬉戏，佛上空飞舞的天乐不鼓自鸣。整个画面表现了西方佛国净土世界。弥勒经变以弥勒佛说法为中心，穿插描绘山喷香气，地涌甜泉，庄稼一种七收，树上生衣，随意取用，路不拾遗，夜不闭户、

龙王洒水、罗刹扫地、人寿八万四千岁，寿终老人自入坟墓，女人五百岁婚嫁等等，展示弥勒世界美妙景象。不同的经变有不同的构图形式。阿弥陀经变、弥勒经变为主体式构图，以佛和菩萨说法会为中心，四周穿插净土世界的各种场景与情节，画面浑然一体。观无量寿经变，东方药师经变，中间以净土世界说法会为主体，两侧以对联形式的立轴画分别表现佛经中的故事，观无量寿经变分别绘画未生怨、十六观；东方药师经变分别绘画九横死、十二大愿。这样的画面主次分明，故事画作为经变画的一部分，为装饰的需要而形成了较为规整的连环画形式。又如维摩诘经变表现维摩居士与文殊菩萨共论佛法，劳度叉斗圣变表现外道劳度叉和佛弟子舍利弗神变斗法，两经变的画面都分成左右，使其各成主体，围绕两方主体人物，交织各种神变故事，内容丰富，引人入胜。经变画这种佛教艺术形式是中国佛教艺术的独创，体现了中国古代艺术家驾驭复杂题材，创作大型经变，宏篇巨制的杰出水平，画家善于通过雄伟壮观的宫殿楼阁，绮丽多姿的山水景致来创造辽阔的境界，同时善于应用丰富灿烂的色彩造成一种金碧辉煌，以此来表现佛国净土的美妙世界。在雄伟壮阔的场景中又注意细致入微地刻画不同的人物。

3、佛教东传故事画　又名佛教史迹画。始于隋、初唐，盛于唐后期。为传自天竺（今印度）、尼婆罗（今尼泊尔），犍陀罗（今巴基斯坦白沙瓦一带）、西域于阗（今中国新疆和田）和中国本土的佛教传说。题材多达数十种，大抵分为佛教感应化现的传说，弘扬佛教的高僧和使臣的神异故事，显示神灵、表征吉凶的佛教瑞像图，佛教圣地和圣迹的传说。如释迦晒衣石、善断吉凶的佛图澄、张骞出使西域求佛名号，犍陀罗国释迦双头瑞像、于阗毗沙门天王与舍利弗决海、中国四大佛教灵山之一的五台山及其圣迹与化现传说。这些看似神奇的传说故事，反映佛教的东传，中国与印度、中亚、西域的文化交流，佛教的中国化。

4、供养人画像　有僧官、僧尼，当地达官贵人、文武官僚、工匠、牧人、行客、侍从、奴婢和善男信女，唐后期张氏归义军政权兴建洞窟中的供养人画像，一家三代，姻亲眷族都依次排列在一起，此时的洞窟成了光耀门庭的家庙。特别是晚唐第156窟场面宏大，结构严谨的“河西节度使张议潮统军出行图”与“宋国河内郡夫人宋氏出行图”乃重要的历史画卷。隋唐时期供养人像逐渐增大，盛唐开始一些大窟中出现等身大像。供养人的形象服饰描绘的细致讲究。

5、装饰图案　隋代图案是北朝“建筑装饰图案”向唐代“织物图案”的过渡时期，以“藻井图案”为其代表，纹样形式多样。唐代是敦煌图案发展的高峰，以藻井图案为代表，装饰多仿绫、锦、绢、绣织物上的纹样，繁缛多样，井内主花纹样有莲花、三兔莲花、交杵莲花、灵鸟莲花、莲花飞天、团花、云头团花、葡萄石榴、宝相花、茶花等等。井外边饰图案主要纹样有卷草纹、半团花纹、团花纹，各种几何纹、回纹、菱格纹、灵鸟石榴卷草纹、百花蔓草纹等，造型丰满，结构严整，色彩华丽。

壁画艺术经过隋代的探索，唐代臻于娴熟精湛。唐前期人物丰浓，肌胜于骨，色彩富丽，线描采用自由豪放的兰叶描，绘画呈现一派雄浑健康，生机勃勃的气派。吐蕃占领时期，色彩明快清雅，线描精细柔丽，人物性格刻画细腻，构图严密紧凑，形成精致淡雅的风格。至晚唐出现公式化的趋向，开始缺少意境和情趣。

三、五代、宋、西夏、元时期石窟艺术

晚唐武宗、后周世宗两次灭佛使佛教遭到沉重打击；佛教各宗派已日趋衰落；唐中叶以后经济重心开始南移；海上丝绸之路兴起，陆上丝绸之路趋渐衰弱，上述诸多因素影响下，敦煌石窟佛教艺术也呈衰退趋势。但五代、宋时期统治瓜（今安西县），沙（今敦煌市）的曹氏归义军政权经济、政治、外交、举措得当，宗奉佛教，设置画院与伎术院，形成了院派特色，石窟佛教艺术仍显繁荣景象。西夏、元时期受到中原绘画艺术与藏传密教艺术的影响，也不乏精品佳作。

（一）洞窟建筑形制

继承晚唐旧式，主要流行主室正壁开龛，和中心设方形佛坛的殿堂窟，五代、宋时期中心佛坛窟规模超过前代。此时还保存了宋代干德八年（970）、开宝九年（976）、太平兴国五年（980）等纪年的木构窟檐四座，它们是第427、431、444、437窟。西夏、元时期殿堂窟出现了多层圆形佛坛的形式，如莫高窟第465窟、榆林窟第3窟等。

（二）彩塑

多遭严重破坏，仅存五代第261，宋代第55窟，西夏第246数窟彩塑。塑像题材与风格承唐代之余绪，但已缺乏唐塑之神韵。第55窟主像塑弥勒佛像三身，表现“弥勒三会”，西夏第491窟塑供养天女，都是新题材。

（三）壁画

1、五代、宋时期仍以大幅经变为主，题材内容大都一如前代，随着洞窟规模扩大，有的洞窟经变规模之大，入画内容之多，超过前代。第220窟后唐绘新样文殊、第76窟宋代绘千手千眼观世音菩萨广大圆满无碍大悲心陀罗尼经变、八大灵塔变等，都是新题材。但经变种类数量渐趋减少，画面格式化现象日益严重，画面榜题增多，几乎每个画面的内容，均插以墨书榜题，借助榜题文字，说明所绘内容。至西夏、元时期，大部分传统题材经变的种类进一步减少，有的已绝迹，画面更趋格式化。受中原两宋画风之影响，榆林窟第2、3、29窟所绘水月观音、文殊变、普贤变，无论人物造型、山石云气，线描赋色、结构布局、意境神韵都是不可多得的艺术佳作。与此同时受藏传密教艺术的影响，曼陀罗、五方佛、明王、金刚等藏传佛教题材增多。出现藏密绘画艺术的新因素、新技法。

2、佛教东传故事画

五代、宋、西夏时期进一步发展，共有40多个洞窟绘画。瑞像画以单幅大画绘于洞窟前室通向主室的甬道顶部，如莫高窟第98、454窟牛头山瑞像及大型圣迹图。还出现经变式故事画，与其它经变同绘于一壁，如五代莫高窟第72窟的大型刘萨诃和尚因缘变相图，组合30多个内容，描述了北魏圣僧刘萨诃一生的神异事迹，又如五代第61窟五台山化现图，为莫高窟最大的佛教圣迹图。以五峰为主体，组合五台山数百里内灵异化现，佛教圣迹及城市关隘、店铺、道路共一百九十余处于一壁，自上而下描绘了天界、神和人交接界、人间现实世界，是一幅独特的以现实与想象结合的地图，内容丰富，意境深远，也是一幅难得的山水画。

3、尊像画　五代、宋时期出现了大幅四大天王、天龙八部、八大龙王、毗沙门天王赴哪吒会等护法题材，宋、西夏时期大型供养菩萨行列，十六罗汉图。

4、本生、因缘、佛传故事画　数量虽不多，却都是鸿篇巨制，绘于五代、宋一些大型洞窟壁面下部，以大面积连屏表现。

5、供养人画像　五代、宋时期数量进一步增加，形象更为高大。曹氏归义军政权一门五代及其姻亲、显官、属吏，还有与曹氏联姻的于阗国王、王后，甘州回鹘公主，均与入壁。如五代第98窟供养人像达160多身，组成宏大的队伍，显赫其身份，于阗国王像高达2.92米。至西夏、元时期，出现了党项羌、回鹘族、蒙古族供养人像，有国师、贵族、官员，体格魁梧，身材高大，身着不同民族的服饰。

6、图案艺术已趋式微　纹样过于规整和程序化。五代图案继承唐代余风，多绘团龙藻井，井心莲花中多绘团龙，井外多卷草纹，回纹边饰。宋与西夏浮塑施金的团龙藻井，有一龙、二龙、四龙、五龙。还有团花藻井，花中画交杵和法轮，井外边饰以回纹、卷草纹、白珠纹为主，元代除沿袭西夏遗风，还有井心绘六字真言，大日如来等，图案艺术也反映了世俗对佛教艺术的影响，以及藏传密教的影响。

五代至宋初，即曹氏政权前期的壁画艺术，犹存唐代余风。山水画、故事画、肖像画，巨幅壁画有独特成就，在画院画师或画行画匠的带领下，使公式化的经变形成了统一风格。壁画人物肌肉丰腴、设色热烈、线描豪放有变化，但失之粗糙简率。至宋代，即曹氏政权后期，经变内容更趋贫乏空洞，人物神情呆板，千篇一律，色彩单调贫乏，线条柔弱无力，缺乏艺术生命力。

西夏壁画初期，继承曹氏画院规范，后来在进一步汉化基础上，产生了兼有中原风格和党项民族特征的人物造型。

元代艺术为迥异的两种风格，一种以莫高窟第3窟千手千眼观音、第61窟炽盛光佛为代表，采用铁线描、折芦描、游丝描、丁头鼠尾描等多种线描造型，设色清淡典雅，这是中原传入的汉密风格；另一种以莫高窟第465窟萨迦派壁画为代表，人物形象有印度、尼泊尔人特征，铁线描挺拔秀劲，色彩多用青、白、绿等色，敷色厚重，这种线描和色彩并重、神秘、怖畏、冷艳的风格，来自藏传密教。

四、敦煌石窟艺术的珍贵价值

敦煌石窟艺术，大多以佛教经典为依据，但佛国世界的创造，与现实生活发生密切关系，要摄取现实生活为素材，佛国世界只是现实世界的反射。历经一千年创造的敦煌石窟艺术，某种意义上表现了一千年古代社会的生活，展示了一千年内涵丰富的文化。所以敦煌石窟不仅是辉煌灿烂的艺术宝库，而且也是极其珍贵的文化宝库。我们从历史、艺术、科技三个方面简述敦煌石窟的珍贵价值。

（一）历史价值

敦煌石窟营造及其历史过程，敦煌的悠久历史，当地有影响的世族与大姓，以及敦煌同周围民族与西域的关系，在历史中没有或很少记载。敦煌石窟有成千上万个供养人画像，其中有一千多条还保存题名结衔。供养人像和题记，生动、丰富、真实地提供了许多历史状况和历史线索。使我们了解了与敦煌历史、敦煌石窟营建史有密切关系的阴、索、李、翟、张、曹等各世家大族的史事，他们相互间盘根错节的关系，他们与周围各少数民族政权的复杂关系，他们营造敦煌石窟的史实。都是研究张、曹归义军统治时期敦煌历史的珍贵资料。还使我们了解不同历史时期，拓拔鲜卑、吐蕃、吐谷浑、回鹘、党羌、蒙古等少数民族政权在敦煌的活动，各民族间错综复杂的关系及他们的文化艺术；反映了唐代的仪卫制度、奴婢制度、吐蕃官制、归义军政权的管制等。

本生、佛传、福田经变、弥勒经变、宝雨经变、楞伽经变及供养人题记，可帮助我们了解古代经济生活的状况。如农牧业方面，有耕作、收获、捕渔、家畜饲养、狩猎。庄园收获图和寺院收获图，告诉了我们唐代“庄园”与“寺院”经济的消息。手工业方面有锻铁、酿酒、制陶、纺线、织褐、皮匠、制鞋、画匠、伎匠、塑匠、纸匠、木匠、石匠、打窟人、金银匠、弓匠、踏碓师。商业方面有屠房、肉坊、酒肆、旅店、金银行、木行、弓行等。据藏经洞文献记载，称“匠”者共有二十余种。将壁画与藏经洞文献结合研究，可反映出古代敦煌地区手工业和商业的面貌。

法华经变、涅槃经变提供了古代军队操练、出征、征伐、攻守的作战图，及兵器装备的宝贵形象资料。

敦煌壁画中保存有属于体育属性的资料，如骑射、射靶、马技、跃马、相扑、角力、举重（举象、举钟）、奕棋、投壶、武术、游泳、马球、蹴踘等。

敦煌是丝绸之路的“咽喉之地”，过往胡商、汉贾必经之地，也是从事丝绸贸易与中转之地。壁画中描绘了中原与西域商人在丝绸之路上东来西往，相望于道的景象。如北周第296窟福田经变，一边是高鼻深目的胡商，牵着载有货物的骆驼，另一边是骑马的中国商人，赶着满载货物的毛驴，相遇在桥上。同时也透出了古丝绸之路经商贸易的艰难险阻的消息。如隋代第420窟法华经变，商队赶着满载丝绸的骆驼和毛驴，路遇大批武装的强盗，商队的财货被抢劫一空；唐代第45窟观音经变，一群胡商赶着毛驴，载着丝绸在山谷中遇到了强盗。

丝绸之路既是贸易之路，也是外交往来、文化交流之路。敦煌壁画也有图像的记载，如唐代第323窟描绘了出使西域的西汉使臣张骞；五代、宋第98、454窟描绘了出使印度的唐代使臣王玄策；中唐、五代、宋的第231、237、98、61、72窟描绘了西行求法和活跃于河西走廊的名僧刘萨诃，莫高窟第126窟、榆林窟第2、3、29窟刻画了唐僧玄奘西天取经的事迹，东来传教的著名僧人安世高、康僧会、佛图澄在唐宋的第323、9、108、454窟也有描绘。

古代社会生活的衣食住行、生老病死、婚丧嫁娶等民情风俗场景在壁画中无处不见。盛唐到西夏时期的弥勒经变普遍绘画了嫁娶图，表现了佛经所言，弥勒世界人寿八万四千岁，“女人年五百岁，尔乃行嫁”的内容。图中表现了唐宋时期敦煌地区广泛流行两种不同的婚俗，一种是受汉人传统文化的影响，男方行聘娶婚，即男方行聘，迎娶新娘，回家成婚；另一种是西域民族风俗，男就女家行礼，行入夫婚。壁画中的嫁娶图细致地表现了婚礼场面的设置：在庭院搭设帐篷，宴请宾客的礼席，围设新婚夫妇拜堂的帐帷和新婚夫妇居住的青庐。还表现了婚礼仪式的全过程：新郎迎亲、乐舞助兴、拜堂成礼、莫雁之礼、共入青庐，举行洞房同牢合卺之礼。又如自北周至宋代的故事画微妙比丘尼、善事太子入海品、佛传、涅槃经变、表现了古代的丧葬习俗，描绘停棺为亡人举哀，出殡送葬、殡葬的丧葬过程；还描绘了行后土之祭，构置坟茔（修筑坟墓四周围墙）、设圹埋葬、地面起坟（堆土堆）的土葬埋葬方式。

敦煌石窟的彩塑和壁画，大都是佛教内容：如彩塑和壁画的尊像，释迦牟尼的本生、因缘、佛传故事画，各类经变画，众多的佛教东传故事画，神话人物画等，每一类都有大量、丰富、系统的材料。还涉及到印度、西亚、中亚、新疆等地区，可帮助我们了解古代敦煌以及河西走廊的佛教思想、宗派、信仰、传播，佛教与中国传统文化的融合，佛教中国化的过程等等，对研究敦煌地区佛教史和中国佛教史都是极其宝贵的资料。

（二）艺术价值

敦煌石窟营建的一千年历程，时值中国历中上两汉以后长期分裂割据，走向民族融合、南北统一，臻于大唐之鼎盛，又由颠峰而式微的重要发展时期。在此期间，正是中国艺术的程序、流派、门类、理论的形成与发展时期，也是佛教与佛教艺术传入后，建立和发展了中国的佛教理论与佛教宗派，佛教美术艺术成为中国美术艺术的重要门类，最终完成了中国化的时期。敦煌石窟艺术，绵延千年，内容丰富，数量巨大，其艺术形式既继承了本土汉晋艺术传统，吸收南北朝和唐宋美术艺术流派的风格，又不断接受、改造、融合域外印度、中亚、西亚的艺术风格，向人们展示了一部佛教美术艺术史及其中国化的渐进历程。又是中国艺术与西域艺术往来交流的历史记载。对研究中国美术史和世界美术史都有重要的意义。

从中国绘画美术的门类角度看，敦煌石窟壁画中的人物画、山水画、动物画、装饰图案画都有千年历史，自成体系，数量众多的特点，都可成为独立的人物画史、山水画史、动物画史、装饰图案画史。特别是保存了中国宋代以前即10世纪以前如此丰富的人物画、山水画、动物画、装饰图案的实例，这是世界各国博物馆藏品所未见的。

敦煌壁画中有音乐题材洞窟达200多个，绘有众多乐队、乐伎及乐器，据统计不同类型乐队有500多组，吹、打、拉、弹各类乐器40余种，共4500多件。敦煌藏经洞文献中也有曲谱和其它音乐资料。丰富的音乐图像数据，展现了近千年连续不断的中国音乐文化发展变化的面貌。为研究中国音乐史，中西音乐交流提供了珍贵资料。

敦煌石窟大多数洞窟的壁画中几乎都有舞蹈形象。有反映人间社会生活、风俗习尚的舞乐场面和舞蹈形象，如西域乐舞、民间宴饮和嫁娶舞乐；有经变中反映的宫廷和贵族燕乐歌舞场景；有天宫仙界的舞蹈形象，如飞天的舞蹈形象，供养伎乐等。还有藏经洞保存的舞谱及相关资料。舞蹈艺术是无法保留的时空艺术，古代的舞蹈形象，我们现代人已知之甚少，就敦煌石窟舞蹈形象的珍藏而言，堪称舞蹈艺术的博物馆，保存了无数高超的舞蹈技巧和完美的舞蹈艺术形象，代表了各时代舞蹈发展的面貌及其发展历程。

敦煌石窟艺术中有十分丰富的建筑史资料。敦煌壁画自十六国至西夏描绘了成千成万座计的不同类型的建筑画，有佛寺、城垣、宫殿、阙、草庵、穹庐、帐、帷、客栈、酒店、屠房、烽火台、桥梁、监狱、坟莹等等，这些建筑有以成院落布局的组群建筑，有单体建筑。壁画中还留下了丰富的建筑部件和装饰，如斗拱、柱坊、门窗、以及建筑施工图等。长达千年的建筑形象资料，向我们展示了一部中国建筑史。可贵的是，敦煌建筑资料的精华，反映了北朝至隋唐四百年间建筑的面貌，填补了南北朝至盛唐建筑资料缺乏的空白。此外，不同时期，不同形制的800余座洞窟建筑，五座唐宋木构窟檐，以及石窟寺的舍利塔群，都是古代留存至今的宝贵建筑实物资料。

（三）科技价值

本生、佛传故事画、弥勒经变、法华经变，有许多耕获图，表现一种七收的内容。图中展现了北周到西夏600多年间敦煌地区农业生产的面貌，使我们了解当时农业生产的全过程：农夫一牛拉犁、二牛拉犁（二牛抬杠）耕地，妇女持装籽种的篮子播种，头戴笠帽、手持镰刀的农夫，收割成熟的庄稼，男子抡连枷打场，男子以木杈、木锨，女子用簸箕、扬篮扬场等。壁画中还逼真地描绘了各种农业生产工具，除上述提到的工具之外，还有直辕犁、曲辕犁、三脚耧犁、铁铧、耱、耙、锄、铁锨、扁担、秤、斛、斗、升，特别是盛唐第445窟弥勒经变中出现的能调节耕作深度的曲辕犁形象，为我们提供了当时最先进的农耕工具的唯一的珍贵图像数据。

敦煌作为中西交通的枢纽，在壁画上不仅留下了商旅交往的活动情景，还留下了宝贵的交通工具的形象资料。他们有牛、马、驼、骡、驴、象、舟、船、车、轿、舆、辇等。常用的交通工具车辆类型各异，牛车有“通幰牛车”、“偏幰牛车”、敞棚牛车，马车有驷车、骆车，还有骆驼车、童车、独轮车等，特别是保存了中国为世界交通工具做出独有贡献的独轮车、马套挽具（胸带挽具和肩套挽具）、马蹬、马蹄钉掌等珍贵的图像数据。

西魏第285窟、北周第296窟五百盲贼得眼皈依故事画，表现了骑着战马的骑兵，与身穿裤褶的步兵（强盗）作战的场面。画面上画出了马铠，它是保护战马的防护装备，古称具装，或具装铠。第285窟马铠的形制齐全，从保护马头的“面帘”，到保护马鞍后尻部的“寄生”一应俱全。反映了汉代已有的具装，到北朝时期已发展为完备成熟的保护装备。马铠的产生和发展是中国为世界军事装备所做的独有贡献。敦煌保留了珍贵的图像数据。

隋至西夏的尊像画、药师经变中的佛、菩萨、弟子手中及供桌上绘画了玻璃器皿，有碗、杯、钵、瓶、盘等器型，它们呈透明、浅蓝、浅绿、浅棕色，器型、颜色与纹饰表现出西亚萨珊风格或罗马风格，说明了这些玻璃器皿是从西亚进口的。壁画不仅反映了古代玻璃工艺的特点，还反映了中西的玻璃贸易。

百科全书式的敦煌藏经洞文献

公元1900年6月22日（清光绪二十六年五月二十六日），敦煌莫高窟下寺道士王圆箓在清理今编第16窟的积沙时，于无意间偶然发现了藏经洞（即今第17窟），从中出土了公元4—11世纪的佛教经卷、社会文书、刺绣、绢画、法器等文物5万余件。这一震惊世纪的发现，为研究中国及中亚古代历史、地理、宗教、经济、政治、民族、语言、文学、艺术、科技提供了数量极其巨大、内容极为丰富的珍贵资料，被誉为“中古时代的百科全书”、“古代学术的海洋”。

敦煌文献中，大约百分之九十是佛教文献。现存敦煌佛经中最早的写卷是日本中村不折所藏的《譬喻经》，经末题记云：“甘露元年三月十七日于酒泉城内斋丛中写讫”。“甘露元年”即前秦甘露元年，公元359年，这也是藏经洞敦煌文献的最早记年。佛教经典中，经、律、论三类经典应有尽有，而最有价值的则是禅宗经典和三阶教经典。敦煌文献中还发现了迄今为止最早的《六祖坛经》，对于慧能禅宗思想的形成十分重要，与宋代以后的《坛经》多有不同。敦煌文献中也保存了不少三阶教经典，如《三阶佛法》、《三阶佛法密记》、《佛说示所犯者法镜经》、《三界佛法发愿法》等，它的发现，为佛教研究增添了新的内容。

敦煌佛经还有不少藏外佚经（即《大藏经》中未收佛经），不仅可补宋代以来各版大藏经的不足，还为佛教经典和佛教史的研究打开了新的门径。敦煌佛经中还有不少被认为是中国人假托佛说而撰述的经典，即所谓“伪经”，这些疑伪经反映了中国佛教的特点，是研究中国佛教史的宝贵资料。敦煌文献中的梵文、古藏文、回鹘文、于阗文、吐火罗文及与汉文对照的佛经，对摸清汉译佛经的来源以及考证佛经原文意义作用很大。敦煌文献中各类佛经的目录也不少。此外，敦煌佛经，尤其是隋唐时期的写经，由于校勘精良、错讹较少，对校勘唐以后的印本佛典也大有裨益。

敦煌文献中还有一批寺院文书，其中包括寺院财产账目、僧尼名籍、事务公文、法事记录以及施入疏、斋文、愿文、燃灯文、临圹文等，是研究敦煌地区佛教社会生活不可多得的材料。

敦煌是古代佛教圣地，道教的发展远不如佛教，但在唐朝前期，由于统治者推崇老子，道教一度兴盛起来，因而，在敦煌文献中也保存了为数不少的道教典籍。敦煌文献中的道教经卷约有500号左右，主要为初唐至盛唐的写本。而纸质优良、书法工整、品式考究则是敦煌道教文献的一大特色。

除佛教、道教文献外，敦煌文献中还保存了有关摩尼教、景教文献，为我们了解古代中西文化交流提供了重要历史证据。

敦煌文献中的历史、地理著作、公私文书等，是我们研究中古社会的第一手资料。以史籍而言，敦煌文献中除保存了部分现存史书的古书残卷外，还保存了不少已佚古史书，这些史籍不仅可补充历史记载的不足，而且可订正史籍记载的讹误。敦煌文献中的一批地理著作，也十分引人注目，这些已亡佚的古地志残卷，是研究唐代地理的重要资料。敦煌文献中还有关于西北地区，特别是敦煌的几种方志，更为史籍所不载，如《沙州都督府图经》、《沙州伊州地志残卷》、《寿昌县地境》、《沙州地志》等，对敦煌乃至西北历史地理的研究十分重要，每一件都是弥足珍贵的史料。

关于归义军统治敦煌的历史，在两《唐书》、《资治通鉴》、以及新、旧《五代史》、《宋史》等正史中记载都非常简略，且错误很多，人们对这段历史的情况只能零星的了解。敦煌文献中有关这段历史的资料在上百种以上，数十年来，学者们根据这些资料，基本搞清了这段历史，从而使这段历史有年可稽，有事足纪，千载坠史，终被填补。

敦煌文献中还保存了大量中古时期的公私文书，这些未加任何雕琢的公私文书，是我们研究中古时期社会历史的第一手资料。这些公私文书，都是当时人记当时之事，完全保存了原貌，使我们对中古社会的细节有了更深入的了解，对研究中古社会历史至关重要。

敦煌文献中保存的大量古典文学资料更为引人注目。它包括《诗经》、《尚书》、《论语》等儒家经典及诗、歌辞、变文、小说、俗赋等，文学作品除文人作品和某些专集、选集的残卷外，大多都是民间文学作品。

敦煌文献中的儒家经典，最具学术价值的是它对今本儒学典籍的校勘价值。其中《古文尚书》是我们今日所见到的最古的版本，东汉经学大师郑玄所着《论语郑氏注》，更是失而复得的可贵资料，郑玄注《毛诗故训传》，南朝徐邈《毛诗音》则最为诗经研究者所重视。

敦煌文献中保存的诗歌数量很多，其中尤以唐五代时期为最多，大致包括佚存的唐代诗人之作、敦煌本地诗人之作、释氏佛徒之作、敦煌民间诗歌几个方面。敦煌佚存的唐代诗人之作，最著名的是韦庄的《秦妇吟》和《王梵志诗》。敦煌歌辞，过去一般称为曲子词，除少数文人作品外，大多数来自民间，作者几乎渗透于社会的各个阶层。在这些歌辞中，值得一说的是《云谣集杂曲子》的发现，这个集子编选了30首作品，从时间上看，明显早于传世的《花间集》、《尊前集》，为研究词的起源、形式及内容，提供了宝贵的材料。敦煌歌辞由于作者的广泛性，极大地影响了题材内容和创作风格，使得它的题材内容丰富多样，艺术风格多姿多彩。另外，一些民间小唱如《五更转》、《十二时》、《十二月》、《百岁篇》、《十恩德》等，也属于敦煌歌辞这一范畴。变文是敦煌文学中最引人注目的一部份。所谓变文，是一种韵文和散文混合在一起用于说唱的通俗文学体裁。变文作为一种新的文学体裁，过去竟不为世人所知，幸赖敦煌变文的发现，才使这一问题水落石出，从而解决了中国文学史上许多悬而未决的问题。敦煌文献中的话本小说主要有《唐太宗入冥记》、《秋胡小说》、《韩擒虎话本》、《庐山远公话》等，为后世白话小说的发展开拓了道路。敦煌俗赋有《韩朋赋》、《晏子赋》、《燕子赋》、《丑妇赋》等，是古代辞赋通俗化的产物，和文人赋有明显区别。此外，还有如讲经文、因缘、押座文、佛赞、偈颂等文体的作品中，也有不少文学性很强的佳作。

敦煌文献中还保存了一些重要的语言学资料，如《玉篇》、《切韵》、《一切经音义》、《毛诗音》、《楚辞音》、《正名要录》、《字宝》、《俗务要名林》等。

敦煌文献中的科技史料，则是中国科技史上的一支奇葩。科技资料主要有数学、天文学、医药学、造纸术和印刷术等方面的内容。数学方面有《九九乘法歌》、《算经》、《立成算经》等，这些都是我国现存算术中最早的写本，是研究中国数学史的重要史料。天文学方面，有《二十八宿次位经和三家星经》、《全天星图》、《紫微垣星图》等，它表明我国天文学在当时已处于世界领先水平，同时也为我国天文学和天文学研究提供了不可多得的资料。古代，天文和历法是密不可分的，敦煌历日大部分是由敦煌自己编制的，其中《宋雍熙三年（986）丙戌岁具注历日并序》已引用了西方基督教的星期制。医学类的文献，目前所知，至少在60卷以上，如果再加上佛经中的医学内容，则有近百卷，大致可分为医经、针灸、本草、医方四类。这些医书不仅为传世医书的校勘提供了较为古老的版本，同时，出于这些医籍中保存了一些久已失传的诊法、方药，提供了一些不为人所知的内容。不仅对医学史研究有意义，而且在今日临床医学中也有一定参考价值。敦煌文献保存4—11世纪连续不断的纸张样本，是研究造纸术的活材料。敦煌文献中的唐咸通九年（868）《金刚般若波罗蜜经》，是现存最早的雕版印刷品，也是中国发明印刷术的实证。这些科技史料的发现，再次向世人证明中国科学技术在古代居于领先地位。

敦煌文献中除大量汉文文献外，还有相当数量的非汉文文献，如古藏文、回鹘文、于阗文、粟特文、龟兹文、梵文、突厥文等，这些多民族语言文献的发现，对研究古代西域中亚历史和中西文化交流有不可估量的作用。

敦煌文献还保存了一些音乐、舞蹈资料，如琴谱、乐谱、曲谱、舞谱等，这不仅使我们能够恢复唐代音乐与舞蹈的本来面目，而且将进一步推动中国音乐史、舞蹈史的研究。

敦煌石窟和敦煌文献的丰富内涵和珍贵价值，不仅受到中国学者的极大重视，而且吸引了世界许多国家的众多学者竞相致力于对它的研究，遂在本世纪形成了一门国际显学——敦煌学，在20世纪国际人文社会科学领域内大放异彩。

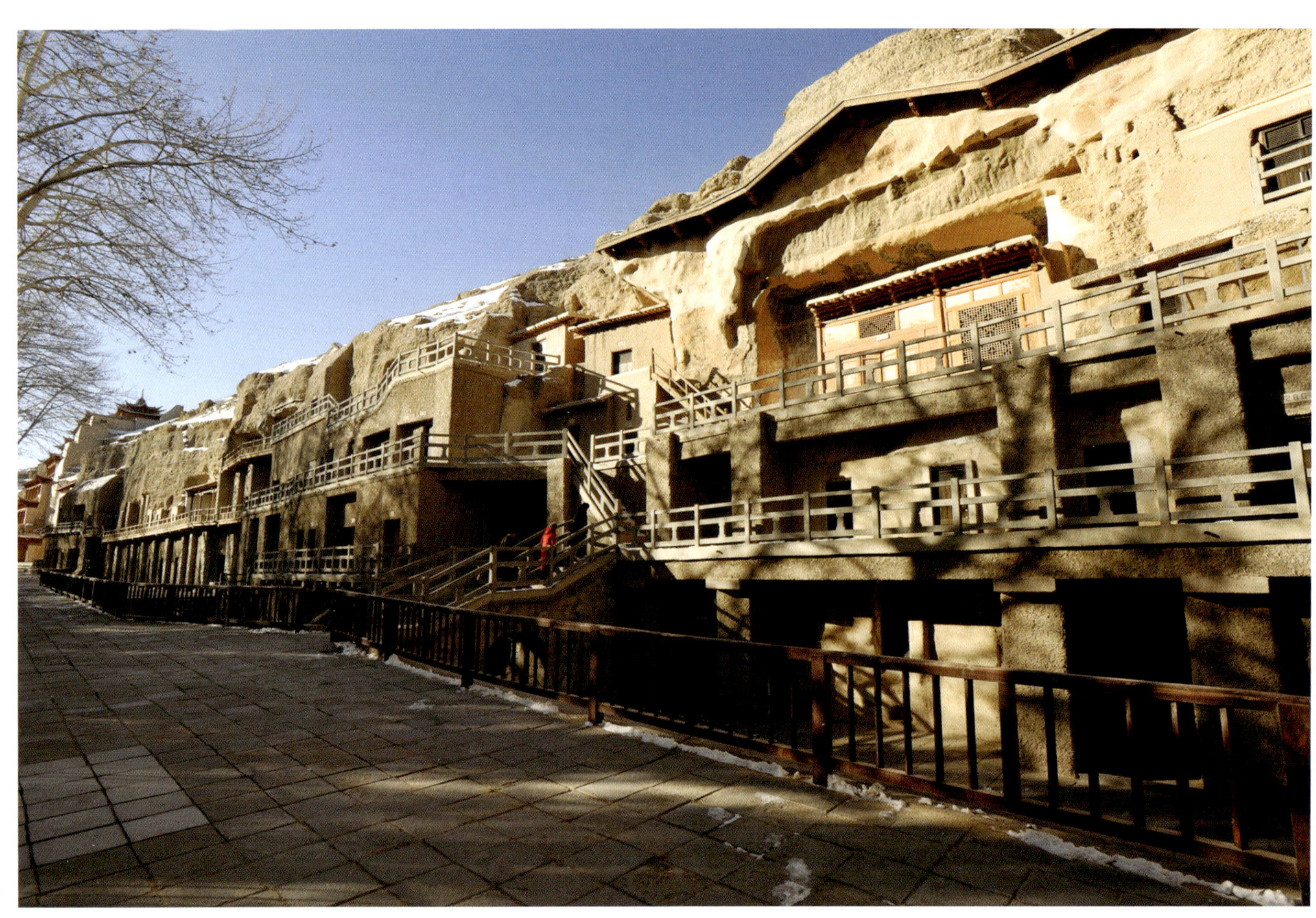

Exterior view of the caves at the Mogao Grottoes. Photo by Perry Hu, 2012. 莫高窟洞窟外景，胡维智摄

Mogao Caves 432 and 45 at Dunhuang: Ritual Art and Architecture
敦煌莫高窟432窟、45窟介绍 - 仪式艺术与建筑

Annette L. Juliano
朱安耐

Introduction

Situated at the far western end of Gansu province just 25 km outside the oasis town of Dunhuang, the 492 surviving Mogao Grottoes, more popularly known as the Caves of the Thousand Buddhas (Qianfodong千佛洞), preserve one thousand years of Chinese Buddhist art—painting, architecture, and sculpture of unparalleled magnificence dating from the early fifth to the fourteenth century. The cultural ramifications of this repository, strategically positioned at the beginning and end of the Silk Road, reach far beyond the borders of China and reverberate throughout the development of Buddhist art in Asia.

Dunhuang and the Mogao Grottoes remained largely unknown in the West until the late nineteenth century, when European explorers, most notably Sir Aurel Stein, reached the hinterlands of Central Asia (Chinese Turkestan) and far northwest China. For most of the twentieth century, Dunhuang was well known in scholarly circles but not to the broader public. Even by the late 1970s, during my own first visits to this extraordinary site, it was still a tiny desolate town filled with traders and their camels; a single barracks-style hotel accommodated the few foreign or Western visitors to the windswept cliffs, where the resident caretakers and Chinese scholars of the Dunhuang Academy struggled to document and preserve the caves from the relentless onslaught of the desert dunes.[1] Since the 1980s, this situation and the town itself have been transformed as an increasing number of exhibitions worldwide focus on the exoticism of the Silk Road and the role of Dunhuang, heightening awareness of and fascination with these caves. Traveling to Dunhuang has also become far less arduous with the original three-day train trip from Lanzhou, Gansu, replaced by a one-hour flight to the new airport. Now, more than two hundred thousand visitors a year from throughout the world make the journey to Dunhuang and the Mogao Grottoes.[2] The town of Dunhuang has become a tourist destination booming with hotels, restaurants, and shops. As Professor Roderick Whitfield commented, "even Stein might be surprised to see the caves today, besieged by tourists."[3] This greater ease of travel coupled with modern digital imaging techniques satisfies the needs of tourists and armchair travelers alike as well as those of scholars on site or half-way around the world. Once obscure, Dunhuang studies have emerged as a separate, internationally well-recognized field of scholarship.[4]

When visitors arrive, they are immediately stunned by the harsh beauty of the desert and then overwhelmed by the contrast with the splendors hidden in the semi-darkness of the caves that dot the 1,700-meter length of the cliff. Entering a cave for the first-time, one leaves behind the monochromes of the searing desert and the rock cliff; inside, walls, ceiling, and sculpture shimmer with brilliantly rich colors, particularly lapis, turquoise, and cinnabar. The visitor stands enthralled among apparitions—near life-size sculptured images of Buddhas, bodhisattvas, monks, and guardians set against masterfully painted visions of Amitabha's Pure Land (also referred to as Sukhavati, a "land of bliss" or paradise) covering the walls. This same sense of awe was experienced by the often quoted fifteenth-century Persian emissary to China's Ming court who remarked that the Dunhuang Buddhist murals were "of such character that all the painters of the world would be struck with wonder."[5]

This explosion of interest in Buddhist art and the Silk Road among scholars, art lovers, and museum visitors in the West and in Asia has spurred a proliferation of exhibitions, some geared for general audiences, others for more scholarly inquiry.[6] Galleries are filled with all types of Buddhist imagery, fragments of Buddhist wall murals, sculptures, and other Buddhist paraphernalia excavated from foundations of lost temples or drawn from private and museum collections.[7] Much of this material had been retrieved from temples destroyed over time by political and religious turmoil, pulled from cache burials hastily dug during Buddhist persecutions, or removed from cave shrines. Such exhibitions certainly provide opportunities to see and to admire Buddhist "works of art," often of exceptional beauty. At the same time, however, these paintings and statuary exist in isolation, lacking the religious and spatial context in which they were intended to function. Sculptures and wall paintings from cave temples—such as Mogao, as well as Yungang 云冈, Maijishan 麦积山, or Xiangtangshan 响堂山, to name only a few—present nearly insurmountable challenges. In their original context, hollowed out of the cliff or mountainside, the caves created ritual architectural spaces in which wall paintings, sculptures, inscriptions, and banners were integral to the conception of the physical structure and the religious ceremonies performed within.

For the organizers of exhibitions focused on Buddhist works of art from cave temples, the contextualized environment can seldom be the major consideration and is often only partially addressed with site photographs and accompanying videos.[8] Caves, carved into the living rock, like all religious architecture, be it a church, mosque, or synagogue, define a sacred space that structures meaning and the relationship between the human and spiritual or divine realms. The cave serves as a mediating space which enables human beings to experience transcendent realities temporally and spatially by engaging all the senses.[9] Walking into a cave allows the visitor not only to see but also to experience the space and its interrelationship with the effect of light, whether natural or from oil lamps, the sculpture and the painting, and the offerings left in worship.[10] This China Institute exhibition about the Dunhuang caves attempts to convey a somewhat fuller sense of the cave temple experience by combining replicas of the main architectural features, sculpture, and some paintings from two caves with original works of art and sutras.

Organized by the Dunhuang Academy and China Institute Gallery, this approach departs from a more traditional art historical methodology by structuring the exhibition around replicas, a hybrid approach not without controversy and tilted toward an educational explication. In the end, neither replicas nor stereoscopic production nor the digital wonders of virtual reality can as yet replace the visceral and tactile engagement of actually being present in the cave. Still, it is hoped that this exhibition strategy will allow viewers to interact more deeply and directly with the cave temple and experience the use of such sacred spaces for Buddhist practice by the faithful—enriching the time-honored art historical approach of stylistic and iconographic analyses.

Each of the two galleries contains a modified full-scale replica of a Dunhuang cave shrine reflecting important differences in architectural plans, iconography, and style. The earlier example is a partial replica of Western Wei dynasty (535–556) Cave 432 (cat. no. 30); it features a central stupa-pillar, the ritual architectural form that dominated fifth and sixth-century cave temples. Although this is an incomplete replica of the cave, it serves as an effective introduction to cave temple spaces and aspects of the Buddhist religion and practice. Dated some two hundred years later, high Tang dynasty (705–781)[11] Cave 45 is presented in a more complete replica (cat. no. 32) and represents a sharp contrast with the architecture, décor, and iconography of Cave 432. It is a main-hall type cave shrine with a single focal point, a niche at the back filled with seven life-sized images—the Buddha, monks, bodhisattvas, and guardians—standing before a painted group of bodhisattvas. Outside the niche, facing walls depict the Pure Land of Amitabha on the one side and Avalokiteshvara (Ch., Guanyin) and the rescue of the faithful, scenes drawn from the Lotus Sutra, on the other. The truncated pyramidal ceiling above helps capture a fuller sense of the later cave shrine experience.

Cave 432, Western Wei (535–556)

As described more fully in Fan Jinshi's essay in this publication, Dunhuang gained prominence and stability during the Eastern Han (25–220) and particularly during the Northern and Southern Dynasties period when north China was controlled by the Tuoba. An off-shoot of the Xianbei tribe, the Tuoba formally established their kingdom, known as the Wei, in 386. By 439, this expanding kingdom had unified all of the north, including Dunhuang in the far northwest, under their banner in the Northern Wei dynasty. Originally established as a garrison during the Western Han (206 BC–9 CE) to protect access to the Western Regions, procure the famed Ferghana horses, and prevent incursions of the Xiongnu tribes, Dunhuang soon grew into a major commercial and Buddhist center where a steady stream of caravans began and ended their Silk Road trade. Chinese populations from the heartland were forcibly re-located to Dunhuang and to other military garrison cities in Gansu province, blending Chinese traditional culture, including Confucian and Daoist teachings, with Buddhism.[12] Buddhist monks journeyed from

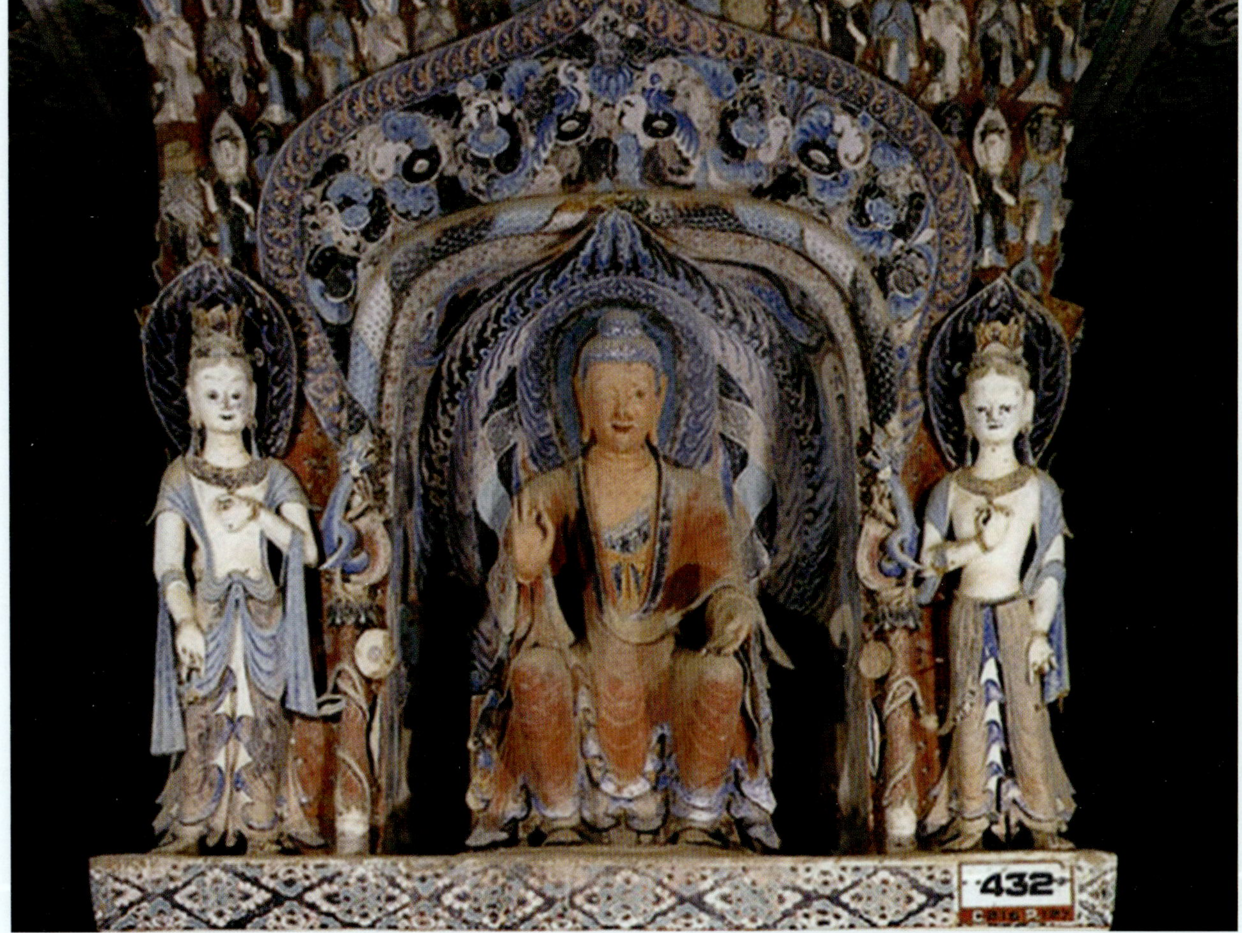

Fig. 1. Seated Shakyamuni Buddha and two bodhisattvas on the east face of the central stupa-pillar of Mogao Cave 432. Western Wei dynasty (535–556)

India and Central Asia to preach the Buddhist Law at this emerging cultural crossroads, undoubtedly carrying with them sutras and small portable images, while Chinese Buddhists endured the reverse pilgrimage westward, seeking the source of the Buddha's teachings in India.

The Northern Wei reigned over a unified north until 535, when, weakened by internal struggles between the ruling house and opposing tribal aristocracy, the kingdom split into two short-lived rival dynasties, the Eastern and Western Wei, with the Western Wei maintaining control of Dunhuang in Gansu as well as Chang'an in Shaanxi.[13] Although their rule lasted for only twenty-two years, at least ten caves were constructed under the patronage of the Western Wei.

Cave 432, which dates to the Western Wei, belongs to the distinctive group of cave temples in Gansu from the second half of the fifth century and at Dunhuang from the sixth century extending into the early seventh century (Northern Wei through Sui). These share what is referred to as the "central stupa or pillar plan" (see cat. no. 30, illus. 30-1).[14] Built on an east-west axis, the cave is accessed by an east-facing entrance and a narrow passage through the cliff face to its large rectangular interior space. The interior layout consists of two sections delineated by the ceiling.[15] In the front section of the room or about a third of the space, the ceiling rises to a peak across the main axis to form a gabled ceiling, described in Chinese as *ren*-shaped人字, and then it becomes flat; the flat ceiling signals the beginning of the back section or large main hall (two-thirds of the space) dominated by a square central pillar, the visual and ritual focus of the cave. Reaching from floor to ceiling and square in cross-section (ca. 12 ft. or 3.6 m high and 7 ft. or 2.1 m square), this central pillar is divided into two parts: a plinth below and sculptural elements above. The high plinth, wide at the base and narrowing as it rises from the floor, is decorated with painted images of Buddhas and bodhisattvas, *chintamani* (flaming wish-granting jewels), and floral patterns which were repainted in the later Xixia, or Western Xia, dynasty (990–1227). At about the center of the pillar, the plinth ends with a protruding molding decorated with floral medallions. This molding forms a base that supports a plethora of very high and low-relief stucco sculptures against painted backgrounds on the pillar's four sides.

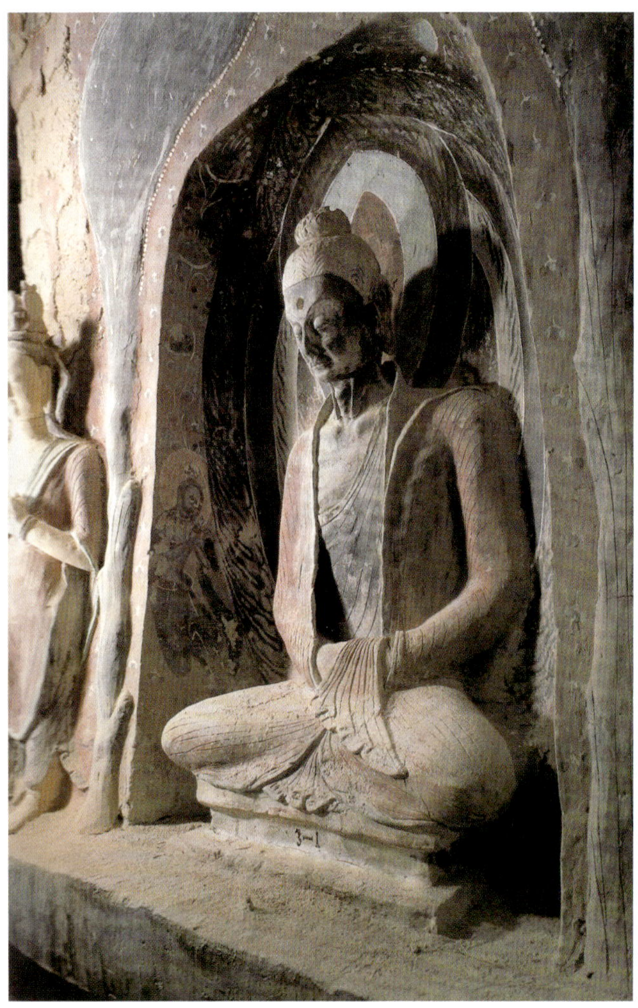

Fig. 2. Figure of emaciated Buddha from the west face of the central pillar in Mogao Cave 248. Northern Wei dynasty (386–534). After Dunhuang wenwu yanjiusuo, comp., *Dunhuang Mogaoku* (Beijing: Wenwu chubanshe, 1981), vol. 1, pl. 80

The pillar's east face directly aligns with the narrow entrance corridor and would be the first sculptural icon seen by the devotee or visitor: a single large niche houses a seated Buddha in the "pendant legs position" or "European posture" flanked by standing bodhisattvas (fig. 1); above, small bodhisattvas sit or kneel in reverence (see cat. nos. 9–12). The other three sides—north, west, and east—have two levels: the lower level has a seated Buddha in *padmasana* or meditation posture flanked by standing bodhisattvas and smaller kneeling figures, and the upper level has a similar configuration but with a smaller seated Buddha flanked by two bodhisattvas on each side rather than one and with fewer kneeling bodhisattvas.[16]

It is not always possible to specifically identify which manifestation of the Buddha is represented by the sculptural images on the four sides of the pillar. The largest Buddha on the east face sits in a "pendant leg position" with the right open hand raised in the *abhaya* (do not fear) mudra and the left open hand fingers resting on his knee in the *vara or varada* (charity and compassion) mudra often identified with Shakyamuni, the historical Buddha and founder of the religion, or with Maitreya, Buddha of the Future. He sits ensconced in a niche against a richly painted background, his red robe falling in almost symmetrical regularly-spaced folds over his body; his head is framed by a halo and his body by a flaming mandorla edged with white beaded borders; the tip of the mandorla extends out over the edge of the niche towards the curved, low-relief Indian-style pointed arch above. Framed by a band filled with four-petaled palmettes, small heads and sometimes torsos emerge from the centers of lotus pods, presumably belonging to those reborn and released from the cycle of suffering and rebirth.[17]

Squeezed into every available space near the top of the niche on either side of the Buddha's mandorla are *apsaras*, flying immortals (飛僊 *feixian*) or heavenly celestials (天人 *tianren*), celebratory figures who fly about with bare torsos, wearing *dhoti* and trailing scarves as they dance vigorously, play music, and carry offerings; their elongated and V-shaped pose is typical of the earlier style of Northern Wei. Just below stand two haloed bodhisattvas reflecting strong Central Asian influences. A dragon frames the niche—its thick, tubular reptilian body is wrapped across the top of the niche and ends on each side after passing through a large lotus leaf—and stands on top of a pillar wrapped with a lotus vine and open blooms.

On the west face of Cave 432's pillar, the larger figure on the lower level depicts the emaciated fasting Buddha, a difficult vision of a gaunt suffering Shakyamuni enduring penance;[18] this pairing is similar to those on the east and west faces of the central pillar in Northern Wei Cave 248 (fig. 2).[19]

The function and symbolism of these central stupa or pillar caves have been much debated with no definitive conclusion although a consensus has emerged. Actually, the two interpretations overlap: one emphasizes the structural, since such massive central pillars provide additional structural support for caves carved from the sandstone at Dunhuang and weakened by erosion from unrelenting sandstorms; the second stresses the symbolism of the stupa, in particular its *yasti*, a central pole representing the *axis mundi* or cosmic or world mountain, which serves as a conduit from the world of man to the spiritual world.[20] Other representations of the *axis mundi* were embodied in the early Chinese ritual buildings of the *mingtang* type based on Chinese cosmology, again connecting the world of man and the world of the gods, and used to satisfy the ritual requirement that the emperor perform an annual sacrifice to Heaven.[21] Here, in the Buddhist space, the *axis mundi* can be considered almost a universal symbol, offering an appropriate structure for the devotee to practice circumambulation or *pradaksina* (to walk to the right), by circling the pillar clockwise.

This architectural feature of the central pillar arrived in China at least by the mid-fifth century and to date has been found in smaller cave sites tucked into the foothills of Gansu's Qilian mountains, including Jintasi 金塔寺 (Golden Pagoda Temple; fig. 3), Wenshushan 文殊山 (Manjushri Mountain), and Matisi 马蹄寺 (Horse Hoof Temple).[22] Possible antecedents for the use of such pillars and their implications have been proposed from the cave temples at Kizil and Kumtura to as far back as the Ajanta caves and *chaitya* halls of India. A concept as fundamental as that of the world mountain or world tree would easily acquire multi-layered interpretations and reflect the mix of diverse sources and influences flowing into northwest China from the Western Regions and interacting with traditional Chinese ideas and practices from north China.[23]

The central pillar or stupa was most likely associated with the ritual of circumambulation, the clockwise circling of a sacred object or space. This ritual was a central part of a pilgrim's observance at holy sites; for Buddhists, the stupa was the most important venue, but the rite could be performed around the perimeter of a cave interior or a large temple incorporating several sites. Walking around a stupa or central pillar can be considered an act of prayer or reverence done in repentance or for the accrual of merit "to ensure a better prospect for one's family and progeny."[24] Also, while walking, the devotees make a clear-minded connection with the transcendent qualities vested in the objects, structure, and

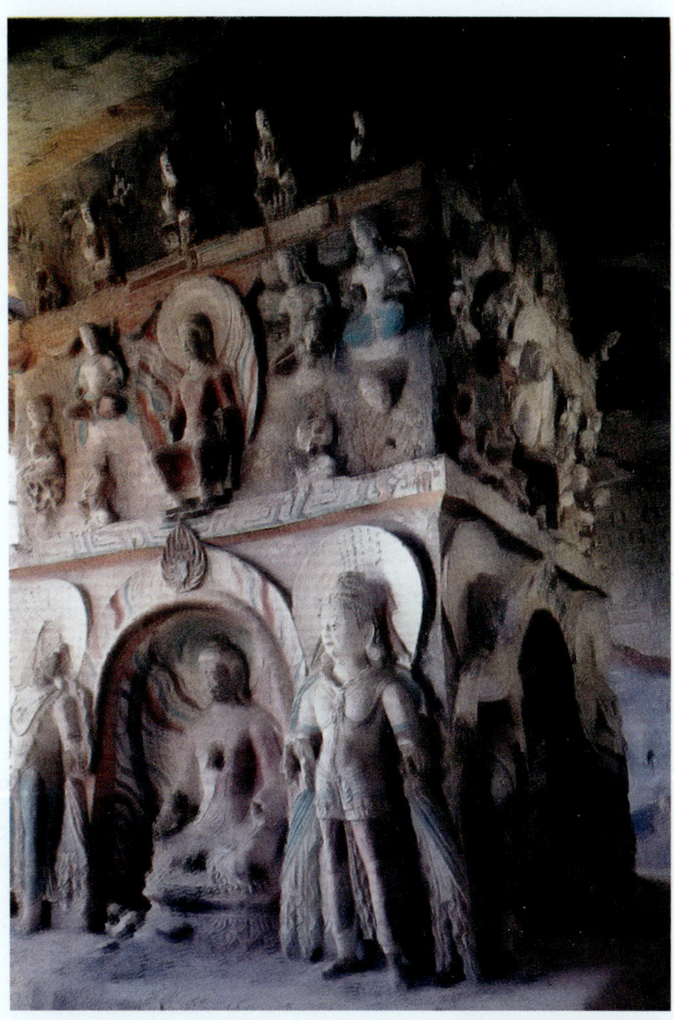

Fig. 3. East face of the central stupa-pillar in the Western Cave of Jintasi, outside the city of Zhangye, Gansu. Period of the Sixteen Kingdoms, Northern Liang dynasty (398–439). After Zhang Baoxi, ed., *Gansu shiku yishu diaosu bian / Grotto Art of Gansu Sculpture* (Lanzhou: Gansu meishu chubanshe, 1994), pl. 39 (bottom left)

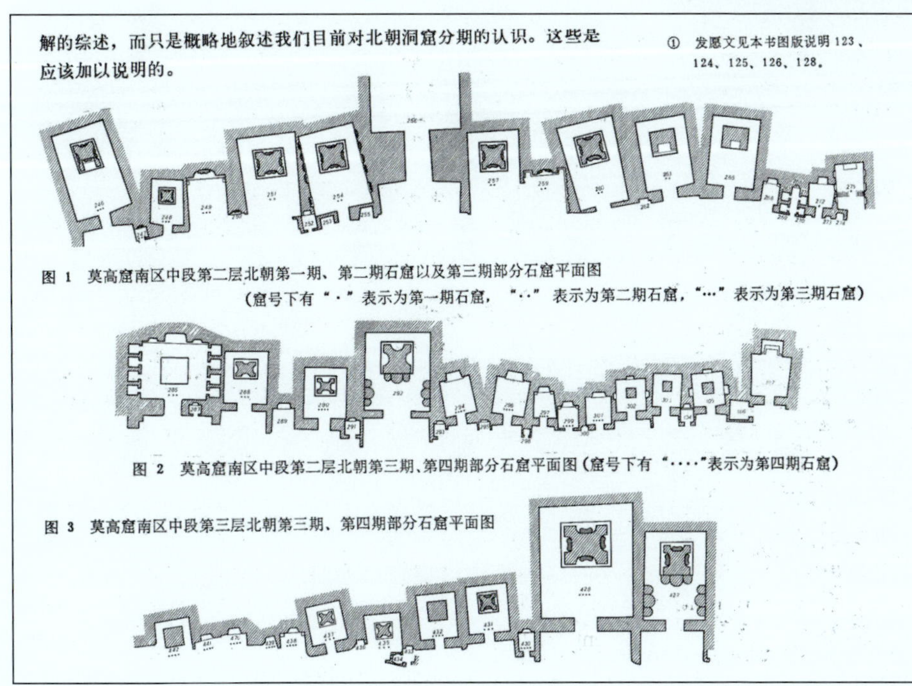

解的综述，而只是概略地叙述我们目前对北朝洞窟分期的认识。这些是应该加以说明的。

① 发愿文见本书图版说明 123、124、125、126、128。

图 1 莫高窟南区中段第二层北朝第一期、第二期石窟以及第三期部分石窟平面图
（窟号下有“·”表示为第一期石窟，“··”表示为第二期石窟，“···”表示为第三期石窟）

图 2 莫高窟南区中段第二层北朝第三期、第四期部分石窟平面图（窟号下有“····”表示为第四期石窟）

图 3 莫高窟南区中段第三层北朝第三期、第四期部分石窟平面图

Fig. 4. Plans of Northern Dynasties caves with central stupa-pillars having two and three tiers of images at the Mogao Grottoes. After Dunhuang wenwu yanjiusuo, comp., *Dunhuang Mogaoku* (Beijing: Wenwu chubanshe, 1981), vol. 1, p. 185, figs. 1–3

images that one aspires to achieve. At the same time, although this merit-accruing practice is well attested to in India, there is no indisputable evidence to indicate that circumambulation formed part of the Buddhist practice in Gansu caves—except for the fact of the central pillar and the commentary of the monk Dharmaraksa who translated the *Lotus Sutra* in 286 and apparently practiced circumambulation assiduously (fig. 4).[25]

As mentioned above, the main element of Cave 432 (replica, cat. no. 30) is the central stupa-pillar; almost all the other parts of this cave, missing from the replica—the walls, ceiling, and base of the stupa-pillar—were repainted by the Tibetan Tangut tribes that established the Western Xia dynasty and controlled part of Gansu and what is today Ningxia. With only the central pillar and the sculpture and paintings on the four faces, it is impossible to evoke in the gallery more of the contextual experience of entering Cave 432. However, given the considerable similarities between Cave 432 and a number of other Northern and Western Wei caves that were not as extensively refurbished and repainted, the Dunhuang Academy chose to provide two examples from these related caves: a painting of the famous Golden Deer Jataka (also known as the Deer King or Ruru Jataka) composition from the Northern Wei Cave 257 (replica, cat. no. 29) and a painting of heavenly musicians in *trompe l'oeil* balconies from the Western Wei Cave 288 (replica, cat. no. 31). Comparisons with other Northern (Caves 248, 254, 259) and Western Wei caves (Caves 249, 288) provide the possibility of some judicious speculation about what had likely been originally painted on the walls of Cave 432. The imagery, architectural plan, and artistic styles of these related caves were comparable, and all shared a completely standardized program.

It is likely that most of the paintings on the north, south, and west walls of Cave 432 were dominated by the Thousand Buddha motif (also visible in the high Tang Cave 45 [replica, cat. no. 32, illus. 32-16]). In rare instances,

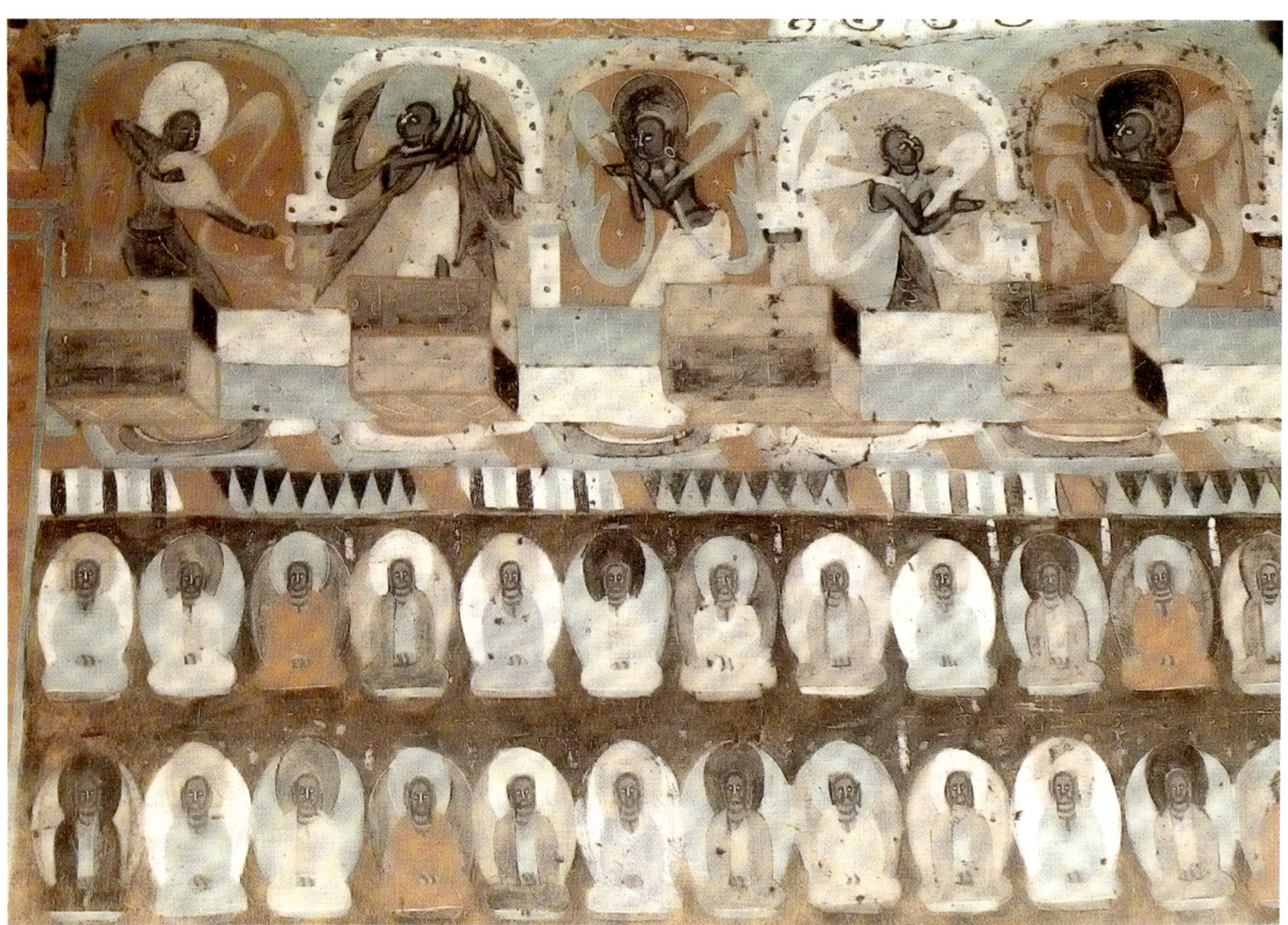

Fig. 5-a. Thousand Buddha pattern below celestial musicians in Mogao Cave 251. Northern Wei dynasty (386–535). After Dunhuang wenwu yanjiusuo, comp., *Dunhuang Mogaoku* (Beijing: Wenwu chubanshe, 1981), vol. 1, pl. 4

small Buddhas made in very low relief of unbaked clay mixed with straw and painted were attached to the central pillar in place of the kneeling bodhisattvas (see cat. nos. 13 and 14), but not in Cave 432.[26] The usual motif consists of registers of seated Buddhas in meditation and in the lotus posture; often the wall is divided into a grid of horizontal and vertical lines with one Buddha filling each square of the grid. To maintain the repetitive and uniform nature of the pattern, a stencil or pounce may have been used. Sometimes, this repetitive Thousand Buddha pattern will be punctuated with a large painted preaching Buddha or small niches with projecting Chinese-style roofs filled with single sculptural images of seated bodhisattvas or pensive Buddhas. This repetitive pattern can be found painted on walls and ceilings of Dunhuang caves dating throughout the Tang dynasty (618–907). In these caves, the Thousand Buddhas symbolize the enormous numbers of Buddhas that existed through the eons in the Past and the Future, while the sculptural images on the pillars or in central niches refer to the present; Mahayana thought postulates not just one Buddha but many Buddhas throughout the universe (figs. 5-a and 5-b).[27]

Several scholars have written about what role the Thousand Buddha pattern may have played in devotional practices, particularly meditation and visualization. This repetitive pattern provided settings for the advanced practice of visualization techniques involving the mental construction of an eidetic image, with the eventual goal of the practitioner learning to visualize a chamber full of Buddhas.[28] In Cave 254, the cartouches next to many of the Buddha images held names which correspond to those in the *Sanjie sanqian foming jing* (*Sutra on the Three Thousand Buddhas of the Three Kalpas),* the past and those in the future.[29] Circumambulating in the present and chanting the names of the Thousand Buddhas parallels the experience of *samsara*—cycle of growing old, becoming

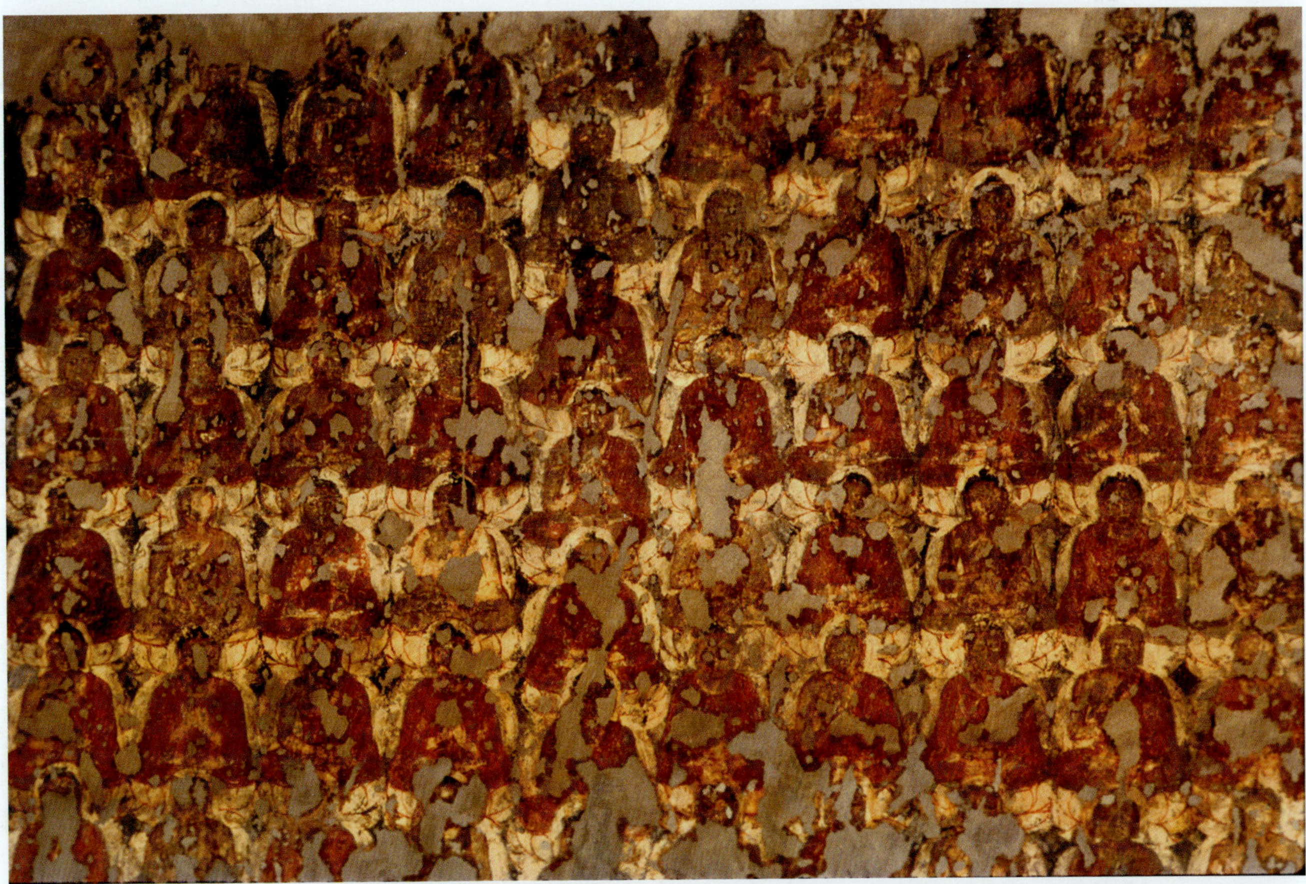

Fig. 5-b. Detail from *Miracle of Shravasti*, depicted on the right hand wall of the ante-chamber of Cave 2, in Ajanta, India. Early 6th century. This is one of the great miracles performed by Shakyamuni at the ancient city of Shravasti. "To silence the skeptics who did not believe the word of the Buddha, he manifested himself miraculously before them in a thousand different forms." After Bernoy K. Behl, *The Ajanta Caves: Ancient Paintings of Buddhist India* (paper edition: New York: Thames & Hudson, 2005), p. 119. Photo by Bernoy K. Behl

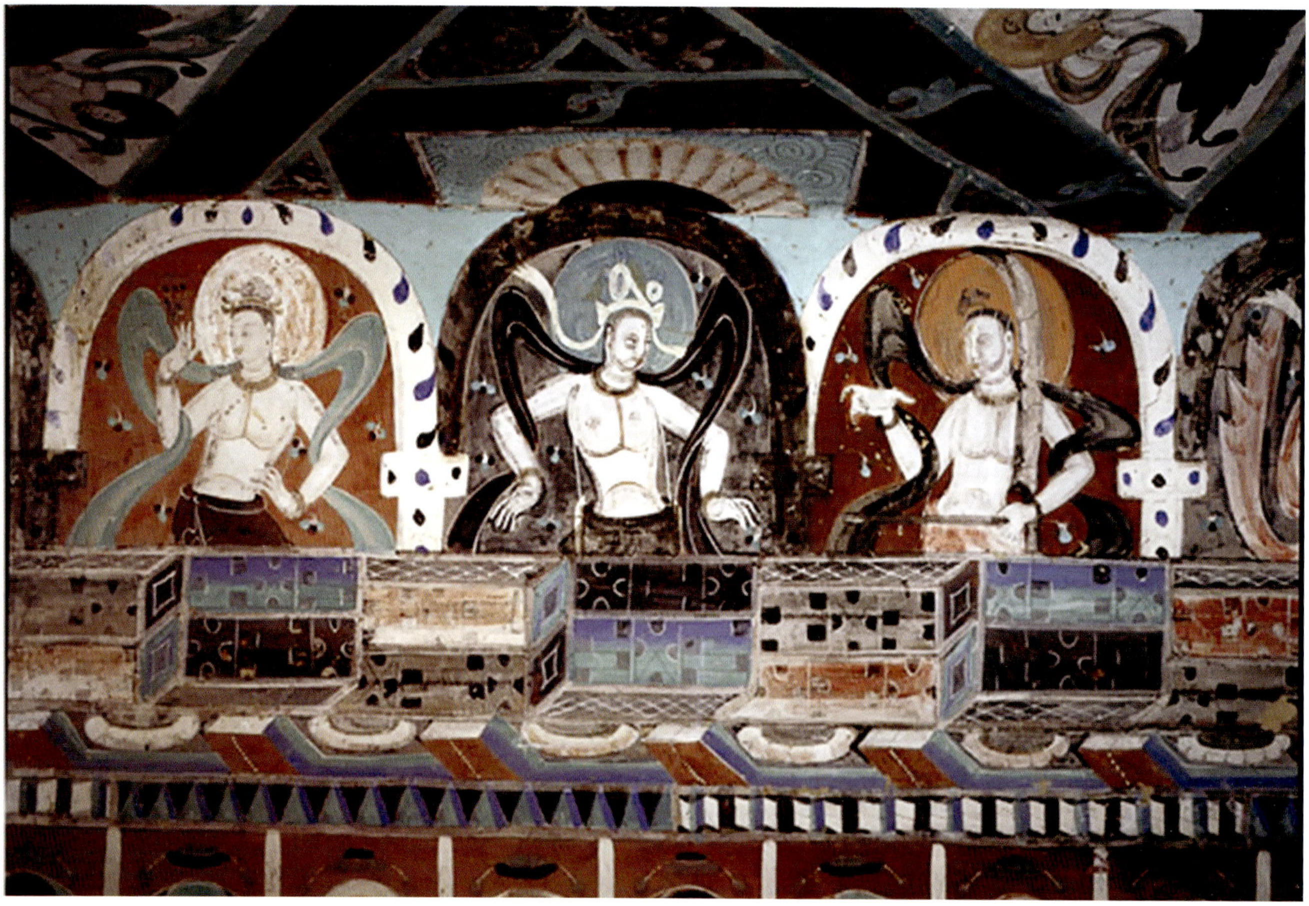

Fig. 6-a. Heavenly musicians from a border running along the top edge just below the ceiling on the walls of Mogao Cave 288. Western Wei dynasty (535–556). After Dunhuang wenwu yanjiusuo, comp., *Dunhuang Mogaoku* (Beijing: Wenwu chubanshe, 1981), vol. 1, pl. 109

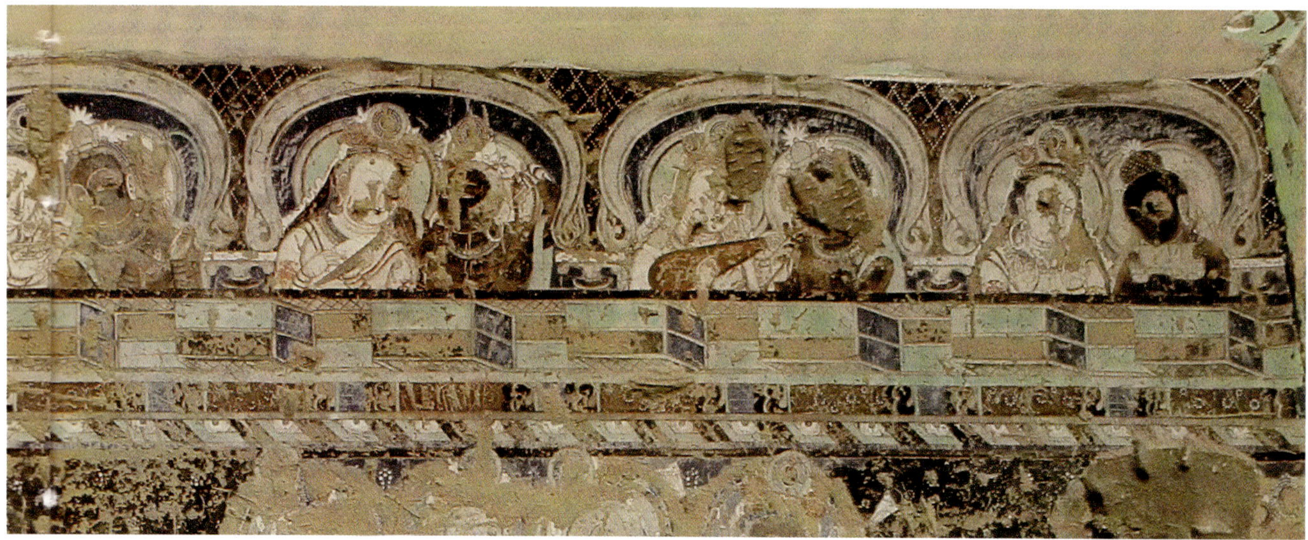

Fig. 6-b. Detail from a mural in Cave 38 (ca. 4th–5th century), from the Buddhist caves near the township of Kizil, in Baicheng county, about 65 miles (105 km) west of the oasis town of Kucha, Xinjiang. After *Kezier shiku* (Beijing: Wenwu chubanshe 1989), vol. 1, pl. 99

ill, dying, and rebirth. Hopefully, performing these devotional practices helped one to accrue merit and thus to affect past and future lives.[30] Cave 432 articulates in art and architecture, and thereby re-enforces for the faithful, the process and obstacles the Buddha endured to achieve the goal of enlightenment.

Three other painted iconographic elements commonly found in central pillar caves are the square ceiling motif called a *tianjing* or *zaojing* covering the ceiling around the central pillar,[31] heavenly musicians tucked in balconies at the edge of the ceiling, and jataka stories of the Buddha's previous lives. Assuming that the north, south, and west walls were covered with the Thousand Buddha pattern, a painted border similar to that from Western Wei Cave 288 (replica, cat. no. 31) would have run along the very top edge of the walls just below the ceiling. Like that border it would have depicted heavenly musicians and / or bodhisattvas with looping scarves standing in niches behind colorfully patterned *trompe l'oeil* balconies clearly of Central Asian inspiration (figs. 6-a and 6-b).[32] The lower middle part of the same wall, at about eye-level, would have had a horizontal row of paintings describing jataka stories, which being far more than fairy tales were taken seriously for their moral and spiritual teachings. The painting in Cave 257 which tells the story of the beautiful nine-colored deer (Ruru Jataka) and its extraordinary compassion is an innovative narrative composition; elements of the narration are separated by diagonal lines of triangular mountains, and the development of the story is constructed in two narrative strands which end in a middle scene (see replica, cat. no. 29).[33]

Cave 45, High Tang (705–781)

Divided for more than three centuries, China was finally reunified by successors of the Northern Wei Tuoba Xianbei under the banner of the Sui dynasty. Although only three decades long, from 589 to 618, this new regime under the powerful leadership of Yang Jian, known as the emperor Wendi (r. 589–610), ardently supported Buddhism and further strengthened the link between Dunhuang in the far northwest and Chang'an, the re-established imperial capital of China. Almost immediately upon reunification, an imperial envoy of the Sui arrived at the Mogao cave site and commissioned a new cave.[34] Buddhism, now well established with a devoted following among the peasants, nomadic populations, and privileged classes, helped heal the factionalism and regionalism of the past centuries by providing a unifying ideology. At the same time other Sui innovations, including a new legal system, laid the foundation for the achievements of the ensuing Tang empire.

In 618 the Sui dynasty fell to the Tang dynasty, whose rulers expanded westward into Xinjiang (Chinese Central Asia) and beyond, to Samarkand; they moved south into Afghanistan and northern Pakistan. Trade both by land along the flourishing Silk Road and by sea routes grew, transforming the imperial capital of Chang'an into a worldly metropolis of two million that attracted monks, merchants, soldiers, entertainers, and diplomatic delegations from all over Asia. A hallmark of Tang art and the vitality of Tang culture was the emergence of a cosmopolitan artistic style—a synthesis of a myriad of foreign influences and Chinese aesthetic values. Achieving the peak of their popularity and importance, the Buddhist religion and Buddhist art reached new heights of elegance and sophistication manifested in the construction of an impressive number of cave temples during the first half of the eighth century in what is known as the high Tang period (705–781), represented by Cave 45 in the exhibition. Although Mogao was geographically remote from the capital of Chang'an, its art was strongly influenced by the styles current at the capital. Fortunately for the history of Buddhist art, the magnificently painted murals, decoration, and sculpture remain relatively intact in the hundreds of Tang caves opened there; this treasure trove preserved what is an important reflection and record of the destroyed masterpieces from the large monasteries that once stood in the capital Chang'an.

In dramatic contrast to the central stupa-pillar plan of the sixth-century Cave 432, high Tang Cave 45 is an excellent example of the "assembly-hall-like" space designed mainly for devout Buddhists to gather and worship; this architectural plan became popular and dominated cave construction from this period onward (see cat. no. 32 [replica], and Appendix 1). This open rectangular hall contains one niche, filled with seven splendid life-sized images (ca. 6 ft. or 1.8 m) beautifully painted, preserved, and positioned in the center of the back wall opposite the entrance (see p. 5, fig. 5). A robustly modeled Buddha image, seated in a lotus posture on an octagonal, stepped pedestal, dominates the alcove space, his presence exuding serene and compassionate power; his right hand is raised in the *abhaya* (do not fear) mudra and the left, with palm and fingers down, displays the *bhumisparsha* mudra (gesture of touching the earth), calling the earth to witness his unshakable resolve. The indented mid-section of the pedestal refers to Mount Sumeru, the world mountain connecting the phenomenal world with the spiritual realm.

Fig. 7. Detail of the young monk Ananda, one of the figures on the south side of the niche in west wall in Mogao Cave 45. High Tang period (705–781)

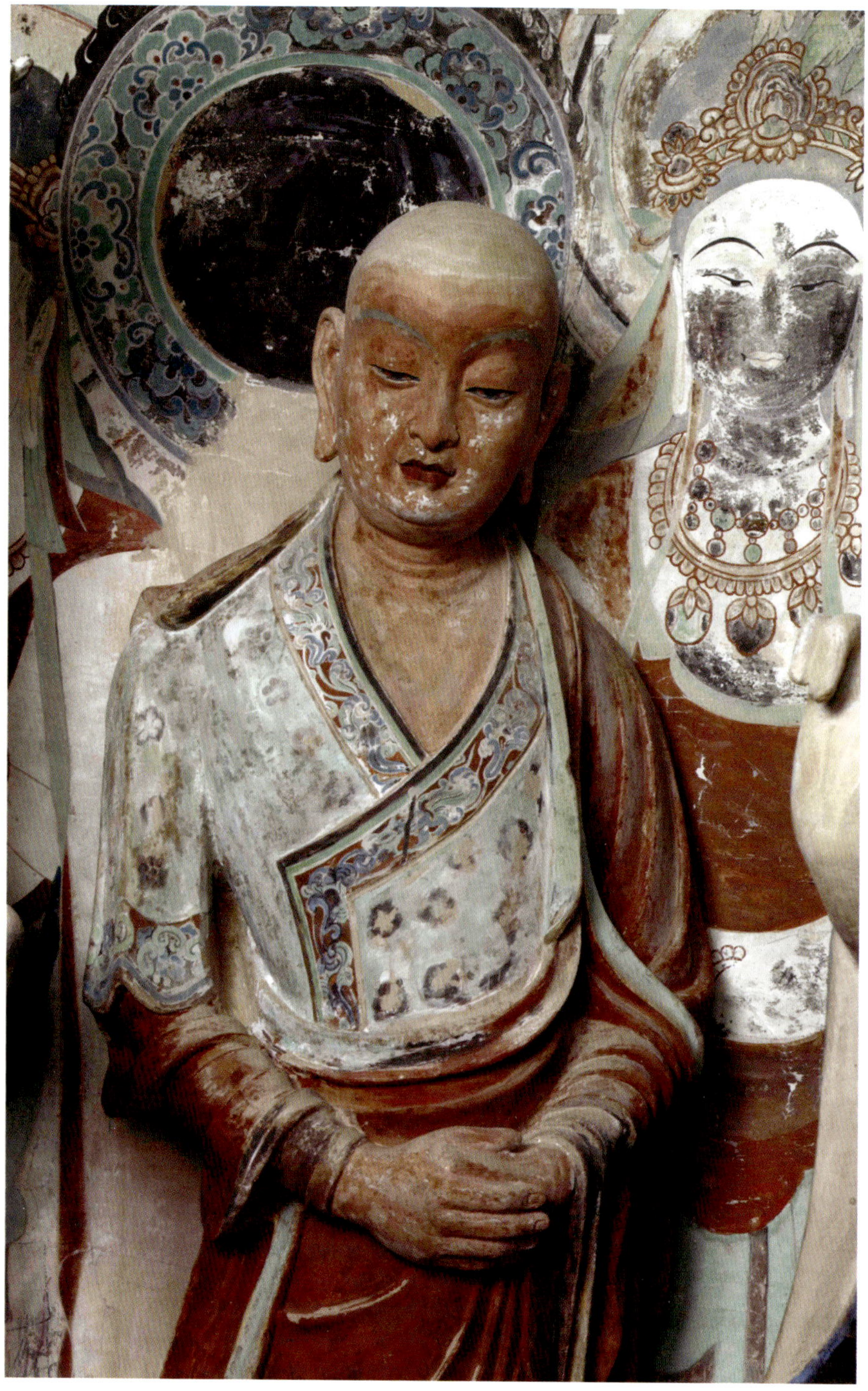

Flanking the Buddha in Cave 45 are his two best-known monk disciples; Ananda, the youngest, stands at his right, and Kashyapa, the oldest, on his left. Both wear luxuriously patterned robes with gilded edges, reflecting the prosperity at the height of the empire. Sculpturally, both are compelling and skillfully rendered portraits capturing Ananda's youthful expressive face and gentle contemplative nature (fig. 7) and Kashyapa's knowing but care-worn eyes and stubbled chin above the emaciated body of an ascetic. Next to the monks are two classic eighth-century bodhisattvas standing bare-chested in an S-curve posture with one out-thrust hip emphasizing the rounded and sensuous but solid forms of the body (see cat. no. 32, illus. 32-3 and 32-4). Facial features of these feminized images recall Tang court beauties with their full round faces, high arched eyebrows, and sharply defined, bow-shaped plump lips. At the outer edges of the niche, two *dvarapalas* dressed as generals in full military armor stomp on demon figures; their wrath is caught in clenched fists, which probably originally held weapons, and in their bulging eyes and fierce, exaggerated grimaces. These are two of the Four Heavenly Kings who protect the Buddhist universe.

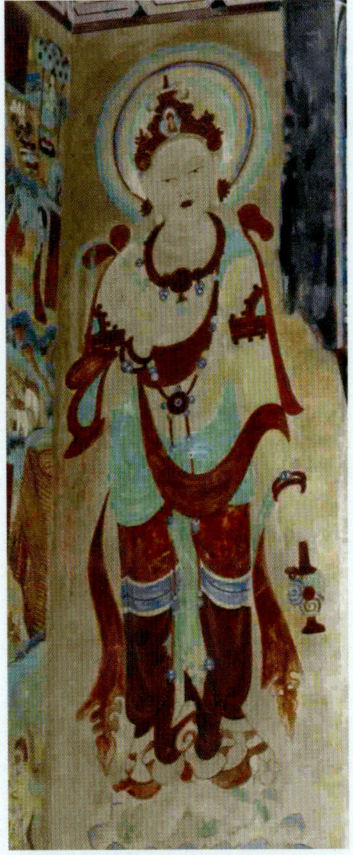

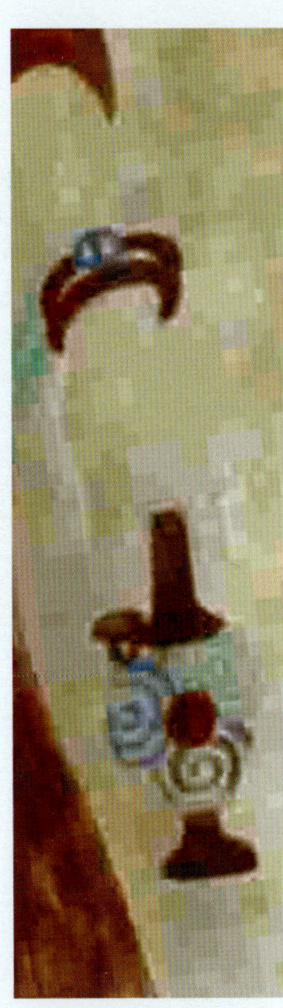

Fig. 8. a) Image of Avalokiteshvara holding a *kundika* bottle and lotus flower on the west wall, south of the niche in Mogao Cave 45. Mid-Tang period (781–848). b) Detail of *kundika* bottle held by Avalokiteshvara

On the side walls just outside the niche are two very popular and widely known bodhisattvas; on the left/south side is painted a life-size Avalokiteshvara, and on the right/north, Ksitigarbha (Ch., Dizang), the Merciful Helper of the Dead or Saviour from Hell. Probably repainted later when the wall was repaired, both date from the mid-Tang period (781–848) when Dunhuang was controlled and ruled by the Tibetans. Influence from the Tibetan occupiers is visible in the face and crown of Avalokiteshvara, who stands on a lotus flower base and holds in the left hand a long, narrow-necked bottle, known as a *kundika*, containing *amrita* water, the nectar of immortality (fig. 8). The *kundika* (pure-water bottle) is a ritual vessel with an ovoid body resting on a high splayed foot; it has a bulbous spout with a cup-shaped mouth attached to the shoulder.[35] Such vessels, carried by monks for Buddhist rituals of hand washing, were fashioned from glazed pottery, porcelain, or metal and apparently introduced into China from Central Asia and India during the Tang, around the seventh century. Ksitigarbha, a bodhisattva, was so moved by the suffering in the Buddhist hells that he tried to intercede with the King of Hell and vowed not to achieve Buddhahood until all the hells were emptied.[36] Unlike any other bodhisattva, he is depicted as a monk with a shaven head and robe, holding in one hand a wish-fulfilling jewel (see replica, cat. no. 32, illus. 32-15). He is often seen in other depictions also holding a staff festooned with metal rings to alert animals and insects ahead lest he inadvertently harm them.

Behind all the sculptures in the niche, there is a circle of haloed bodhisattvas painted on the wall along with the Buddha's halo and fiery mandorla. The top of the Buddha's leaf-shaped mandorla bends up onto the ceiling, pointing to and overlapping a lavishly painted tableau of the Many Treasures Stupa or Tower, a famous parable from the *Lotus Sutra*.[37] The Many Treasures Stupa itself seems to be floating atop what looks like a magic carpet but is actually a tasseled canopy resting on the green foliage of the jeweled trees of the Pure Land just above the Buddha's head. The magnificently opulent square stupa shows Shakyamuni and the Prabhutaratna (Many Treasures Buddha) seated cross-legged, face to face; a bejeweled pedestal between them supports a *chintamani*. Prabhutaratna, the ancient Buddha who entered nirvana eons ago has returned to bear witness to Shakyamuni's preaching and the *Lotus Sutra*. When Shakyamuni sat at Prabhutaratna's invitation, the pagoda rose into the air to the astonishment of the mesmerized multitudes below (see cat. no. 32, illus. 32-5).[38] As the parable continues, Shakyamuni uses his transcendental power to levitate all the members of the great assembly. The hovering bodhisattvas float in the air, painted on each side of the Treasures stupa. During the high Tang period, the sophistication of the sculpture achieved an exquisite balance between realism and stylization, visible here in the interplay and integration between two- and three-dimensional forms in the niche and its ceiling.

Superbly conceived and fluently painted mural compositions, dating from the high Tang, cover the north and south walls of the assembly hall. On the north wall, a glittering vision of the Pure Land of Ultimate Bliss (Skt., Sukhavati), often described as a paradise, presided over by Amitabha Buddha materializes filled with palaces, musicians, and dancers (see replica, cat. no. 32, illus. 32-11 and 32-13).[39] With the growing popularity of the Pure Land School during the Tang, there was a proliferation of these large-scale paintings depicting Amitabha and other Buddhas in their divine abodes.[40] Rebirth in Amitabha's Pure Land itself involves both the transformation of the deceased into a new being and the miraculous power to facilitate this process.[41] These images reflect the Buddhist belief that when one of their adherents departs from this world, they are placed by Avalokiteshvara in the heart of a lotus and then sent to Amitabha's Pure Land in the West.[42]

The main teaching of the Chinese Pure Land Buddhist tradition involves visualization of the Amitabha Buddha, as well as his attendants and Pure Land, and meditative contemplation (that is, focusing the mind with Mindfulness of the Buddha) through recitation of the name of Amitabha Buddha, to attain rebirth in his Pure Land. The *Amitayurdhayana*

Sutra describes Queen Vaidehi's practice of thirteen visualization methods corresponding to the attainment of various levels of rebirth in the Pure Land. Queen Vaidehi's suffering, which stems from her son's betrayal, is symbolic of all those who have suffered tragedy and injustice; she cries out to Amitabha for help and he teaches her the thirteen subjects, a ladder of meditation, which brings her to higher and higher levels of awareness progressing towards her rebirth.[43] Chinese Buddhists had traditionally viewed the practice of meditation and recitation of Amitabha Buddha's name as analogous or alternative means to achieve enlightenment. In Cave 45, two narrow vertical panels, one on each side of the mural of the Pure Land, are separated from the heavenly vision by a border of five-petaled flowers; the panel on the west end (left side) depicts Queen Vaidehi's meditation practice in a series of small scenes separated and connected by cartouches and landscape elements, mostly trees and mountains (fig. 9).

The ladder starts at the top left and zigzags back and forth as the vignettes move down the wall: first, Vaidehi kneels and visualizes the setting sun; second, followed by water just below; to the right and third, the ground of the Pure Land, depicted as a white rectangular box laying on the ground; and fourth, directly below, the Pure Land's jeweled trees; and so on until the last step. In the twelfth step Vaidehi visualizes her own ascension to the Pure Land, and finally, in the thirteenth step, she visualizes universal salvation, beyond Amitabha Buddha's Pure Land to the other Buddhas throughout the Ten Quarters.[44] The narrow panel running down the right (or east) side provides the circumstances of Queen Vaidehi's suffering (replica, cat. no. 32, illus. 32-13). Their evil son tries to kill his father, King Bimbisara, but the Queen foils the plot and saves the King. When the son finds out, he imprisons her alone, a scene visible near the top of the panel. Her pleas are heard by Amitabha, shown sitting in the Pure Land in the scene above; he descends on a wisp of cloud to teach her the meditation practice which will free her from suffering.

On the south wall, a huge image of Avalokiteshvara dominates the entire composition; originally, before sustaining damage at the bottom, the bodhisattva's image reached from the ceiling to the floor (fig. 10; see replica, cat. no. 32, illus. 32-6). Small narratives with cartouches surround the figure on both sides and chronicle the interventions of Avalokiteshvara, savior of those in distress. In the Western Paradise, the two greatest and holiest bodhisattvas who serve as acolytes to Amitabha are Avalokiteshvara and Mahasthamaprapta. Avalokiteshvara welcomes the faithful to the Pure Land and represents compassion while Mahasthamaprapta symbolizes power and wisdom. Dashizhi, the Chinese name for Mahasthamaprapta, translates as "he who has obtained great force."[45]

Probably the most venerated and worshipped of all the Buddhist deities, Avalokiteshvara was originally male in India but came to be rendered female in China and Japan. Here, the representation is more strongly masculine. The stalwart, straight-bodied figure, typically wearing a *dhoti*, seems to hold a decorated golden bottle in the left hand and a lotus in the right. Looping scarves, necklaces, medallions, and arm bracelets obscure much of the bare chest; the physical presence does not convey to the same degree the characteristic Tang sensuousness of the Avalokiteshvara painted on the west wall and stucco bodhisattvas flanking the Buddha in the niche. The painting is masterful, however, capturing the different textures of layered textiles with remains of gold patterns and transparent scarves draping over shoulders and arms. A small seated image of Amitabha sits in the center of Avalokiteshvara's floral crown, just below an open, brilliant white-petaled lotus flower nestled inside the lavish protective canopy decorated with hanging jeweled tassels and flaming *chintamani*.

Filling the space on both sides of this powerfully dominant image of Avalokiteshvara are skillfully arranged narrative episodes illustrating the miracles this compassionate bodhisattva performed. His Chinese name, Guanyin or Guanshiyin, means "Perceiver of the World's Sounds," specifically the sounds of distress and pleas for assistance. According to the *Lotus Sutra*, Avalokiteshvara intervened for those in peril who single-mindedly called his name.[46] The painted episodes in Cave 45 are identified by cartouches, and the narrative unfolds as the stories flow from one event to the other interwoven with landscape and architectural settings. One tale tells of Silk Road caravans, their pack mules laden with riches, beset by two hundred or more bogus robbers actually sent from small poor kingdoms seeking to fill their coffers. The image shows foreign traders threatened by these robbers escaping "sword and spear" only though the power of Avalokiteshvara (replica, cat. no. 32, illus. 32-7). Below that, a fettered criminal is liberated by his focus on this bodhisattva, as is a man assailed by demons.[47] The viewer moves easily through the scenes, caught up by the rhythm of repeating cartouches and the brilliant turquoise color of the figures' robes. Because no monasteries or temples with mural paintings survived from the Tang capital, extant sutra illustrations and tomb paintings provide invaluable information about Tang landscape and figural imagery.

The decorative programs in Tang period Dunhuang caves were dominated by popular Mahayana teachings of the Pure Land School and the *Lotus Sutra*, the themes and images of which are embodied in large-scale mural

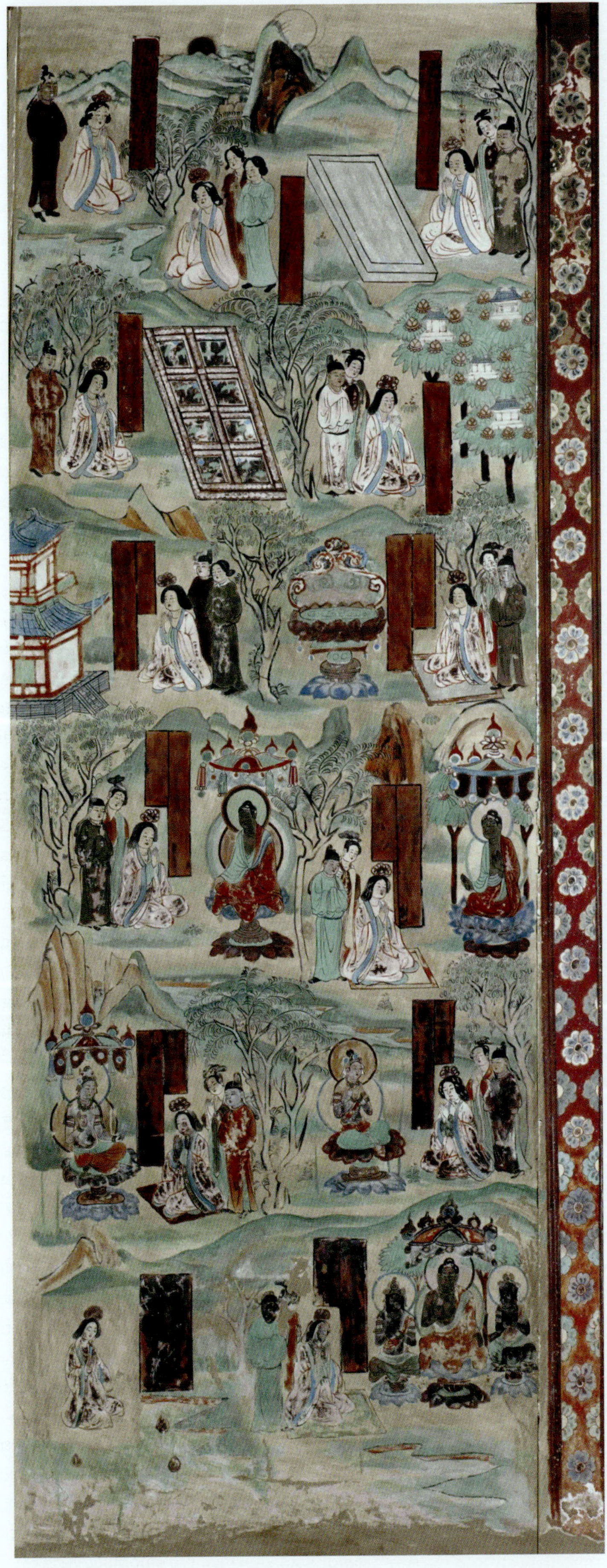

Fig. 9. The Thirteen Meditations of Queen Vaidehi, left panel of the mural on the north wall of Mogao Cave 45. High Tang period (705–781). After Dunhuang wenwu yanjiusuo, comp., *Dunhuang Mogaoku* (Beijing: Wenwu chubanshe, 1981), vol. 3, pl. 138

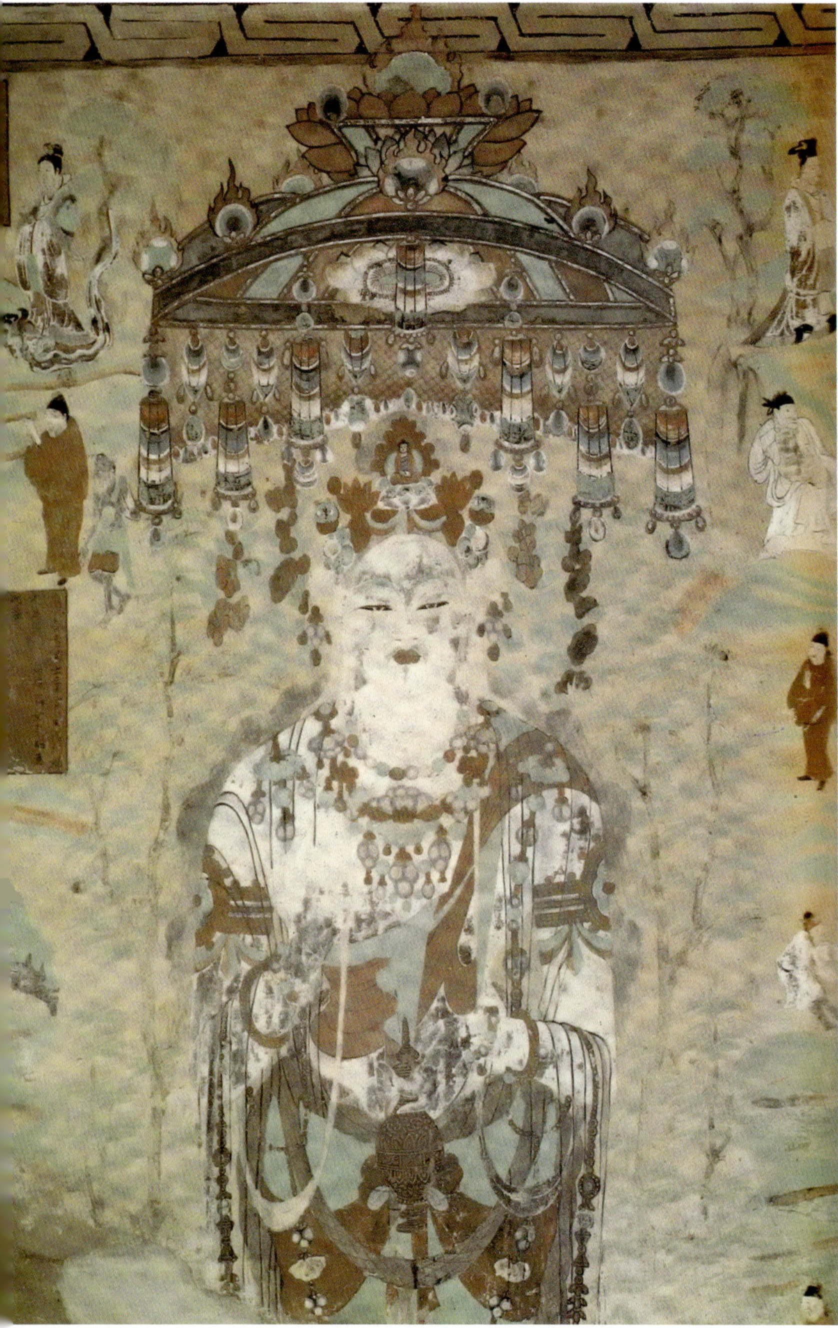

Fig. 10. Detail of large Avalokiteshvara figure in the mural on the south wall of Mogao Cave 45. High Tang period (705–781). After Dunhuang wenwu yanjiusuo, comp., *Dunhuang Mogaoku* (Beijing: Wenwu chubanshe, 1981), vol. 3, pl. 135

paintings, especially from the high Tang period. Older Buddhist themes such as jataka tales were allotted much less space, with one exception. The Thousand Buddha pattern retained a significant and continued presence perhaps as an expression of the multiplicity of Buddhas in the cosmology of the Mahayana doctrines. Pure Land doctrines and the *Lotus Sutra* emphasize visualization and meditation or "mindfulness" as important pathways to transformation in Amitabha's Pure Land. In Cave 45, the Thousand Buddhas cover the slanted surfaces of the truncated pyramidal ceiling typical of high Tang Dunhuang cave architecture (see replica, cat. no. 32, illus. 32-16). Directly in the center, the pyramidal walls meet and form a recessed square referred to as a *zaojing* (藻井) which contains an elegant floral medallion with a border of repeated heart designs. The four sloping ceiling walls together with the *zaojing* form a square canopy symbolizing heaven. The Tang passion for floral medallions is also evidenced in the stamped clay bricks that originally paved cave floors (cat. nos. 23–26). The *zaojing* is framed by double borders filled with classical high Tang floral vines and medallions; an outer border contains a row of stylized lotus petals and a row of overlapping triangles featuring what might be a jewel or bead at each tip. All are painted in vibrant colors. Beyond the triangles an uneven rippling edge on all four sides suggests the movement of fabric, perhaps a canopy. Overall, the form and decoration of the ceiling transform the space of Cave 45 into a dramatic almost theatrical experience.

In Cave 432, the central stupa-pillar plan structures an experience quite different from that in the later open assembly hall of Cave 45. The large stupa-pillar in the square main chamber leaves only a narrow pathway around the chamber, making it virtually impossible to avoid walking around the pillar, clockwise if following the ritual of circumambulation. One sees the Buddha images on all four sides at eye level and above. Small kneeling bodhisattvas in relief (see, for example, cat. nos. 8–12) are tucked next to and behind the arch over the Buddha's head, forcing attention upward to the ceiling. The circumambulator moves from the light flooding over the east face through the cave entrance to the darkness of the west face, which depicts the ascetic, painfully emaciated Buddha struggling on his path to enlightenment, and back to the light again. The act of circumambulation has several layers of meaning and intent, including the acquisition of sufficient merit to end one's suffering; the experience of past, present, and future; and the release from *samsara*, or the cycle of birth, life, death, and rebirth. This ritual walking prepares the practitioner, depending on his or her level of spiritual development, for a form of meditation known as *guan*, or "visualization meditation."[48] *Guan* required visualizing every aspect of the Buddha's body (the artistic images, painted or sculptured, assisted the devout to focus). Circumambulation, along with walking one round, or hundreds, prepares the devout's unattached or "empty" mind to fill with visions. The Mahayana canon emphasized the making of images or donating of funds for the purpose as a way of gaining merit. On the side walls, the Thousand Buddha pattern reinforced the drumbeat of time expressed through the chanting of the names of the Buddhas, while jataka tales of the Buddha's own journey through many lives to achieve the goal of enlightenment offered reminders of the cycle of *samsara*.[49]

The large scale of the open assembly hall space of Cave 45, the life-size sculpture, and the wall mural exemplify the power and grandeur of the Tang dynasty, which peaked in the first half of the eighth century, and highlight the enormous popularity of the Western Pure Land of Amitabha. Since the Mahayana canon emphasizes compassion and help for others on the path to Buddhahood, the laity had a far more active role than earlier, requiring larger communal assembly spaces. Here, the devout could practice circumambulation while experiencing the physical presence of the sculptural images and the magnificent visions in the painted murals. The tableau of the Western Pure Land depicts a remarkable place of beauty that surpasses all other realms, a place presided over by Amitabha and two acolytes, Avalokiteshvara and Mahasthamaprapta, and inhabited by many gods surrounded by music, flowers, fruits, wish-granting trees, and rare birds. Yet this Pure Land is recognizable as a more extraordinary and perfect version of our terrestrial world without the troubles. In addition, the presence of Avalokiteshvara on the opposite wall suggests solace, compassion, and an offer of protection. The configuration of Cave 45 allows the faithful to experience the Pure Land on earth.

One sutra relates that "one ought to kneel before the image with palms together and recite the mantra seven or more times. In this way, many sins would be cleansed."[50] The devout, alone or with others filling the hall, while walking or sitting, can practice one or all three forms of meditation: Mindfulness of the Buddha, that is, calling Amitabha to mind by repeating his name to cultivate peaceful emptiness; repeating the Pure Land Dharani, a kind of mantra or recitation; or Visualization of Amitabha, the thirteen steps depicted on the left side of the Pure Land mural in Cave 45.[51] The experience of these magnificent large-scale spaces with brilliant colors and fantastic magical images surely played a role in inspiring and strengthening faith.

The numerous Buddhist holy days and festivals were celebrated by temple visitors bearing offerings of prayers, incense, fruits, flowers, and donations. Commonly, banners inscribed with sacred writings were strung across the cliffs, and other fabrics were hung inside the caves, often as altar valences across the niche (see cat. nos. 16 and 17); but few have survived.[52]

Hopefully, this exhibition, which incorporates replicas into an approximate representation of their original physical context, allows the viewer to enjoy a richer more multi-faceted experience with perhaps a new awareness not only of how the art related to the sacred spaces of the caves but also how the religion may have been practiced. Still, aspects of the viewer experience of the cave temples as a sacred space cannot be fully replicated in this gallery or indeed anywhere; always absent will be the inescapable presence of the sacred site itself—a cliff wall honeycombed with caves looming overhead and stretching into the distance—and the overwhelming impact of physically entering and walking through spaces carved so deeply into living rock. This journey inward, both literal and metaphoric, enhances the numinous power of the cave spaces.[53]

Buddhism has a strong devotional orientation, especially among the laity, with many Buddhists regularly visiting holy sites and undertaking pilgrimages to make offerings and pray. Any attempt to understand how the Buddhist religion was practiced in these caves presents the same difficult challenges as comprehending what the Buddhist imagery in the cave represents and logically demands turning to the obvious primary sources—the sutras or texts themselves. In the words of Eugene Wang, "In fact, although Buddhist imagery seemingly results from the transfer of the textual into the pictorial or sculptural media, the art is rarely, if ever, a direct illustration of the sutra. Between the word (text or sutra) and image, a discontinuity, a metaphorical or symbolic space, exists."[54] In the world of image making, it is in this virtual space that the creative imagination of the artist acts as the mediator, conjuring up representations of the Buddhist teachings and universe. To understand the ancient practice of the Buddhist religion, we have descriptions in sutras or texts discussing, for example, the rite of circumambulating or proper behavior in front of the image of Amitabha. Again, however, a space exists between the words and the actual rites; within this space, adaptations and changes occurred as the religion spread to China, shaped by variant local cultural value systems and the level of spiritual development of the practitioners. Ultimately, despite the evidence of the caves and their contents and the surviving texts, any contemporary discussion of practice and process regarding Buddhist devotional worship in the fifth or ninth centuries in China involves a considerable degree of speculative interpretation.

NOTES

1. Fan Jinshi, Director of the Dunhuang Academy, gives a brief but useful overview of the founding of the academy and its work in her foreword to Roderick Whitfield, Susan Whitfield, and Neville Agnew, *Cave Temples of Mogao: Art and History on the Silk Road* (Los Angeles: The Getty Conservation Institute and the J. Paul Getty Museum, 2000), p. v. A useful source of information is also the Dunhuang Academy's website, http.//enweb.dha.ac.en. There are a legion of publications concerning the site of Dunhuang in many languages, providing photographs and documentation of the caves. One of the most recent in English, again by Fan Jinshi, provides an overview of the caves and sites as well as identifying and explaining Buddhist iconography, *The Caves of Dunhuang* (Hong Kong: London Editions, 2010).

2. Whitfield et al., *Cave Temples of Mogao*, p. v.

3. Roderick Whitfield and Anne Farrer, *Caves of the Thousand Buddhas: Chinese Art from the Silk Route* (London: The Trustees of the British Museum, 1990), p. 16.

4. Ibid., p. 16.

5. K. M. Maitra, trans., *A Persian Embassy to China: Being an Extract from Zubdatu't Tawarikh of Hafiz Abru* (1934; repr., New York: Paragon Book Reprint Corp., 1970), p. 39; also in Whitfield and Farrer, *Caves of the Thousand Buddhas*, p. 16.

6. Publications on Buddhist art and the Silk Road are legion, and it is impossible to list even the most significant ones. Any one of the following publications provides extensive references on the subjects—Annette L. Juliano, *Buddhist Sculpture from China: Selections from the Xi'an Beilin Museum, Fifth through Ninth Centuries* (New York: China Institute Gallery, 2007); Susan Whitfield and Ursula Sims-Williams, eds., *The Silk Road: Trade, Travel, War and Faith* (Chicago: Serindia Publications for The British Library, 2004); James C. Y. Watt et al., *China: Dawn of a Golden Age, 200–750 AD* (New York: Metropolitan Museum of Art; New Haven and London: Yale University Press, 2004), pp. 79–89, 89–99; Annette L. Juliano and Judith A. Lerner, *Monks and Merchants: Silk Road Treasures from Northwest China* (New York: Harry N. Abrams, Inc., with the Asia Society, 2010), pp. 119–217; Rajeswari Ghose et al., *In the Footsteps of the Buddha: An Iconic Journey from India to China* (Hong Kong: University Museum and Art Gallery, The University of Hong Kong, 1998). There are extensive Chinese and Japanese multi-volume works providing photographic documents of the painting and sculpture in cave temples: Dunhuang wenwu yanjiusuo 敦煌文物研究所 (Dunhuang Research Institute), comp., *Dunhuang Mogaoku* 敦煌莫高窟 [Dunhuang Mogao caves], Zhongguo shiku 中国石窟 [Chinese cave temples], 5 vols. (Beijing: Wenwu chubanshe, 1981–); Gansu sheng wenwu gongzuodui 甘肃省文物工作队 (Gansu Cultural Relics Work Group) and Binglingsi wenwu baoguan suo 炳灵寺文物保管所 (Bingling Temple Cultural Relics Preservation Institute), comp., *Yongjing Binglingsi* 永靖炳灵寺 / *The Binglingsi Grottoes* (Beijing: Wenwu chubanshe, 1989); Tianshui Maijishan yishu yanjiusuo 天水麦积山石窟艺朮研究所 (Art and Research Institute of the Maijishan Cave Temples at Tianshui), comp., *Tianshui Maijishan* 天水麦积山 [Maijishan Cave Temples at Tianshui] (Beijing: Wenwu chubanse; Tokyo: Heibonsha, 1998), and many others.

7. Juliano, *Buddhist Sculpture*, pp. 1–31. One of the oldest museums in China devoted primarily to stone sculpture, the Xi'an Beilin Museum has assembled pieces locally from Xi'an and Shaanxi province as well as nearby provinces. They have recently unearthed a number of cache burials of monumental Northern Zhou (557–581) sculpture.

8. More recent exhibitions involving stereoscopic photography of caves, combined with photographs and objects have begun moving closer to evoking a more effective sense of context, see Katherine R. Tsiang, *Echoes of the Past: The Buddhist Cave Temples of Xiangtangshan* (Chicago: Smart Art Museum, University of Chicago, 2010). Digital images are available on the website of the Xiangtangshan Caves Project, http://xts.uchicago.edu/, hosted by the The University of Chicago Center for the Art of East Asia. A small but growing number of scholars, like Stanley K. Abe, "Art and Practice in a Fifth-Century Chinese Buddhist Cave Temple," *Ars Orientalis* 20 (1990):1–31, have become interested in the relationship between the Buddhist religion and practice. Eugene Y. Wang's description of the Many Treasures Stupa in Cave 169 at Binglingsi is clearly interested in the art historical and iconographic; but there are moments when his description of the sun flooding into the cave transcends the factual and textual, and one can glimpse the specialness of this place and space, in Eugene Y. Wang, *Shaping the Lotus Sutra: Buddhist Visual Culture in Medieval China* (Seattle and London: University of Washington Press, 2005), pp. 13–18. France Pepper, "The Thousand Buddha Motif: A Visual Chant in Cave-Temples Along the Silk Road," *Oriental Art* 44, no. 4 (1998/9): 39–45, explores the relationship of the Thousand Buddha image and its possible uses by the faithful, especially in chanting.

9. For a very challenging and interesting discussion of the role of architectural space in mediating the relationship between god and man in religious structures, see Thomas Barrie. *The Sacred in-Between: The Mediating Roles of Architecture* (London: Routledge, 2010).

10. Steen Eiler Rasmussen, a famous Danish architect and urban planner, commented in his book that "it is not enough to see architecture; you must experience it"; Rasmussen, *Experiencing Architecture* (Cambridge, MA: MIT Press, 1959), p. 17.

11. Literary scholars divided the Tang dynasty into four periods to describe the development of poetry. High Tang was a designation for the Golden Age of classical Chinese poetry. These periods are defined as much by political events as by stylistic characteristics of the arts. The reign of Xuanzong (712–56) is considered the zenith of Tang imperial power and thus the beginning of the high Tang period. Others see this period as beginning earlier. The Dunhuang Academy uses the following periodization of the Mogao Caves in its English literature: early Tang (618–705), high Tang (705–781), middle or mid-Tang (781–848), and late Tang (848–907). The mid-Tang period begins with the invasion and control of Dunhuang by the Tibetans. In the last phase of the dynasty, Dunhuang is returned to Chinese rule.

12. The four slopes of the truncated ceiling of Mogao Cave 249 are teeming with heavenly creatures, including the Daoist goddess *Xiwangmu*, who rides in a chariot drawn by phoenixes, and her male counterpart, *Dongwanggong*, his chariot drawn by dragons. See Terukazu Akiyama and Saburo Matsubara, *Arts of China: Buddhist Cave Temples, New Researches*, trans. Alexander C. Soper (Tokyo, Japan & Palo Alto, CA,

Kodansha International LTD., 1969), pl. 18, p. 45, p. 209. Susan L. Beningson explores the influence of the symbolic configuration of traditional Han tombs on the shaping of early Buddhist rock-cut temples in Gansu in "Shaping Sacred Space: Studies in the Ritual Architecture and Artistic Program of Early Buddhist Cave Temples and their Relation to Tombs in Fifth Century China" (PhD diss., Columbia University, 2009), UMI 3386118.

13. An excellent view of the dynamic forces shaping north China and the struggle between nomadic military rule and more traditional Chinese-style bureaucratic rule can be found in Mark Edward Lewis, *China Between Empires, The Northern and Southern Dynasties* (London and Cambridge, MA: The Belknap Press of Harvard University Press, 2009), see especially chapter three, "Military Dynasticism," pp. 28–54.

14. The various interpretations of the symbolism of the central stupa-pillar in about 18 extant caves at Dunhuang are discussed in Puay-Peng Ho, "The Symbolism of the Central Pillars in Cave-Temples of Northwest China," in Emily B. Lyle, ed., *Sacred Architecture in the Traditions of India, China, Judaism, and Islam*, Cosmos: The Yearbook of the Traditional Cosmology Society 8 (Edinburgh, Scotland: Edinburgh University Press, 1992), pp. 59–70.

15. See the floor plan of Cave 254 in Pepper, "The Thousand Buddha Motif," p. 39, fig. 1.

16. A Buddha placed on each of the four sides of a central cave pillar or a free-standing stone pillar became popular in the sixth century and may be traced back to Indian and Central Asian precedents. However, the identification of these Buddhas of the Four Directions in Chinese sculpture remains perplexing; see Wang, *Shaping the Lotus Sutra*, pp. 343–45. At the same time, the idea of Buddhas in four directions would certainly be consistent with ancient Chinese cosmological beliefs since at least as early as the Shang dynasty. By the Han dynasty each direction acquired additional layers of symbolism, such as a designated color and representative animal.

17. Although Western Wei Cave 249 does not have a central pillar, the Buddha seated in the main niche shares many similar stylistic elements with the Buddha seated with pendant legs on the east face of the pillar in Cave 432. There is a pointed curved arch painted just above the niche and filled with lush lotus flowers; the heads and torsos of small human figures are visible emerging from lotus flowers, presumably reborn into the Pure Land. See *Dunhuang Mogaoku*, vol. 1, pl. 89.

18. Kurt A. Behrendt, *The Art of Gandhara in the Metropolitan Museum of Art* (New Haven and London: Yale University Press, 2007), no. 46, p. 57. No photo of the emaciated Buddha on the west face of the central pillar of Cave 432 is available.

19. See *Dunhuang Mogaoku*, vol. 1, pl. 80.

20. According to Puay-Peng Ho's analysis, "The architectural form of the central-pillared caves at Dunhuang is different from that at Kizil"; Ho, "The Symbolism of the Central Pillars," p. 63.

21. Ibid., p. 67.

22. For a description and discussion of the Hexi Corridor Buddhist caves, Jintasi, Matisi, Wenshushan, and Tiantishan, see Juliano and Lerner, *Monks and Merchants*, pp. 119–33.

23. Ho, "The Symbolism of the Central Pillars," p. 65.

24. Eugene Y. Wang, "Painted Statue in an Optical Theater: A Fifth Century Chinese Buddhist Cave," *Source: Notes in the History of Art* 30, no. 3 (Spring 2011): 28.

25. Pepper, "The Thousand Buddha Motif," pp. 43–44.

26. One unusual cave, Northern Zhou Cave 428, had hundreds of such small relief Buddhas forming a sculpted Thousand Buddha grid on the north and south walls instead of a painted one; *Dunhuang Mogaoku*, vol. 1, pls. 160, 161.

27. Akira Sadakata, *Buddhist Cosmology: Philosophy and Origins*, trans. Gaynor Sekimori (Tokyo: Kosei Publishing Co., 1997), p. 114.

28. Abe, "Art and Practice," p. 8.

29. Pepper, "The Thousand Buddha Motif," p. 40.

30. Ibid., 45.

31. In the ceilings of many of the fifth and sixth-century caves at Dunhuang are what is called a *tianjing*, "celestial well," a design composed of rotated squares and sometimes a painted circle added at the center; this motif is also known as a *laternendecke*. It is found in the center of the truncated pyramid ceiling or as an overall pattern on the ceiling surrounding a central pillar. This motif, which combines a square and circle, is also found on the ceilings of Han and post-Han traditional tombs in Gansu. It is part of a decorative program of motifs symbolizing the ascent of the soul and its travel to a paradisiacal afterlife through the "celestial well" or "well of heaven." Beningson argues that this concept was carried over from traditional Chinese burial practices into Buddhist cave temples; see Beningson, "Shaping Sacred Space," pp. 24–41. The origins of the *laternendecke* are discussed in Alexander Coburn Soper, "The 'Dome of Heaven' in Asia," *Art Bulletin* 29, no. 4 (December 1947): 225–48. In the Tang dynasty, the central square in the center of the truncated pyramid is called a *zaojing*. It is largely a complex design of floral medallions and sometimes heavenly beings and surrounded by textile like tassels and fringes suggesting a canopy or tent (see replica, cat. no. 32, illus. 32-16).

32. *Kezier shiku* 克孜尔石窟 [Kizil Cave Temples], *Zhongguo shiku* 中国石窟 [Chinese Cave Temples] (Beijing: Wenwu chubanshe, 1989), vol. 1, Cave 38, pls. 101–103.

33. A number of scholars point to such devices in narrative compositions as the diagonal line of mountains as an important contribution to the interest in and development of landscape imagery and painting in the Northern and Southern Dynasties period; see Michael Sullivan, *The Birth of Landscape Painting in China* (Berkeley and Los Angeles: University of California Press, 1962), pp. 145–46. For a very interesting analysis of early narrative structure in Buddhist jataka tales, see Julia K. Murray, "Buddhism and Early Narrative Illustration in China," *Archives of Asian Art* 48 (1995): 23–25.

34. Whitfield et al., *Cave Temples of Mogao*, pp. 20–21.

35. William Watson, *Tang and Liao Ceramics* (New York: Rizzoli, 1984), pl. 141; Bo Gyllensvard, "T'ang Gold and Silver," *Bulletin of the Museum of Far Eastern Antiquities, Stockholm* 29 (1957): 75.

36. Zhiru Ng, *The Making of a Savior Bodhisattva: Dizang in Medieval China* (Honolulu: University of Hawai'i Press, 2007).

37. See Burton Watson, trans. *The Lotus Sutra* (New York: Columbia University Press, 1993), chapt.11, pp. 170–81, and Wang, *Shaping the Lotus Sutra*, pp. 3–12.

38. Wang, *Shaping the Lotus Sutra*, p. 437 n116.

39. Inagaki Hisao, trans., *The Three Pure Land Sutras*, in collaboration with Harold Stewart (Berkeley, CA: Numata Center for Buddhist Translation and Research, 2003). The three major texts of Pure Land Buddhism are the *Shorter Sukhavativyuha Sutra,* also known as the *Amitabha Sutra*; the *Longer Sukhavativyuha Sutra*, also called the *Infinite Life Sutra*; and the *Amitayurdhyana Sutra*, or *Visualization Sutra.*

40. Whitfield et al., *Cave Temples of Mogao*, pp. 79–82.

41. Wang, *Shaping the Lotus Sutra*, p. 372. Eugene Wang exhaustively discusses all aspects and dimensions of the "transformation" process and all the associated phenomena in the section of his book titled "Transformation and the Inconceivable"; ibid., pp. 371–81.

42. Kenneth K. Tanaka, *The Dawn of Chinese Pure Land Buddhist Doctrine: Ching-ying Hui-yuan's Commentary on the Visualization Sutra* (Albany: State University of New York Press, 1990).

43. Alexander Coburn Soper, *Literary Evidence for Early Buddhist Art in China* (Ascona, Switzerland: Artibus Asiae Publishers, 1959), pp. 144–46.

44. Ibid., p. 145.

45. Louis Frédéric, *Buddhism: Flammarion Iconographic Guide* (Paris: Flammarion, 1995), pp. 144–45.

46. Watson, *The Lotus Sutra*, pp. 298–306.

47. Akiyama and Matsubara, *Arts of China,* p. 217, no. 50.

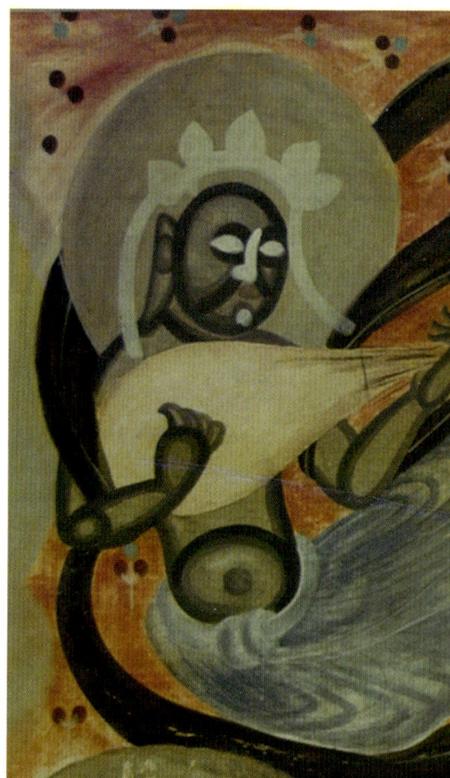

Depiction of flying *apsaras* from Cave 428, Mogao Grottoes. Northern Zhou dynasty (557–580). Replica by Hua Liang.
莫高窟北周第428窟飞天，华亮临摹

48. For the importance of art in strengthening practice by helping practitioners focus their visualization, see Soper, *Literary Evidence*, pp. 188–89. The meditation practiced in Gansu during the fifth and sixth centuries was *guan*, or visualization meditation. For the development of meditation practices in Gansu and the use of images such as the Thousand Buddhas, see two excellent articles: Pepper, "The Thousand Buddha Motif," pp. 39–45, and Abe, "Art and Practice," pp. 1–31, who believes that the early Buddhism developed under the Northern Liang shaped the images of the Northern Wei Caves.

49. Both Eugene Wang and Stanley Abe discuss the character of fifth and sixth-century Buddhism particularly visible in the Dunhuang caves as focused on penance and confessional rituals, concern for past karmic actions, acquiring merit, and meditation practices; Wang, "Painted Statue," pp. 25–32, and Stanley K. Abe, "Mogao Cave 254: A Case Study in Early Chinese Buddhist Art" (PhD diss., University of California at Berkeley, 1989), pp. 29–34.

50. Wang, *Shaping the Lotus Sutra*, p. 437 n110. According to the text preserved in the *Fayuan zhulin* (compiled in 668), this practice would have the result that "One's present life would not be harassed by the myriad mishaps; at the end of one's life, one is reborn in Amitayus's kingdom."

51. Mahayana canon was far more expansive and inclusive than other Buddhist traditions, stressing the capacity of all beings to attain Buddhahood; it moved away from the emphasis on personal individual spiritual development of the monks to greater active participation of the laity. The role of compassion emphasizes helping others and each other along the path.

52. Whitfield and Farrer, *Caves of the Thousand Buddhas*, p. 116, no. 90.

53. John M. Lundquist, *The Temple: Holy Precinct for Sanctuary, Ritual, and Sacrifice*, paperback edition (New York: Thames & Hudson, 2012), p. 104.

54. Wang, *Shaping the Lotus Sutra*, pp. xiii–xxiv, and Annette L. Juliano, review of *Shaping the Lotus Sutra: Buddhist Visual Culture in Medieval China*, by Eugene Y. Wang, *Harvard Journal of Asiatic Studies* 66, no. 2 (December 2006): 568–69.

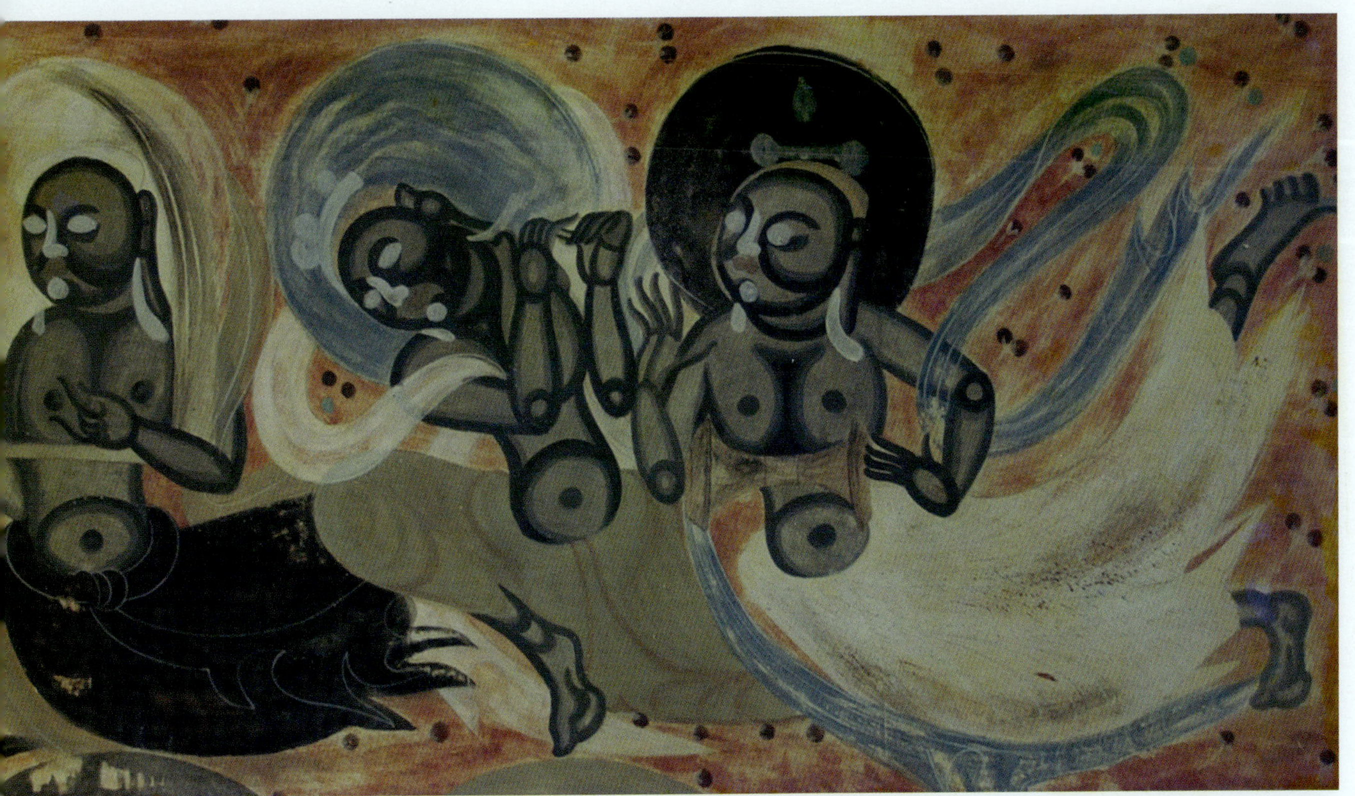

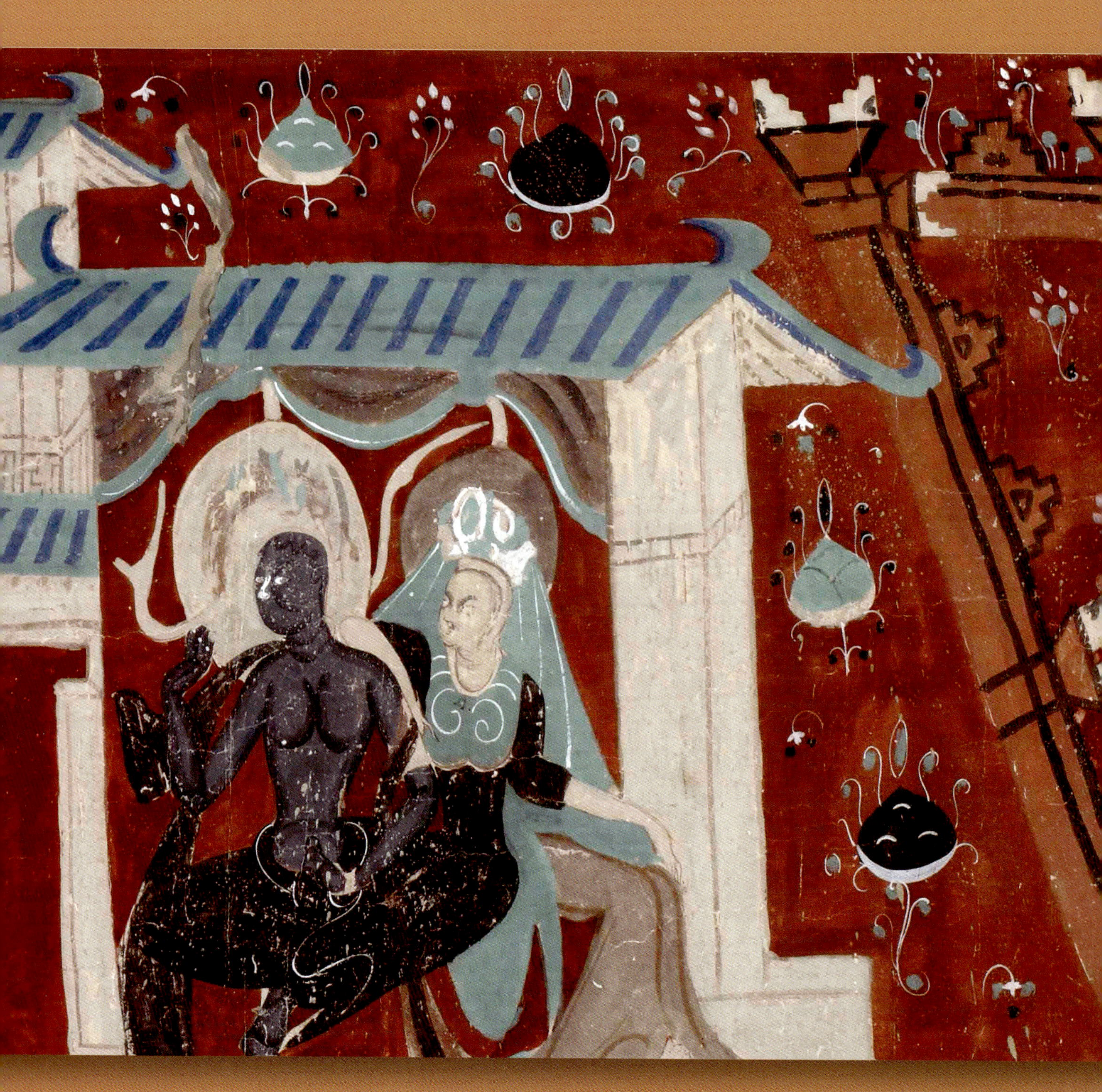

Catalogue 图录

by Lou Jie, Liang Xushu, and Huang Yuanwei
娄婕　梁旭澍　黄苑薇

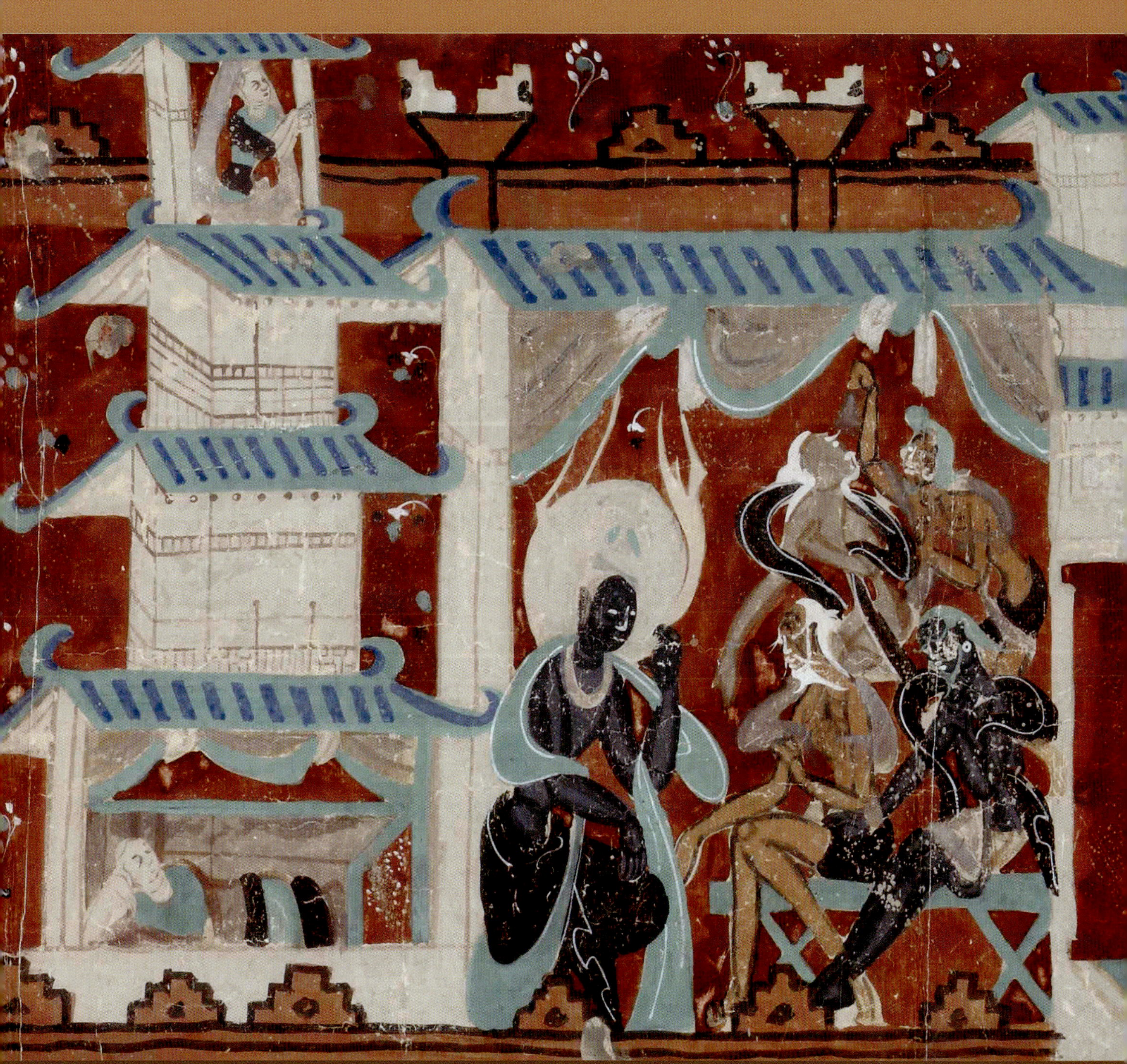

Manuscripts from the Library Cave

The Library Cave (Cave 17) in the Mogao Grottoes, located off the north side of the corridor leading to Cave 16, has an area of about 7.8 square meters. It was originally built between 851 and 867 in the Tang dynasty as a memorial chapel dedicated to an eminent monk. Sometime around the middle of the eleventh century, the monks in the Mogao Grottoes hid their precious collections of manuscripts, ritual objects, prints, and paintings in the cave; they then sealed off the entrance with a wall on which they then painted a mural. It remains a mystery why these relics were hidden here. The most popular theory is that the monks wanted to shelter them from the chaos of warfare. The treasures remained there for almost 900 years.

More than 50,000 manuscripts dated between the fourth and eleventh centuries were found inside the cave. Ninety percent of them are relics from religions that were important at the time: Buddhism, Daoism, Manichaeism, Zoroastrianism, Nestorianism, etc. The other ten percent include a wide range of writings—official and private correspondence, Confucian classics, literature, rudimentary reading materials, social and economic documents (sale contracts, loan and pawn shop documents, accounting ledgers, household registrations), and calendars—covering such subjects as constellations, medicine, weaving, and wine brewing. In addition to Chinese, they were written in Tubo (Tibetan), Khotanese, Sanskrit, Uighur, Sogdian, Turkic, Kuchean, and others. These precious treasures provide abundant information on the social conditions in ancient China and Central Asia and are therefore recognized as an "encyclopedia of the medieval period."

Since the discovery of the Library Cave, research on the manuscripts has gradually broadened in scope to include the grottoes themselves, the history and geography of Dunhuang, and the relics unearthed along the Silk Road. Having become fashionable, Dunhuang studies attract scholarly research and study worldwide.

The discovery of the Library Cave was purely fortuitous. One day in 1900, a Daoist priest named Wang and his workers found a crack on the wall along the corridor of a large cave after clearing the sand. He opened up the wall along the crack and discovered a chamber filled with piles of such priceless cultural relics as manuscripts, books, ritual objects, and so on. The historical information contained in these medieval relics is so valuable that the discovery is recognized as one of the four major discoveries of ancient literature in modern China.

Wang did not realize the value of the relics. After the discovery, he gave them away to officials and friends; moreover, he "sold" a great quantity to foreign treasure hunters for a small price. The remaining manuscripts were transported to Beijing for safekeeping in 1910, but many were lost en route. The greater part of the relics have been dispersed to more than a dozen different countries, including the United Kingdom, France, Russia, Japan, the U.S.A., Germany, and India. Only a very small portion of the manuscripts found in the Library Cave remains in China today. The loss was an unprecedented calamity in Chinese cultural history. (See Appendix 2 for further discussion of this cave and the dispersal of its treasures.)

Overleaf: Scene from the *Deer King Jataka* and *Story of Lady Sumati* (cat. no. 29, detail)
前页：九色鹿本生故事的场景与须摩提女经图（图录编号29，局部）

藏经洞的文物

藏经洞（17窟）位于敦煌莫高窟16窟的甬道北側，面積約7.8平方米，开凿于唐時期（公元851～867年），是一位高僧的纪念窟，何以後來藏有如此多寶物原因未明，很多學者相信是大约在11世纪中叶，莫高窟寺僧为躲避战乱，将该寺多年收藏的珍贵经典、文书、法器、绘画等秘藏在这间斗室，又砌墙封闭窟门，在壁面上重新绘制壁画，密室从此被尘封了近900年。

藏经洞的文物跨越4-11世纪，总计约5万余件。其中90%是宗教文物，涉及佛、道、摩尼、袄（拜火）、景（基督宗教一支）等古代世界重要宗教；其他占10%，内容包罗万象，包括官私文书、儒学经典、文学作品、启蒙读物、社会经济文书（民间买卖契约、借贷典当、账簿、户籍信札）、星宿、历书、医学、纺织、酿酒。文字除中文外，还有吐蕃（西藏）、于阗、梵、回鹘、粟特、突厥、龟兹等文字。这些来自丝绸之路的遺珍，为中国及中亚古代社会面貌提供了大量丰富的宝贵資料，被誉为“中古时期的百科全书”。

藏经洞发现以来，从最初的文献研究逐渐扩展到对敦煌石窟、敦煌史地，以及丝绸之路沿线的出土文物研究，形成了新兴的敦煌学，吸引着中外学者研究探索。

藏经洞的发现是一个偶然：在荒凉的窟區，很多洞内都堆积着流沙，1900年有一位姓王的道士和工人一起清理，有一天在铲除一个大型洞窟甬道的积沙后，洞窟的壁面裂开了一条缝隙，顺着缝隙凿开壁面，有一间小小的密室，室内堆满经卷、文书、法器等各类文物。这些中世纪的文物，蕴藏着珍贵的历史信息，被誉为中国近代古文献的四大发现之一。

藏经洞发现后，王道士并没有认识到文物的珍贵价值，私自取出写经赠送官员、朋友；并把大量文物廉价盗卖给外国尋寶者；1910年文书运往北京保管的途中又不断流散。因此，藏经洞的文物绝大部分流失到英、法、俄、日、美、德、印度等十几个国家，仅有少部分保存在国内，是中国文化史上的空前浩劫。

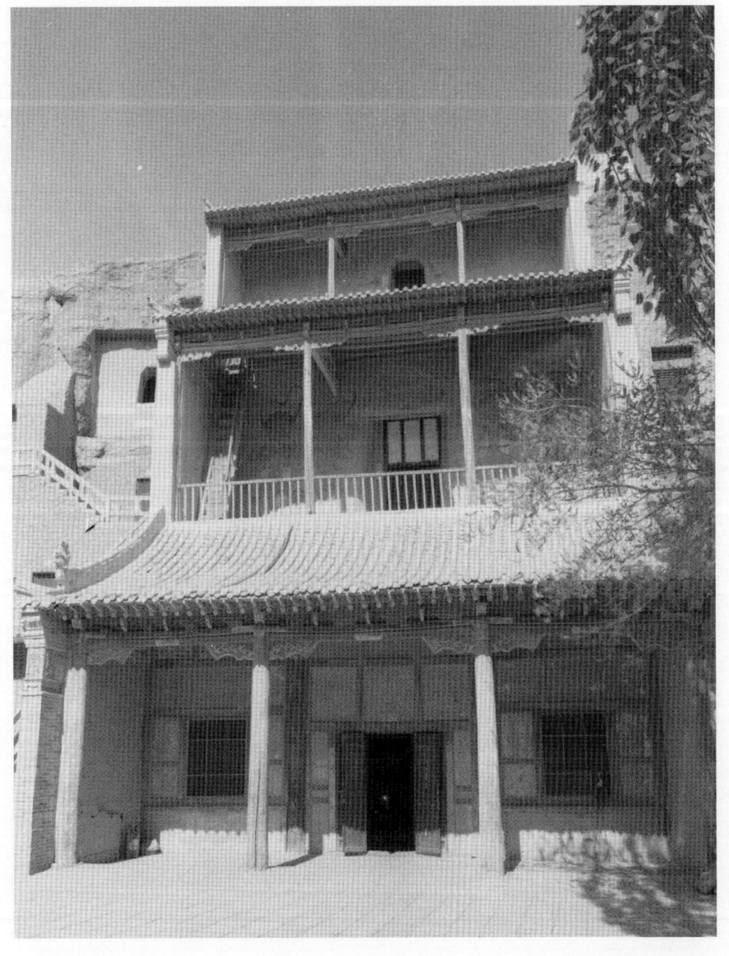

Exterior view of the Library Cave, also known as the "Three-Story Tower" in the 32nd year of Guangxu (1906).
光绪三十二年藏经洞“三层楼”外景

1. Handwritten Buddhist scripture: *Mahaparinirvana Sutra*

Northern Dynasties (386–581)
Ink on paper; 27.5 x 165 cm
Collection of the Dunhuang Academy, D.0227

1、佛經寫本：《大般涅槃经》

北朝（公元386～581年）
纸本，27.5×165厘米
敦煌研究院馆藏编号：D.0227

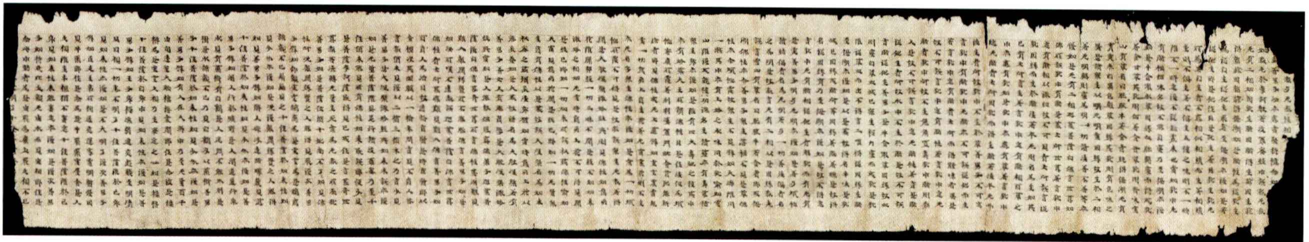

This paper fragment is made of abutilon (Indian mallow), a white and durable material. The skillful square penmanship is in the clerical-regular (*likai*) style, the transitional form from clerical (*lishu*) to regular (*kaishu*) script.

The text is a transcription of "On the Nature of Tathagata," chapter 12 of the *Nirvana Sutra* (or *Mahaparinirvana Sutra*), which was translated from Sanskrit into Chinese by Dharmaksema (385–433). Its main teachings center on the eternity of the Buddha, the meaning of nirvana, and the presence of the Buddha Nature in all beings. It also provides the theoretical basis for the precept of abstention from meat practiced by Chinese monks. It is a very important sutra in Mahayana Buddhism.

Most of the manuscripts found in Dunhuang were written in the Six Dynasties period (3rd–6th century). They preserve in large part the earlier forms of the texts, thus benefiting later generations as a resource for verifying the fidelity of more recent copies.

此為白麻紙，以苘麻製成，潔白堅韌；字体方形，用笔劲健，是隶书向楷书转化时期，称之為隶楷体。所抄《大般涅槃经》為大乘佛教经典，昙无谶（385～433）译自梵本。此經在中國佛教中佔非常重要地位，宣揚佛身常住、涅槃深義、一切众生皆有佛性等，同時也是中国僧侣断肉食素的理論依據。此殘卷所抄錄者為卷十二如来性品。

敦煌本大体均为六朝（公元3～6世纪）写本，保留其较早形态，利於後世校勘。

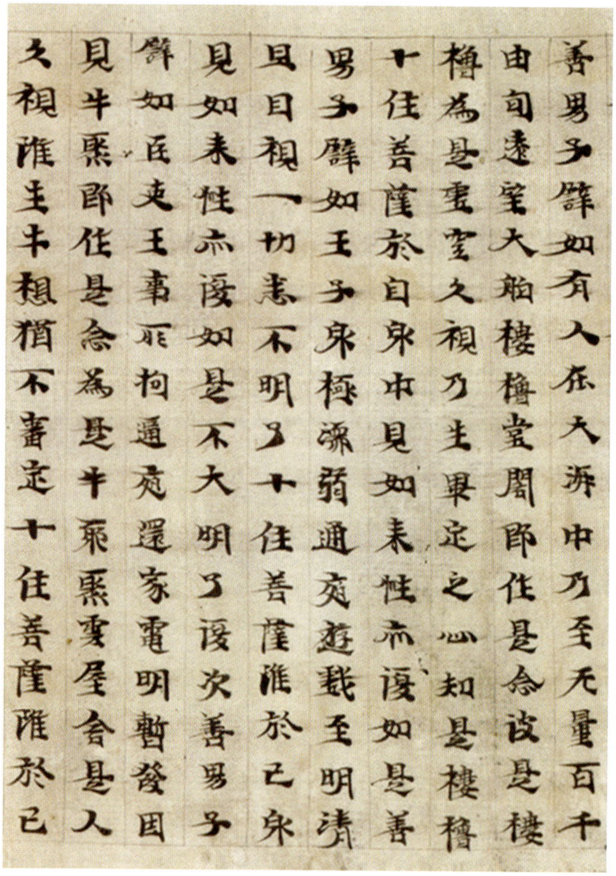

Detail

2. Handwritten Buddhist scripture: *Lotus Sutra*

Northern Dynasties (386–581)

Ink on paper; 24.8 x 66 cm

Collection of the Dunhuang Academy, D.0648

This paper fragment is made of abutilon. The text comes from the *Lotus Sutra,* or *Saddharmapundarika Sutra* (literally, the “Lotus of the Wonderful Law”), a very important Mahayanist scripture which uses an abundance of metaphors to introduce metaphysical concepts and promotes various kinds of religious practices which would lead to the one path of enlightenment. This transcription contains the Parable of the Conjured City, found in chapter 7 of the sutra.

Buddhists believe that making copies of sutras to spread Buddhism has great merit and that copying by hand is also a way of meditation.

2、佛經寫本：《妙法莲华经》

北朝（公元386～581年）

纸本，24.8×66厘米

敦煌研究院馆藏编号：D.0648

此佛经写本為白麻紙。《妙法莲华经》是大乘佛教重要经典，用大量比喻以闡揚形上哲理，提倡各種“乘”（修行途徑）始終會匯歸於一途而成佛。此殘卷是抄錄該經第七品化城喻品。佛教徒相信使佛經廣爲流傳是功德，抄錄也是集中心念的一種修行方法。

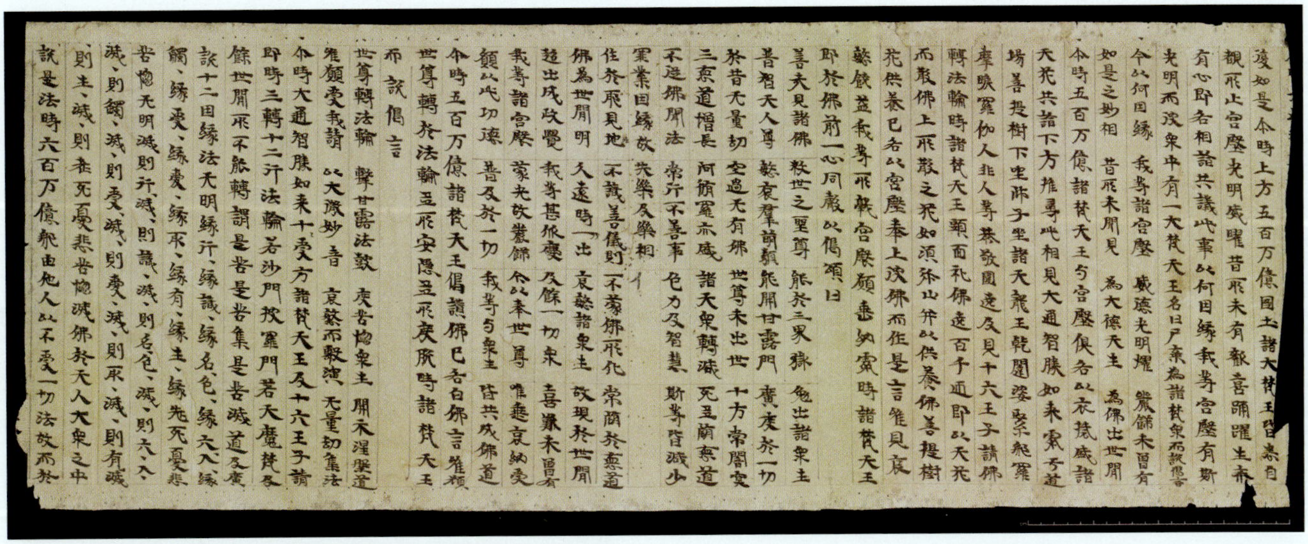

3. Handwritten Buddhist scripture: *Mahabhaisajya Upayakaushalya Sutra*

Tang dynasty (618–907)

Ink on paper; 25.1 x 158 cm

Collection of the Dunhuang Academy, D.0704

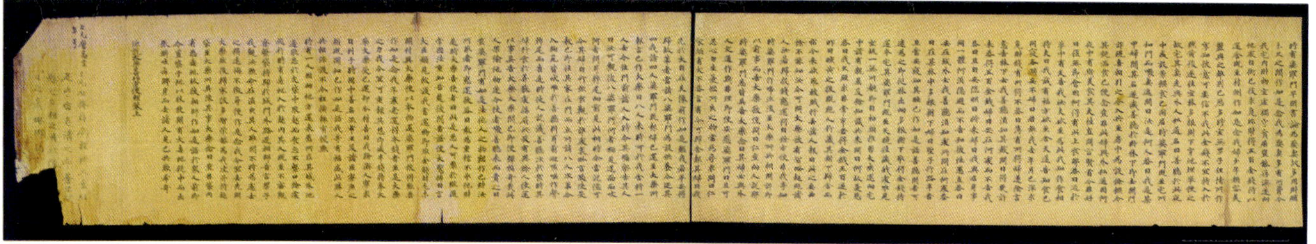

The paper of this fragment had been soaked in a solution made from Amur cork tree bark to give it a yellowish hue. It is of excellent quality, hard and moth resistant. The skillful and neat penmanship is in regular script.

The original sutra would have been in two or three volumes. This transcript is only volume one; it comes from the version of the *Mulasarvastivada-vinaya* translated by Yijing (635–713) in the Tang dynasty. The sutra had not been included in any of the current collections of Buddhist scriptures and was not known until this fragment was discovered in Dunhuang. Therefore, this fragment is an exceedingly valuable document.

This transcript contains two vivid and interesting stories about a wise man called Mahabhaisajya (literally, "Great Medicine") who solved a criminal case and saved a man's life using deductive reasoning techniques. Unfortunately, the other volume(s) have not been found. Therefore, the objective of this sutra is not known.

3、佛經寫本：《佛说大药善巧方便经》卷上

唐（公元618～907年）

纸本，25.1×158厘米

敦煌研究院馆藏编号：D.0704

此佛经写本為硬黄檗纸，製作時以黄檗樹皮溶液泡浸，故纸帶黄色，質料上乘且防蟲。字體為楷书，章法严谨，笔力遒劲，從纸张、字体、墨色、界栏等特征来看，應出自唐代宫廷。

《佛说大药善巧方便经》卷上出自唐义净(615～713)译《根本说一切有部毗奈耶杂事》，現行大藏经均不见收录，幸赖敦煌发现，世人方見此经，是目前唯一發現的一件，珍貴異常。原經應有兩至三卷。此抄本僅有卷上，是两段故事，講述一個名叫大葯的聰明人以推理手法來破案及救人，非常生動有趣，可惜無全文，經中主旨未能稽考。

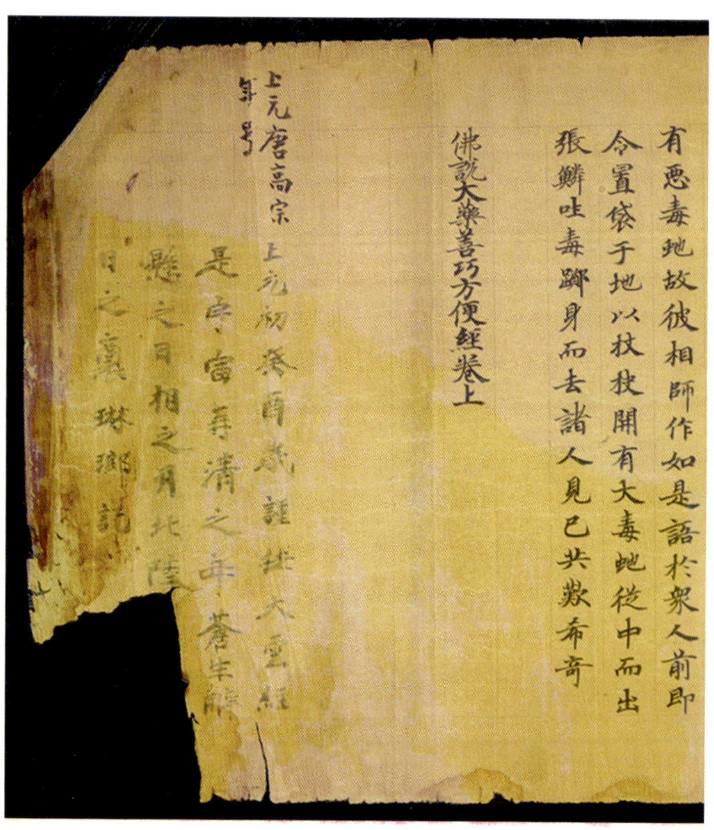

Detail

4. *Wine Transaction Journal*

Northern Song dynasty, 964
Ink on paper; 30 x 105.1 cm
Collection of the Dunhuang Academy, D.0038 & D.0784

The journal had been torn into three pieces: two are kept in the Dunhuang Academy, and the third is in France. Part of a rectangular seal with the words in relief reading *guiyijun jiedushi xinzhuyin*, or "newly cast seal of the Guiyi [Insurrection for the Allegiance] Army and Commissioner [of the Hexi area]," fits this fragment precisely with the segment (P. 2629) now in France.

This document records the wine purchase transactions between April 9 and October 16, 964, by the military government. Dunhuang was the political and economic center of northwestern China, and the local government consumed huge volumes of wine to entertain its guests. Among the 213 purchases recorded in the journal, 34 were for the Uighur envoys from Ganzhou, Xizhou, and Yizhou and for the Khotanese envoys, thus demonstrating the rather intimate relationship between the local government and these rulers.

The wine journal reveals not only the political and economic conditions in Dunhuang at that time, but also details about the units of measurement employed which had never been mentioned in any official historical documents.

4、《归义军衙府酒破历》

北宋，公元964年
纸本，30×105.1厘米
敦煌研究院馆藏编号：D.0038，D.0784

《归义军衙府酒破历》简称《酒帐》，粗白麻紙，现分割为三段：二段保存在敦煌研究院，另一段流失法國。上有四方“归义军节度使新铸印”，印为阳文，法藏段（編號P. 2629）可以缀合。

《酒帐》保存了公元964年4月9日至10月16日共213款支出，均为归义军政府的公费支出。此时的敦煌是西北各地经济文化中心，归义军衙门招待賓客用酒数量巨大；其中有关甘州、西州、伊州、于阗等使者的就有34款，说明彼此關係密切。《酒帐》不但多方面反映出敦煌当时的政治、经济、文化面貌，還提供了历代律历志和礼乐志中很难见到的计量单位的进位：1瓮等于6斗、1斗等于10升、1升等于10合；1角等于15升。

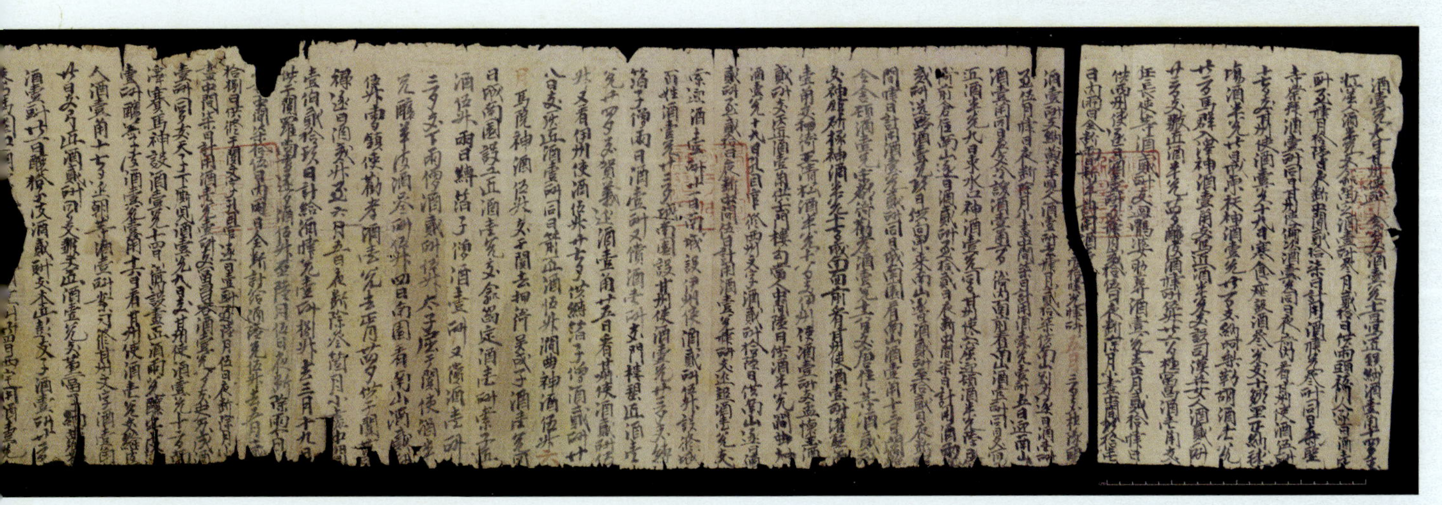

Documents from the Northern Area

From 1988 to 1995, a team dispatched by the Dunhuang Research Academy conducted an archaeological survey and excavations of the previously ignored northern section of the Mogao Grottoes. The largely undecorated caves in this area had been reserved for the use of monks as private accommodations, meditation cells, or funerary chambers. A great number of fragments of sutras and other documents were found, written in such languages as Chinese, Tibetan, Sanskrit, Uighur, Tangut (Xixia), Mongol, and Syriac.

敦煌莫高窟北区出土的文献

从1988年至1995年，敦煌研究所组织了对莫高窟北区的考古发掘。北区大量的洞窟是用来作为僧侣居住、修行和埋葬的处所。考古发掘中发现了许多经卷及文书的残篇，包括了多种语言，如汉文、藏文、回鹘文、梵文、西夏文、蒙文和叙利亚文。

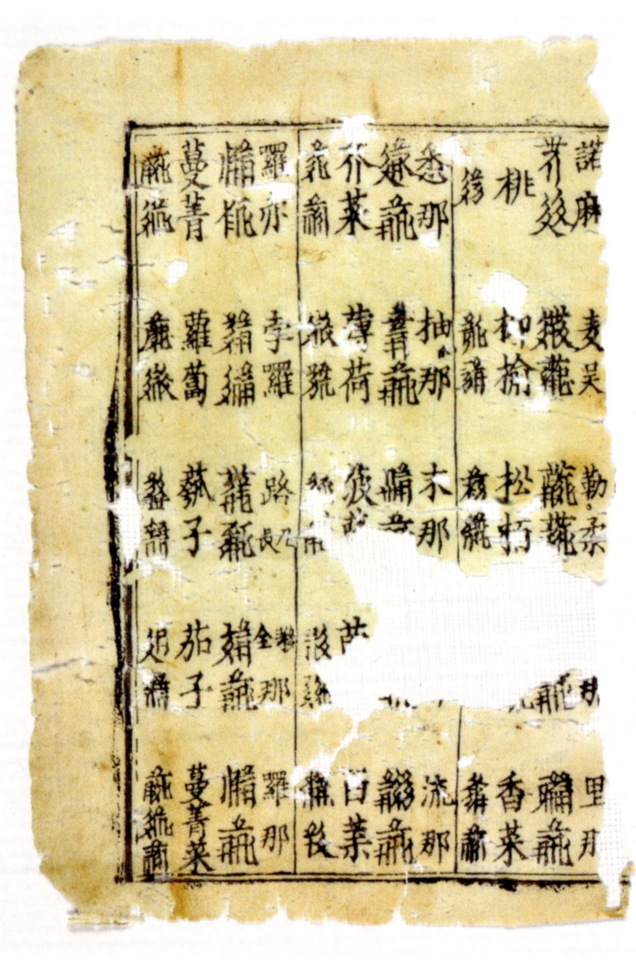

5. *Tangut-Chinese Bilingual Dictionary*

Western Xia dynasty (1038–1227)
Ink on paper; 15 x 21.8 cm
Collection of the Dunhuang Academy, B184:9

This document, excavated from Cave B184 in the Northern Area of the Mogao Grottoes, is slightly damaged, with only one side intact. It was written on soft white jute paper, which has turned slightly yellow and reveals an uneven interlacing of fibers in a horizontal curtain pattern. This woodcut-printed document has a double-line border on the upper, lower, and left sides. It is the verso of page 14 in the *Tangut-Chinese Bilingual Dictionary*. The text belongs mainly to the category "Land Use" (the third and last chapter of the section on Earth). This is the only complete page of this dictionary extant in China, so it is valuable even though fragmentary.

5、《番汉合时掌中珠》

西夏（公元1038～1227年）
纸本，15×21.8厘米
敦煌研究院馆藏编号：B184: 9

该文献于1989年在北区B184窟出土，存一面，略残。白麻纸，泛黄，纤维交织不匀，有横帘纹。纸质柔软。木刻本，上、下左双线边框。为《番汉合时掌中珠》一书中的第14页第2面，内容属“地用下”（地部的第三篇）。这是目前国内仅存的一面比较完整的《番汉合时掌中珠》。虽说仅仅是残页，却弥足珍贵，为国内仅存孤本。

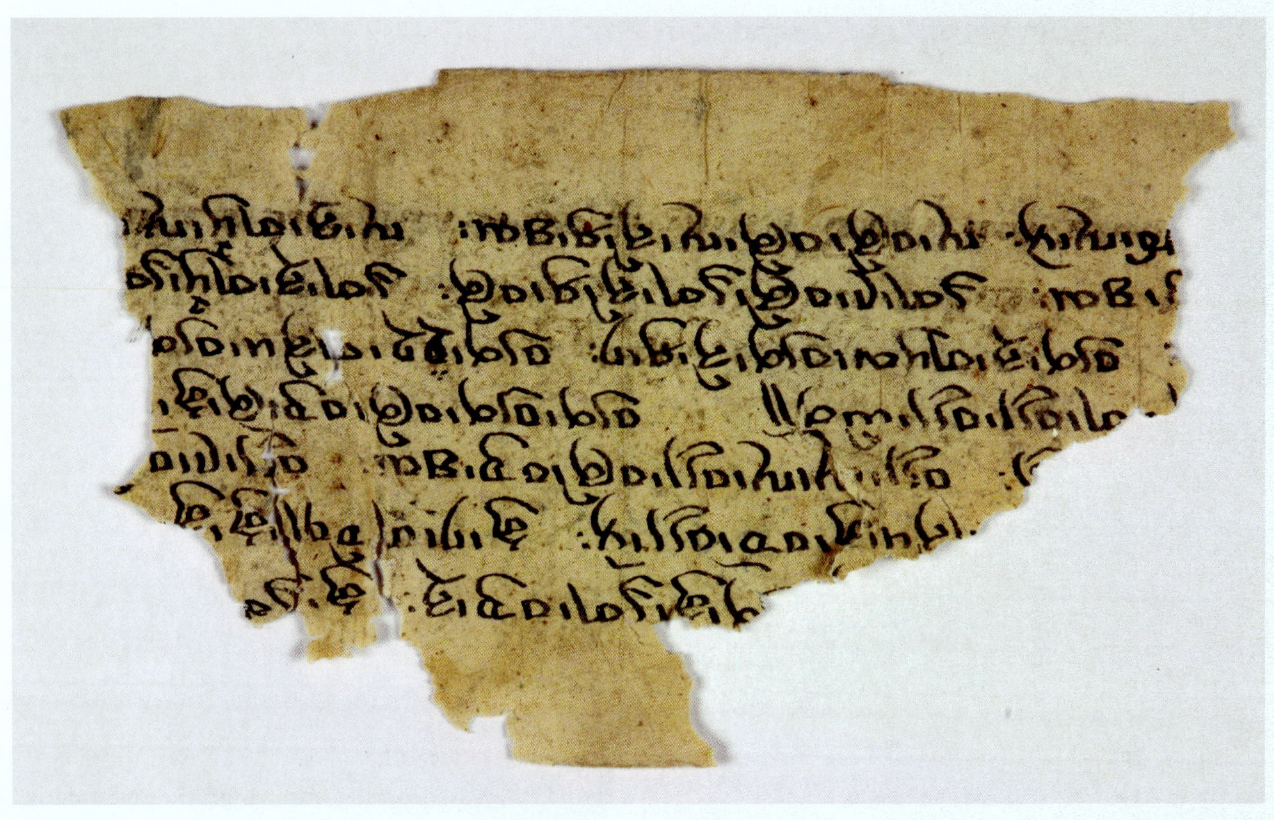

6. Fragment of a document on mathematics written in Tibetan

Yuan dynasty (1271–1368)
Ink on paper; 8.0 x 13.8 cm
Collection of the Dunhuang Academy, B59:10

This document on mathematics, written in a cursive Tibetan script, was excavated from Cave B59 in the Northern Area of the Mogao Grottoes. The text on the front side of this fragment contains the pithy multiplication formula characterized by multiplying two different numbers and then multiplying them again after changing their position. For example, "three times one, one times three equals three" and "two times four, four times two equals eight." It is equivalent to the pithy Chinese formula "one times three equals three, two times four equals eight." The modification in this document is regarded as a kind of innovation and improvement in multiplication formulas. On the document's reverse are some words in the Tibetan language expressing numbers, as well as Tibetan-style numbers which are similar to Arabic numerals. In addition there are abbreviated numbers. It is rare to find this type of document among the Tibetan manuscripts discovered in the Library Cave at Dunhuang.

6、藏文残数学文书

元（公元1271～1368年）
纸本，8.0×13.8厘米
敦煌研究院馆藏编号：B59: 10

在北区B59窟出土一件纸本藏文数学文献。字体为手写草体藏文。其正面内容为乘法口诀。特点是，先将两个不同数字相乘，然后再将它们换位相乘。例如“三一、一三是三”、“二四、四二即得八”，此两句即汉族乘法口诀中的“一三得三”、“二四得八”。这一改进，被看作是对乘法口诀的一种创新和进步。在此件文献的背面，是用文字表示数字的藏文文献，同时又有近似阿拉伯数码的藏式数码。还有缩写数字。为以往敦煌藏经洞所出藏文文献中所不多见。

Clay Images in Low Relief

These molded and painted images are made of clay mixed with fine sand and wheat straw. They were very popular in the early caves of the Mogao Grottoes and served to set off the free-standing Buddha in the main niche. Adhered to the wall by their flat backs, the figures are in low relief on their front. The molded images include Buddhas, bodhisattvas, celestials, lotus flowers, and so on, all colorful and stunning.

影塑

影塑是浮雕式的泥塑，以泥、细砂和麦秸做材料，用泥制模具翻制，并施以彩绘，在敦煌莫高窟前期洞窟中很普遍，主要用于衬托圆塑（立體）主尊。其背面贴于墙壁上，正面为浮雕，造型有佛、菩萨、飞天、莲花等，敷色均衡多姿彩。

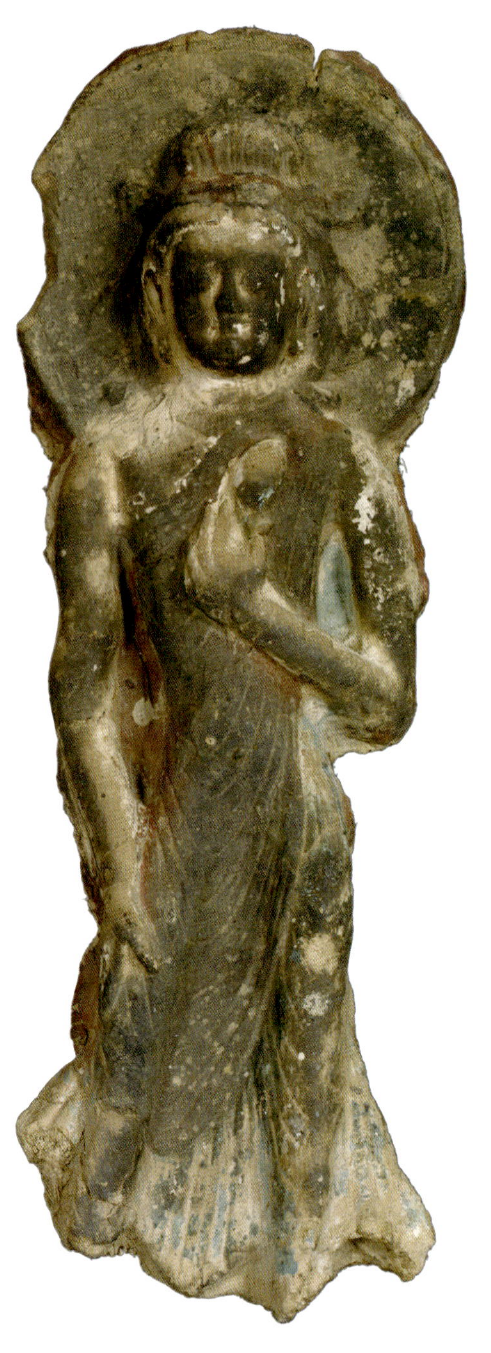

7. Standing bodhisattva

Northern Wei dynasty (386–534)
Painted clay stucco; H. 38.5, W. 11.5 cm
Collection of the Dunhuang Academy, Z.0688

This bodhisattva wears a high chignon. He holds a lotus bud in his left hand. His right hand hangs naturally just touching his robe.

7、立姿菩萨像

北魏（公元386～534年）
彩绘泥影塑，38.5×11.5厘米
敦煌研究院馆藏编号：Z.0688

菩萨梳高髻，左手拈花蕾，右手自然下垂執衣角。

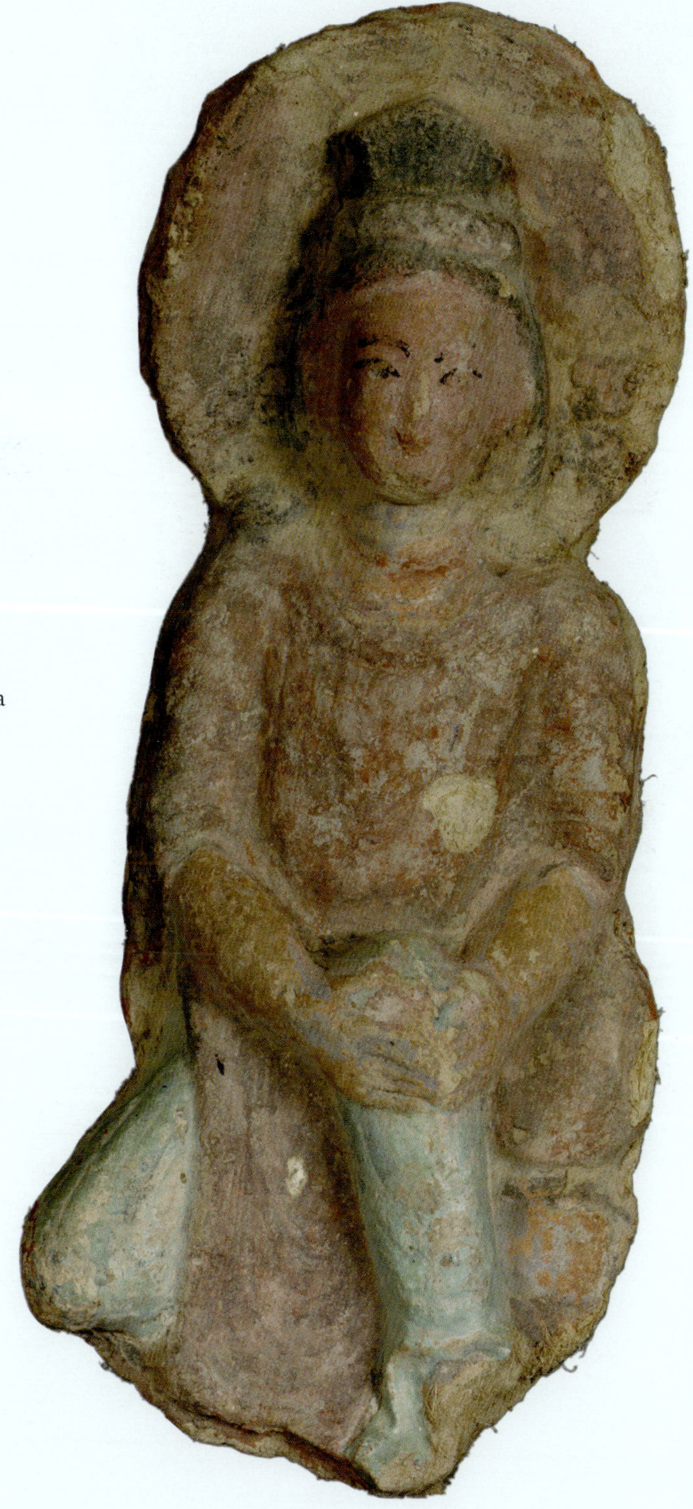

8. Bodhisattva clasping knee*

Western Wei dynasty (535–556)
Painted clay stucco; H. 33, W. 12 cm
Collection of the Dunhuang Academy, Z.0678

This bodhisattva, in a red robe, clasps his bent knee in a naturally relaxed pose.

8、抱膝菩萨像*

西魏（公元535～556年）
彩绘泥影塑，33×12厘米
敦煌研究院馆藏编号：Z. 0678

菩萨着红衣，双手抱膝，神態悠閒。

* Not in the exhibition. 不在展览。

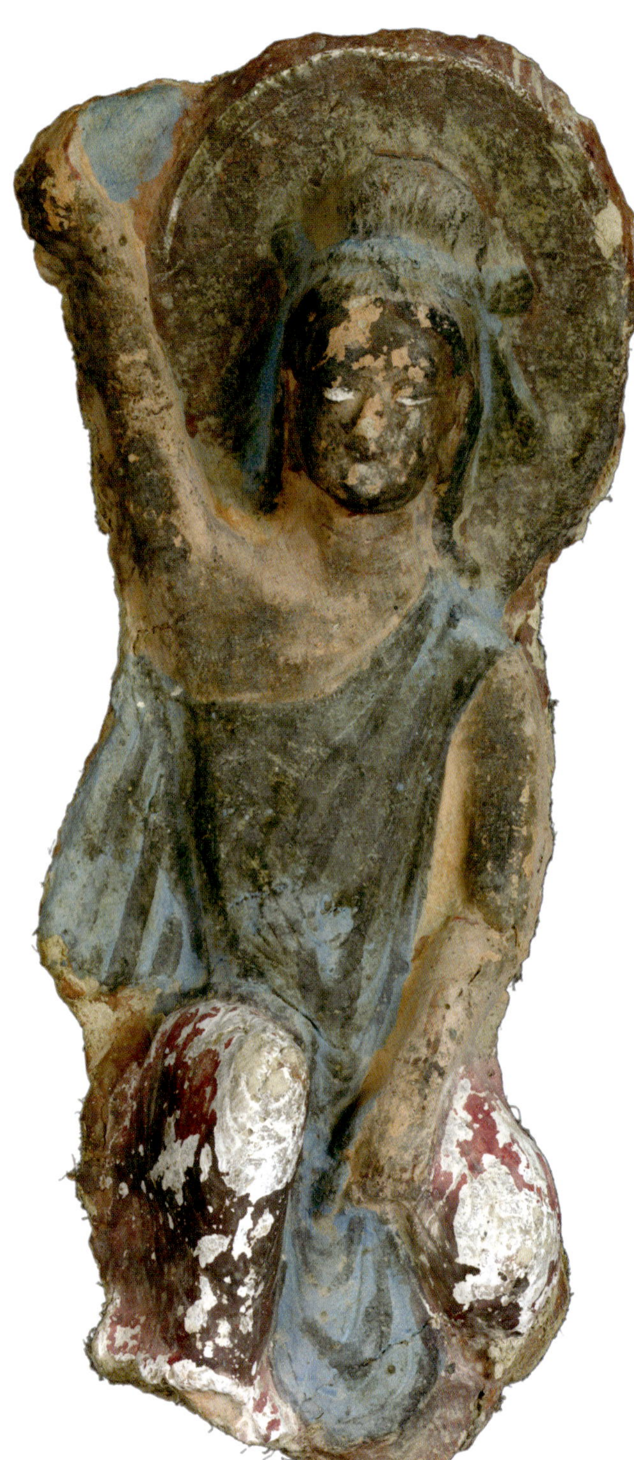

9. Bodhisattva holding aloft a lotus

Northern Wei dynasty (386–534)
Painted clay stucco; H. 34, W. 15.5 cm
Collection of the Dunhuang Academy, Z.0718

The bodhisattva holds a lotus bud in his raised right hand and sits with his legs pendant. He wears a translucent blue robe with his right shoulder bared.

9、举莲菩萨像

北魏（公元386～534年）
彩绘泥影塑，34×15.5厘米
敦煌研究院馆藏编号：Z.0718

菩萨右手高举花蕾，兰色薄纱衣偏袒右肩，双足屈膝作供养。

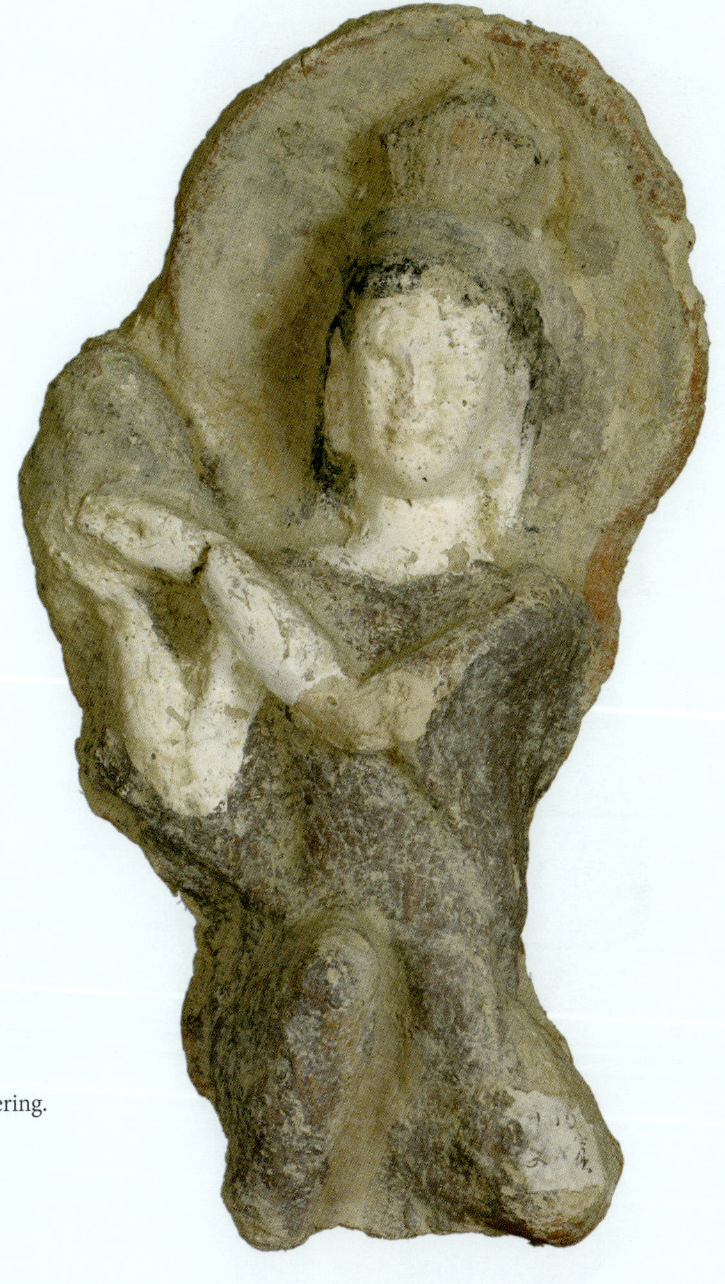

10. Bodhisattva offering a lotus*

Western Wei dynasty (535–556)
Painted clay stucco; H. 29, W. 15 cm
Collection of the Dunhuang Academy, Z.0720

This kneeling bodhisattva is holding a lotus as an offering.

10、捧莲菩萨像*

西魏（公元535～556年）
彩绘泥影塑，29×15厘米
敦煌研究院馆藏编号：Z. 0720

菩萨双手捧莲花、屈膝作供养。

* Not in the exhibition. 不在展览。

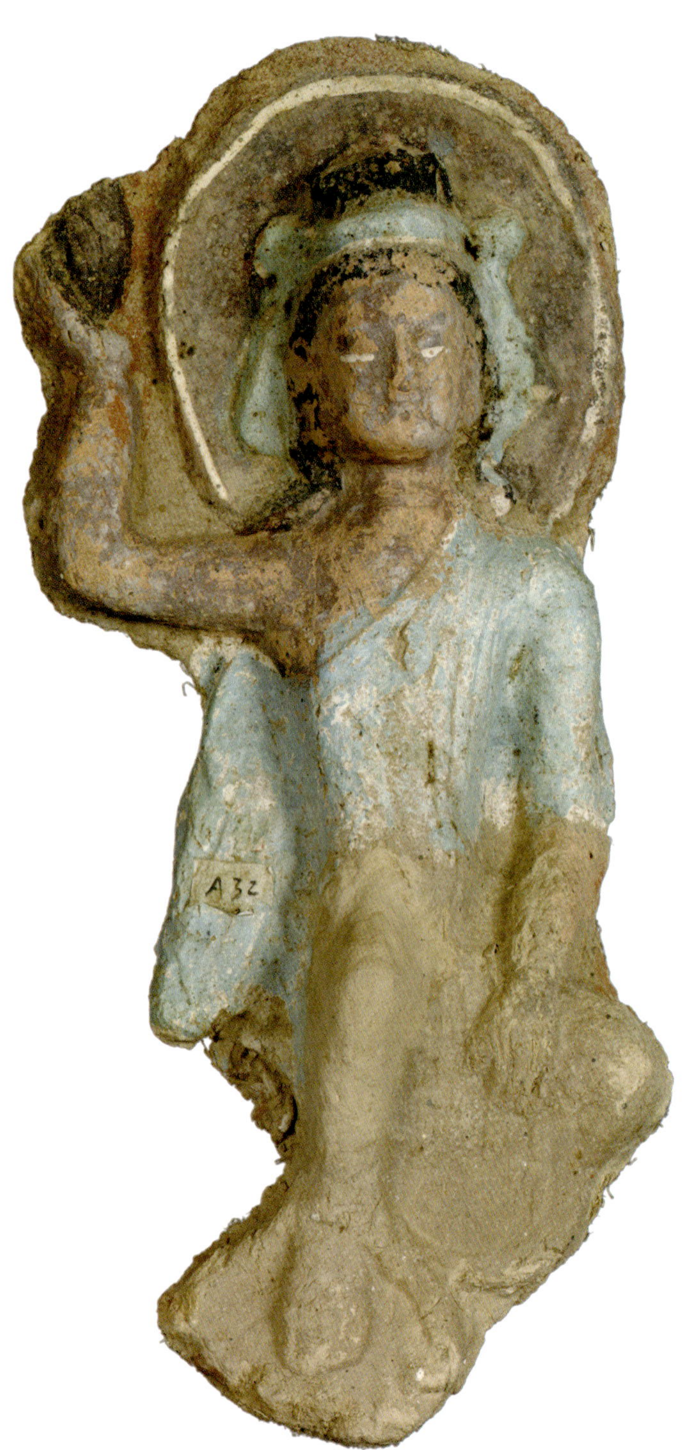

11. Bodhisattva holding up a lotus

Northern Wei dynasty (386–534)

Painted clay stucco; H. 34.5, W. 14 cm

Collection of the Dunhuang Academy, Z.0679

The bodhisattva holds a lotus bud in his raised right hand. He is wearing a translucent light blue robe with his right shoulder bared and a matching headdress.

11、持花菩萨像

北魏（公元386～534年）

彩绘泥影塑，34.5×14厘米

敦煌研究院馆藏编号：Z.0679

菩萨右手高举花蕾，兰色薄纱衣偏袒右肩，与头饰协调统一。

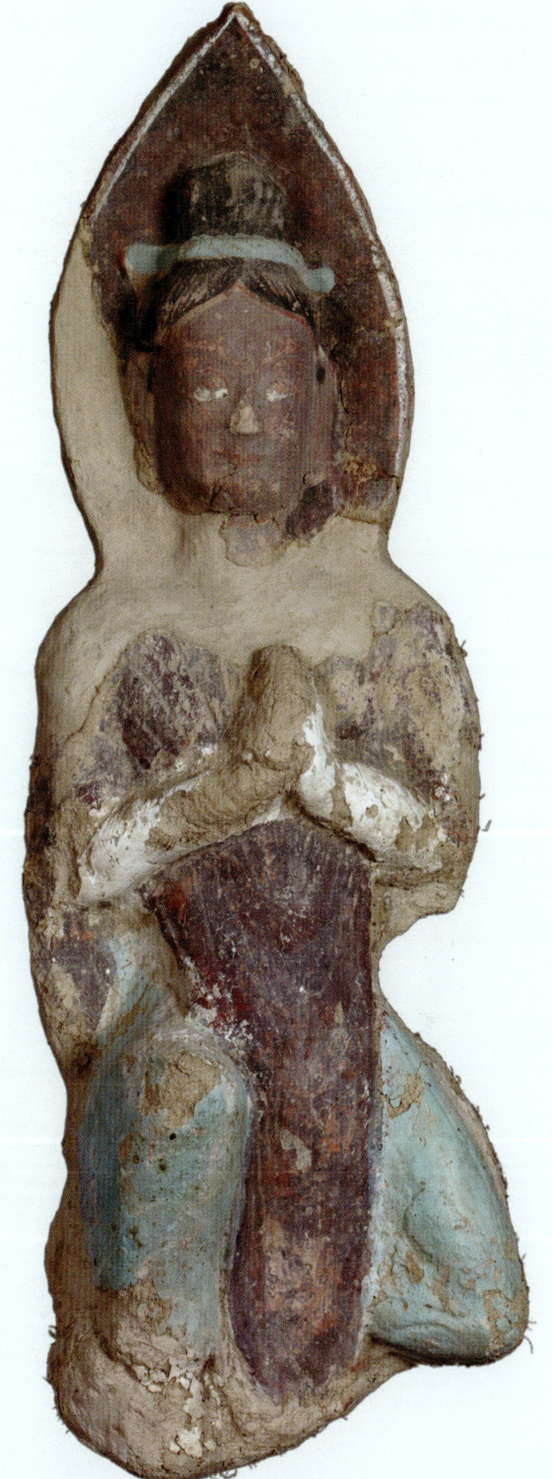

12. Kneeling bodhisattva with palms pressed together

Northern Wei dynasty (386–534)
Painted clay stucco; H. 35, W. 10 cm
Collection of the Dunhuang Academy, Z.0680

This bodhisattva has an almond-shaped nimbus or halo. He kneels with his hands pressed together, indicating that he is listening respectfully or praying. The neck was damaged and has been restored.

12、跪姿双手合十菩萨像

北魏（公元386～534年）
彩绘泥影塑，35×10厘米
敦煌研究院馆藏编号：Z. 0680

菩萨有桃形頭光，双手合十在恭敬跪聽或祈禱的樣子。颈部毁，经修复。

13. Buddha with Chinese characters in nimbus*

Northern Wei dynasty (386–534)
Painted clay stucco; H. 23.5, W. 17.5 cm
Collection of the Dunhuang Academy, Z.0693

This Buddha is sitting in the meditative lotus position. His eyebrows, moustache, and beard are depicted as very thick, unlike the clean-shaven look he is usually given. Inside his nimbus are two Chinese characters *jie yin*, meaning "to receive [someone to the Pure Land]" or "to guide someone to be a Buddhist."

13、接引佛像*

北魏（公元386～534年）
彩绘泥影塑，23.5×17.5厘米
敦煌研究院馆藏编号：Z.0693

佛像结跏趺坐，鬚眉宛然，不像一般剃除鬚髮的佛形象；頭光内有"接引"两漢字（意指帶領往極樂世界或成爲佛弟子）。

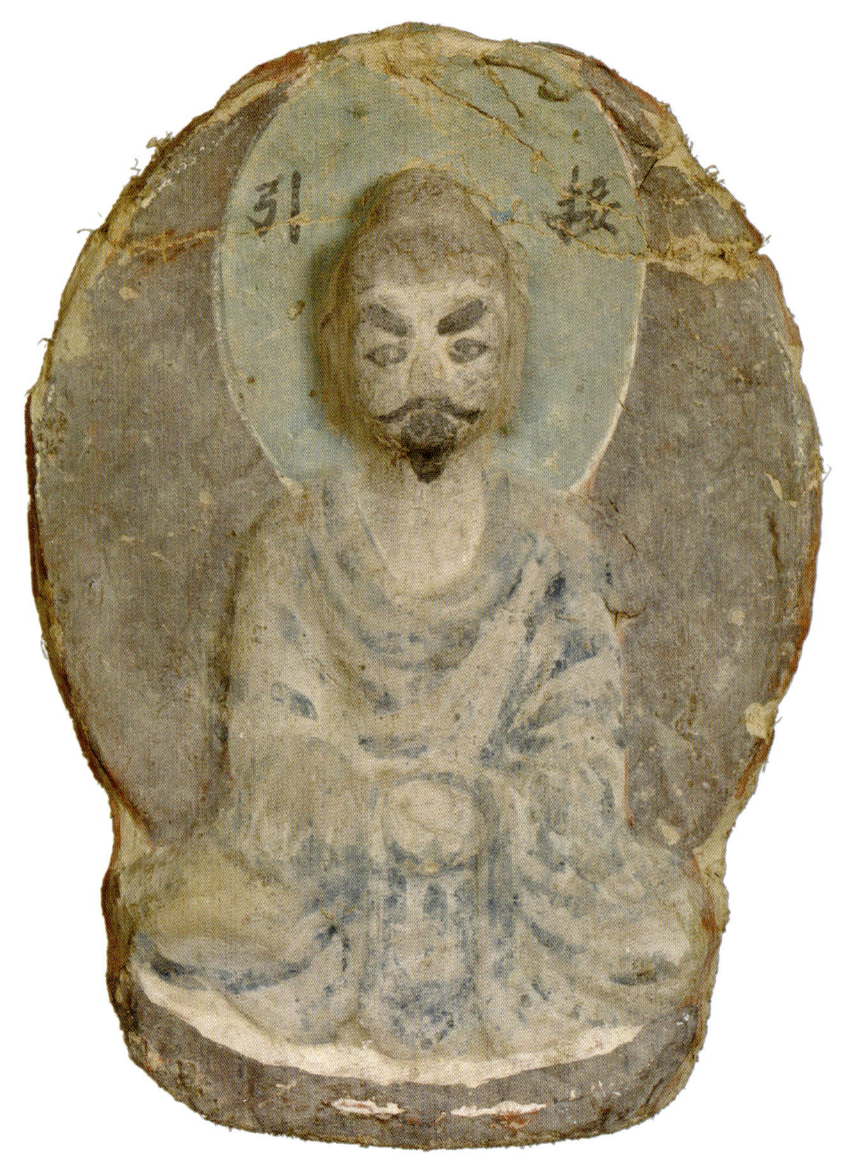

* Not in the exhibition. 不在展览。

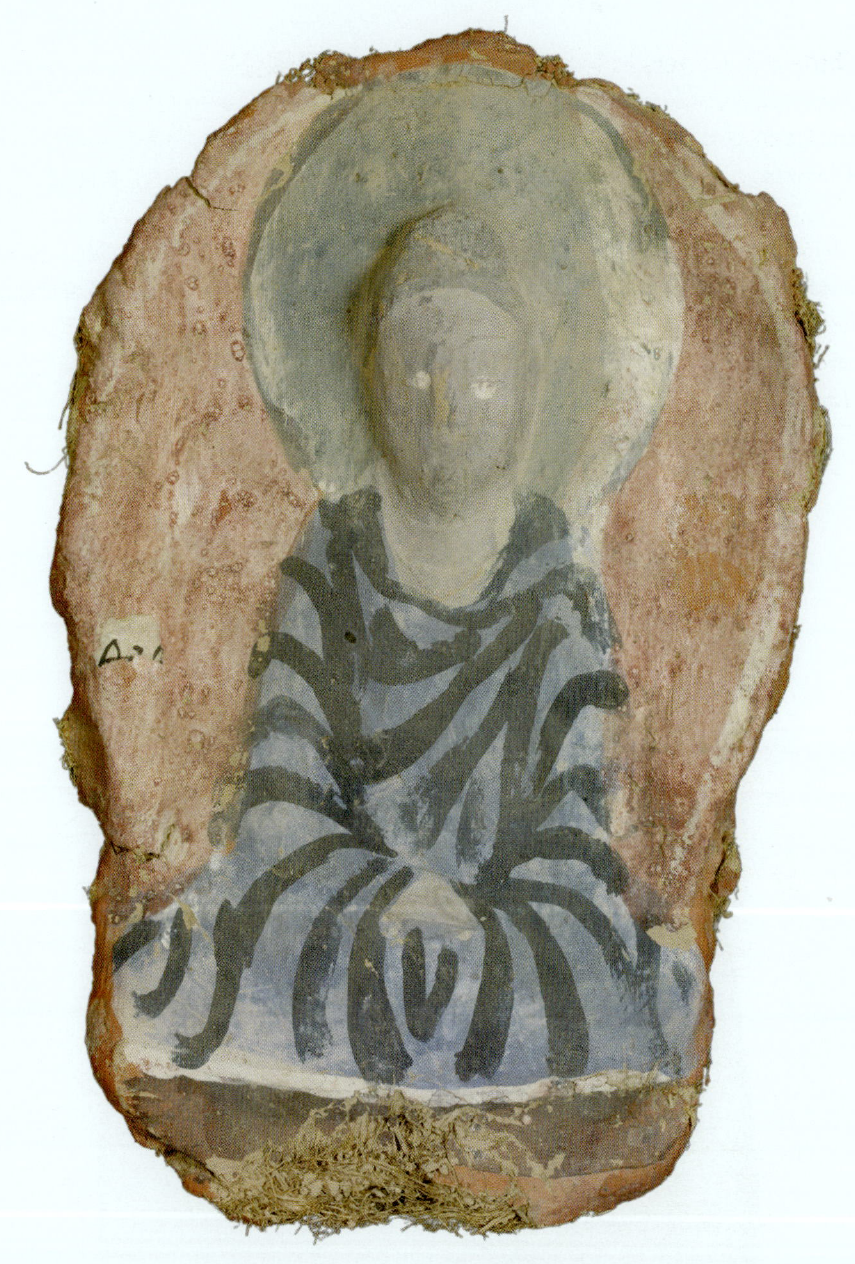

14. Buddha

Northern Wei dynasty (386–534)
Painted clay stucco; H. 24, W. 15.5 cm
Collection of the Dunhuang Academy, Z.0702

This Buddha has a red oval aureole. He wears a blue *kasaya* robe, very different from the more common form in burgundy red, and sits in the meditative lotus position.

14、佛像

北魏（公元386～534年）
彩绘泥影塑，24×15.5厘米
敦煌研究院馆藏编号：Z.0702

椭圆形红底背光，着蓝色袈裟（不同於一般土紅色），结跏趺坐。

15. Standing Buddha

Tang dynasty (618–907)
Painted clay stucco; H. 9, W. 5.4 cm
Collection of the Dunhuang Academy, B142:2

This image was molded in brown clay stucco. The Buddha holds a *mala* (prayer beads) in his left hand and a vase in his right hand, while standing barefooted on the double-lotus base. The rays of his halo and aureole are depicted by radiating raised lines. The parallel folds of his *kasaya* robe form a step-like pattern. Most of the pigments have fallen off, but some red (halo), blue (aureole), and white (Buddha's face, robe, and lotus base) are still visible.

15、立佛像

唐（公元618～907年）
彩绘泥塑，9×5.4厘米
敦煌研究院馆藏编号：B142:2

用红胶泥夹麻脱制而成。佛左手持念珠于胸前，右手持净瓶，赤脚立于雙莲座上。头光背光均由凸起的辐射状线组成，衣纹阶梯状。全像敷彩，现已大部分脱落，但仍可见头光为红色，背光为蓝色，佛面、袈裟及莲座为白色。

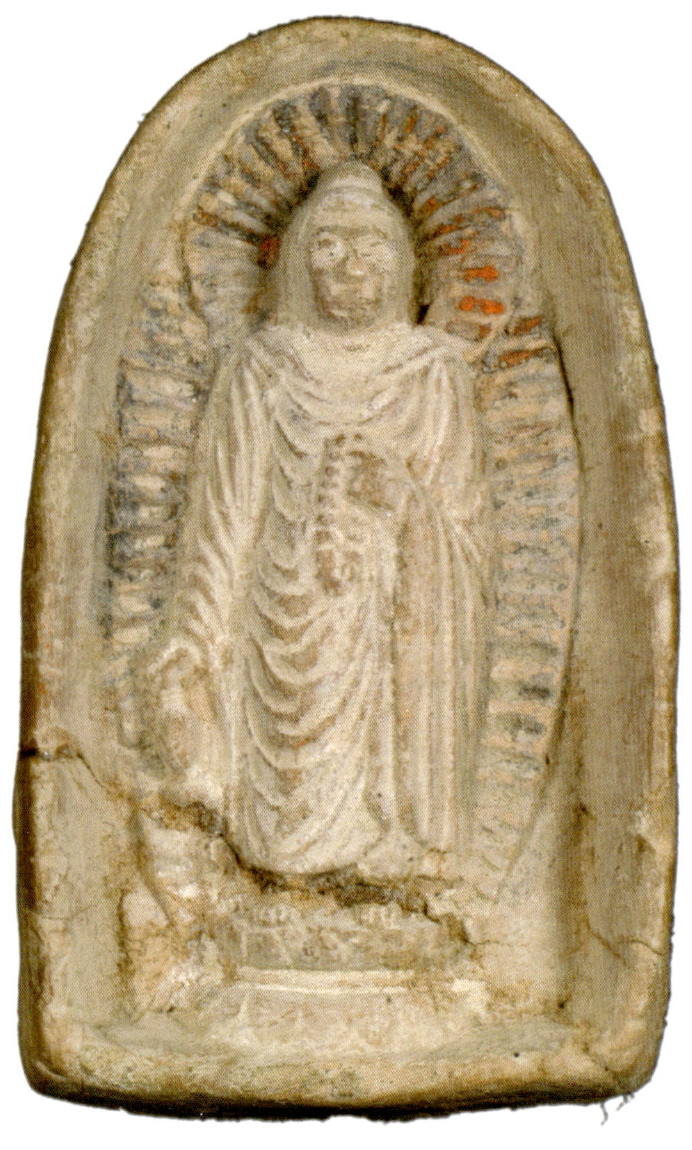

Banners

A Buddhist banner is a kind of offering, derived from the banners used by honor guards of the nobility. Hung from a long bamboo stick, such banners consist of a triangular headpiece, a rectangular body made of one or multiple panels, and a lower end divided into two long streamers. They are held by the immortals, *apsaras*, or courtly attendants depicted beside a canopy or aureole. Since the Tang dynasty (618–907), Buddhists have used them as offerings when praying or making wishes, hanging them beside the Buddha in temples or caves.

In the worship of the Medicine Buddha, offerings of banners and lamps are very important. According to the scripture, one should offer a seven-tiered lamp or forty-nine lamps (seven for each of the seven Medicine Buddhas), raise colorful banners, and so on in order to get rid of bad luck, danger, or disease. Thus, many murals depicting Medicine Buddhas contain scenes of lighting lamps and raising banners.

幡

佛教供具，原是帝王貴族仪仗物。分三部分：幡头、幡身（由数块丝织物连缀成长条）及幡尾（分叉呈燕尾狀）， 悬于竿上，由仙人、飞天或宫廷侍從持执于华盖两侧。唐代以來，佛徒祈福、发愿， 多以此为供品悬于寺庙或佛窟中佛像两侧。在药师佛的信仰中，十分重视幡和灯供养：欲度脱危厄，应造七层之灯，或以四丨九盏灯分供药师七佛前，還有樹立五色綵幡等等， 所以许多药师经壁畫有燃灯、树幡等场面。

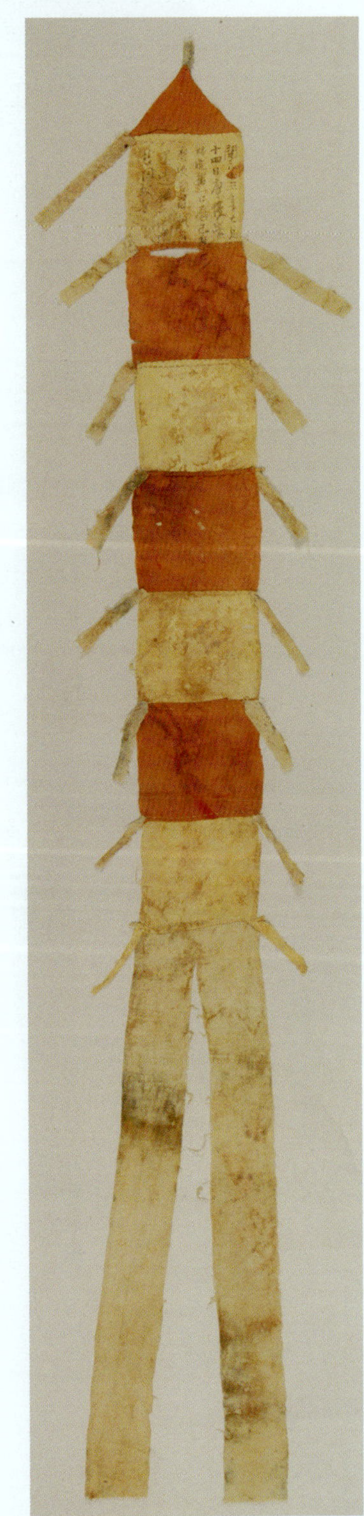

16. Prayer banner

Tang dynasty, 725
Silk; 162 x 15 cm
Collection of the Dunhuang Academy, Z.0003

This banner has a red headpiece and seven square panels alternating in color, with side streamers at each seam (one is missing from the first panel). The headpiece and panels are made of two layers of thin silk, and the lower-end streamers are of raw silk.

The purpose of offering this banner is stated on the first panel of the body: "On the 14th day of the 7th month in the 13th year of the Kaiyuan period [725], I, Upasika [female lay Buddhist] Kang [originally from Central Asia], am offering a banner because of my eye disease. If I recover, I will offer one more to thank Buddha for his compassion."

This banner is a very important source for studying the history of Dunhuang cave building, the culture of different ethnic groups, the Buddhist faith, ancient textiles and weaving skills, and so on.

16、许愿幡

盛唐，公元725年
绢，162×15厘米
敦煌研究院馆藏编号：Z. 0003

幡首为由二层红绢缝制而成；幡身七幅，二色交错相连，每幅都有緣條缀于两侧（其中第一幅缺一条）；幡尾為生绢缝制。

幡身第一幅有发愿文（6行38字）：“开元十三年七月十四日康优婆姨造播（幡）一口为己身患眼若得（损）日还造播（幡）一口保佛慈（因=恩？）故告”。此为康姓（中亞康国人）俗家女弟子为眼疾而造幡，并发愿眼疾治愈后會再造一幡供养，以報佛慈恩（護佑）。

开元十三年幡对于研究莫高窟营建史、民族文化、佛教信仰、古代纺织技术等都有重要价值。

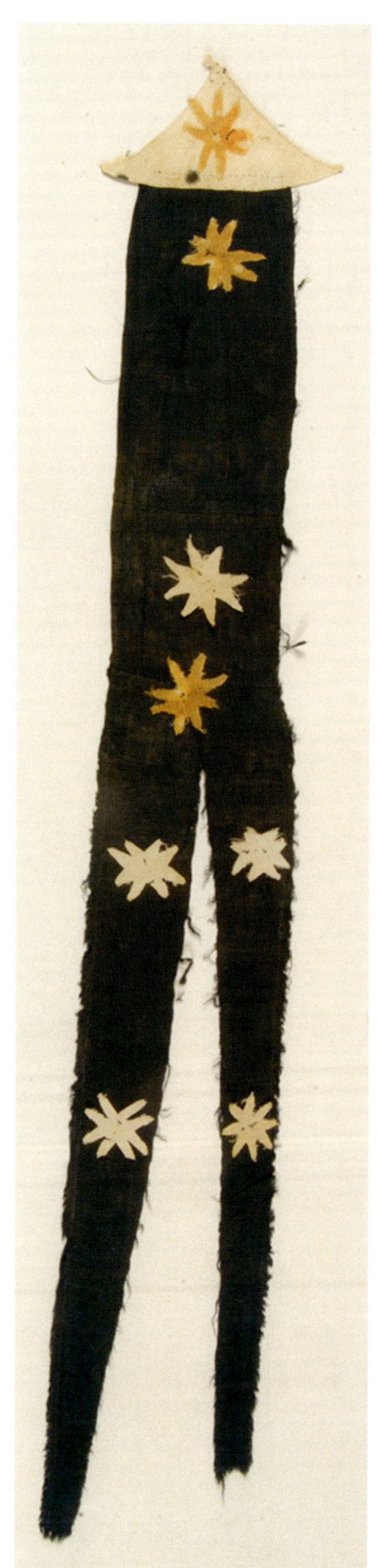

17. Banner with floral appliqués

Tang dynasty (618–907)
Silk; 78 x 9.5 cm
Collection of the Dunhuang Academy, Z.0002

The head of the banner is made of two layers of white thin silk. The body and tail are made of one whole piece of soft, thin silk which was folded twice and then stitched together. Eight eight-petaled silk flowers are attached to the deep blue silk of the banner.

17、缀花绢幡

唐（公元618～907年）
绢，78×9.5厘米
敦煌研究院馆藏编号：Z.0002

幡首为双层白色绢，幡身和幡尾为薄而软的深蓝色绢，是用一块绢分叠三段缝制成。幡上缀饰八瓣花八朵。

Pottery Ware Unearthed in the Mogao Grottoes

While the 492 extant caves in the Southern Area of the Mogao Grottoes served the public, the more than 200 caves in the Northern Area were living quarters, meditation cells, and burial chambers for the monks. The northern caves, which were largely undecorated, yielded such mundane finds as bowls, oil lamps, and coins (see no. 26), among more significant finds, such as the broad range of document fragments (see nos. 5 & 6 above). Some color mixing bowls used by artisans were also found in the Southern Area.

莫高石窟出土的陶器

莫高窟的南区有492个佛窟对公众开放，北区的200多个洞窟则是过去僧侣生活、修行和埋葬的处所，大多数都没有装饰。但是在考古发掘中，发现了陶碗，陶灯，钱币（参见图录26），以及文献残篇（参见图录5、6）。在南区也发现了一些工匠们绘画所用的调色碗。

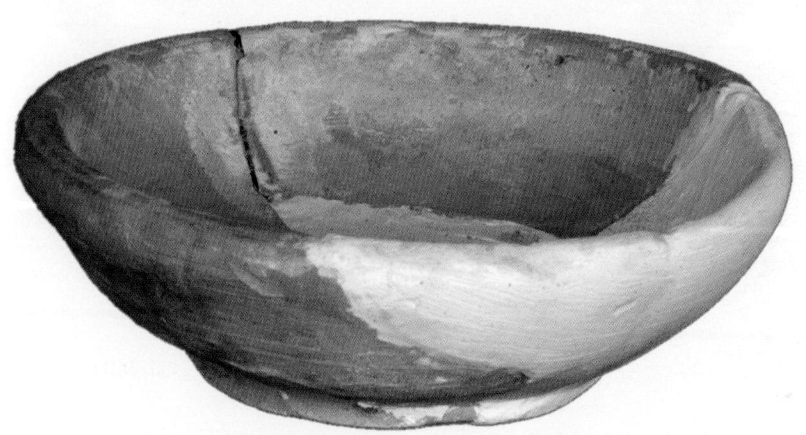

18. Color-mixing bowl

Tang dynasty (618–907)
Pottery; H. 3, W. 10 cm
Collection of the Dunhuang Academy, Z.0900

This bowl was used by artists to mix pigments for painting murals. It had been cracked and was restored with gypsum. However, some green pigment still remains.

18、调色碗

唐（公元618～907年）
陶，3×10厘米
敦煌研究院馆藏编号：Z. 0900

古代画工使用，碗壁缺损，经石膏修补复原。碗内残留绿色颜料。

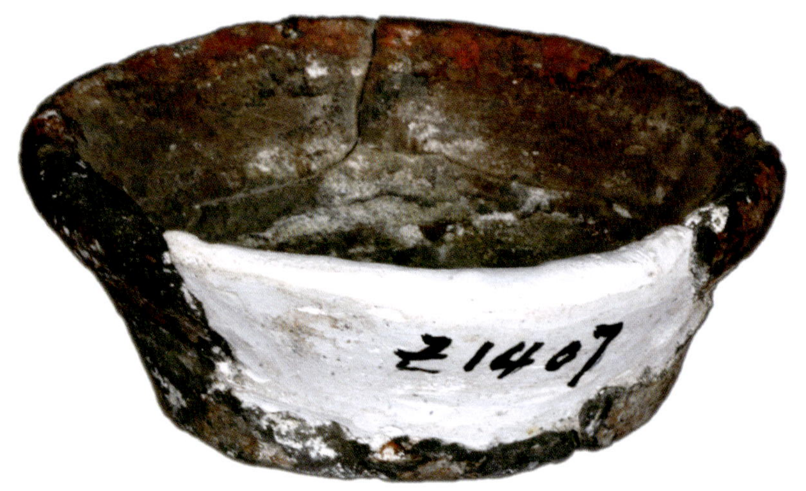

19. Color-mixing bowl

Tang dynasty (618–907)
Pottery; H. 3, W. 8 cm
Collection of the Dunhuang Academy, Z.1407

This bowl was used by artists for painting murals. It had been cracked and chipped and was restored with gypsum. Some red pigment remains visible.

19、调色碗

唐（公元618～907年）
陶，3×8厘米
敦煌研究院馆藏编号：Z. 1407

古代画工使用，有多处断裂纹，缺损一小块，经石膏修补复原。碗内残留红色颜料。

20. Color-mixing bowl

Tang dynasty (618–907)
Pottery; H. 3, W. 8 cm
Collection of the Dunhuang Academy, Z.1408

This bowl was used by artists for painting murals. It had been cracked and chipped and was restored with gypsum. Some yellow pigment can still be seen.

20、调色碗

唐（公元618～907年）
陶，3×8厘米
收藏单位：敦煌研究院　馆藏编号：Z. 1408

古代画工使用，多裂纹，缺损一小块，经石膏修补复原。碗内残留黄色颜料。

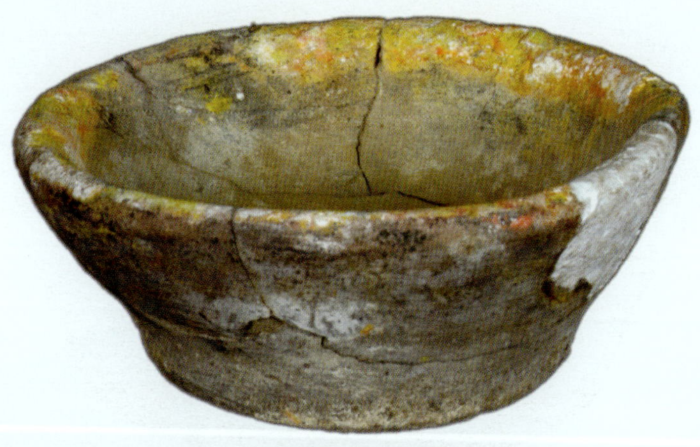

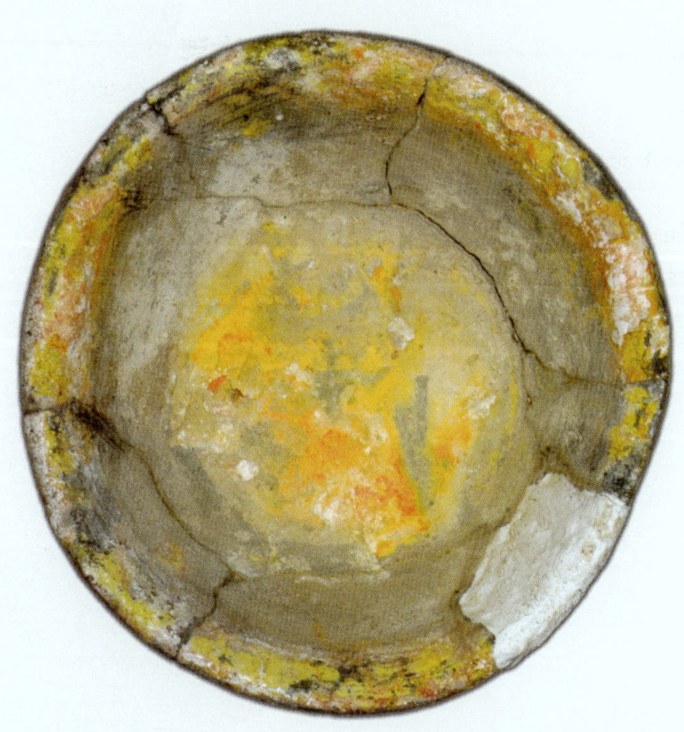

21. Oil lamp

Five Dynasties (907–960)
Clay; H. 2.7, W. 7.7 cm
Collection of the Dunhuang Academy, Z.0832

This bowl-shaped oil lamp and the oil lamp on a stand (no. 22) were both used for illumination by the artists painting or working in the caves.

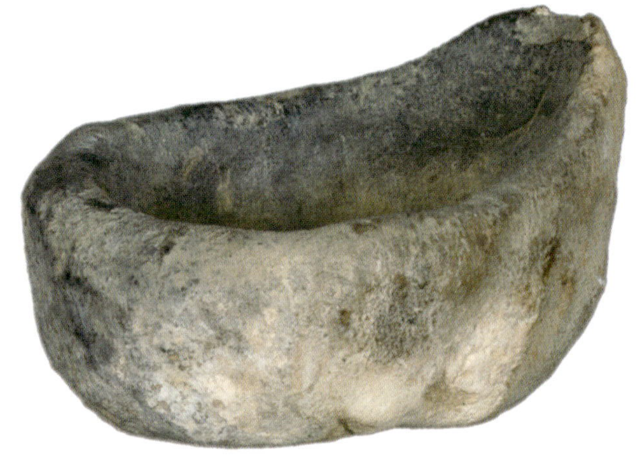

21、油灯碗

五代（公元907～960年）
泥，2.7×7.7厘米
敦煌研究院馆藏编号：Z.0832

此油灯碗和22号的油灯台，都为画工在洞窟绘画和工作时的照明用具。

22. Oil lamp

Five Dynasties (907–960)
Clay; H. 12, W. 12.5 cm
Collection of the Dunhuang Academy, Z.0876-3

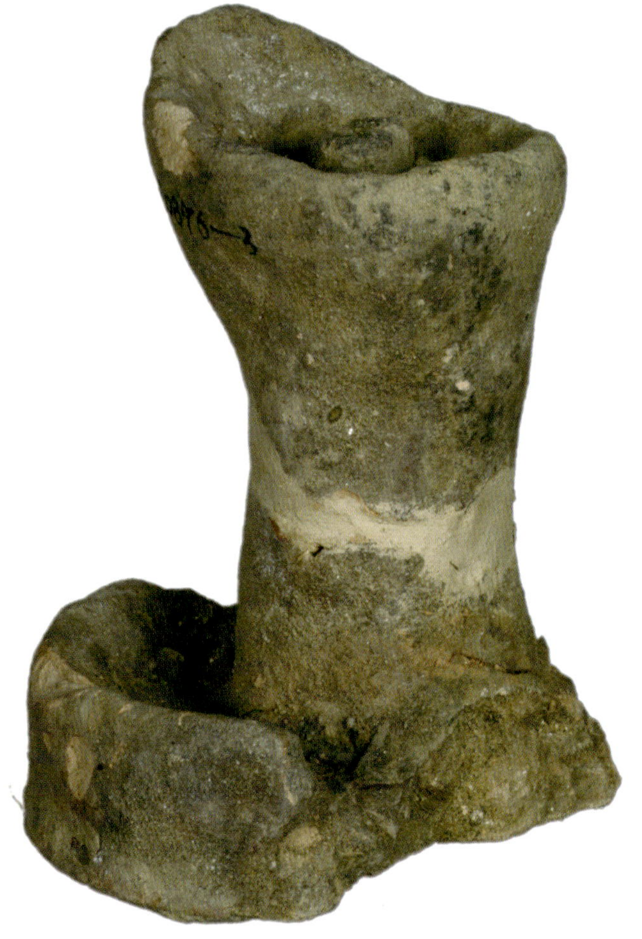

22、油灯台

五代（公元907～960年）
泥，12×12.5厘米
敦煌研究院馆藏编号：Z.0876-3

The Art of Patterned Floor Tiles

These floor tiles found inside or in front of the Dunhuang caves are decorated in low relief. The main patterns usually consist of an eight-petaled lotus combined with other designs, such as vines, scrolling clouds, heart-shaped motifs, flames, or precious beads. Other than floral and geometric patterns, there are also animal designs like horses, lions, and camels. There are as many as eighteen patterns found on the tiles unearthed in front of the caves.

These patterned floor tiles are the valuable products of the highly developed integration of two ancient skills—painting and carving.

花砖艺术

敦煌洞窟内和窟前地面铺设的淺浮雕花砖，一般纹样以八瓣莲花为主，还有蔓草、卷云、桃心、火焰、宝珠等纹。除植物花纹和幾何圖形外，还有动物纹样，如马、狮、骆驼等，仅窟前遗址出土就有十八种之多。這些花砖是古代绘画和雕刻艺术高度结合的珍品。

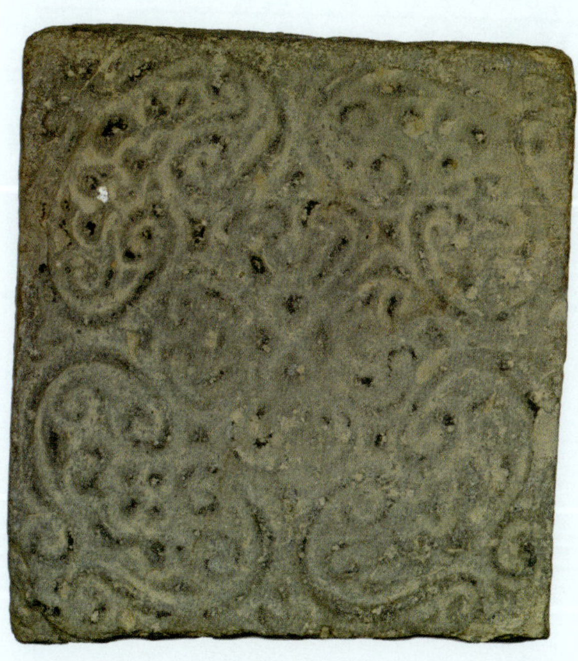

23. Floor tile with pomegranate design

Tang dynasty (618–907)
Clay; H. 33, W. 31, D. 5.5 cm
Collection of the Dunhuang Academy, Z.0069

In the center of the tile is a flower in full blossom with curling petals, surrounded by four pomegranate designs at the corners.

23、石榴纹砖

唐（公元618～907年）
粘土，高33×宽31×厚5.5厘米
敦煌研究院馆藏编号：Z.0069

砖中央为盛开卷瓣花卉，四角为石榴纹。

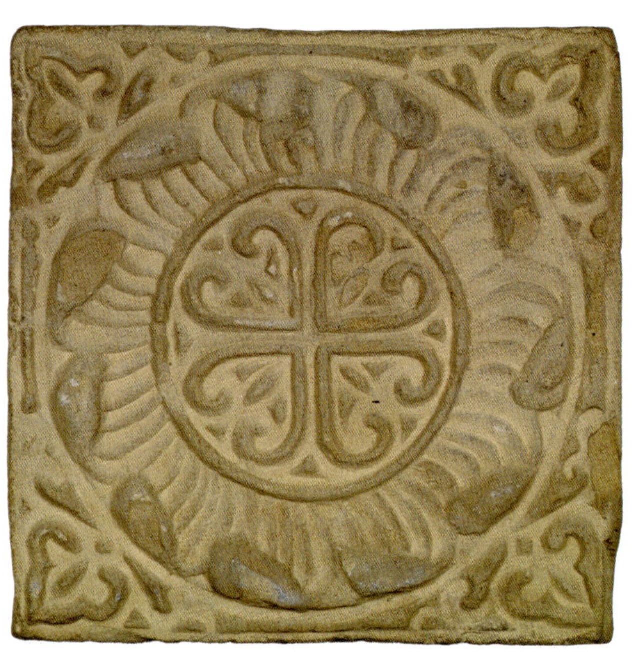

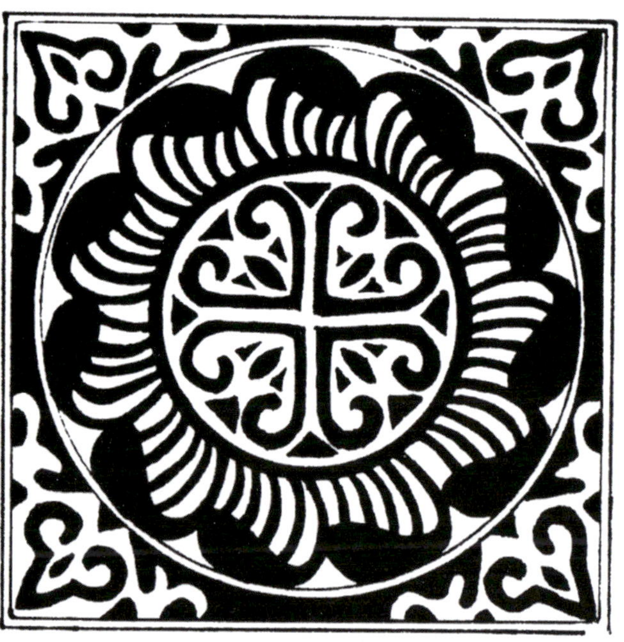

24. Floor tile with eleven-petaled lotus

Tang dynasty (618–907)

Clay; H. 36, W. 35, D. 6.5 cm

Collection of the Dunhuang Academy, Z.1134

The design on this tile is a lotus flower with eleven curling lotus petals and a bud in the center formed by four heart-shaped motifs.

24、桃心十一卷瓣莲花纹砖

唐（公元618～907年）

粘土，高36×宽35×厚6.5厘米

敦煌研究院馆藏编号：Z.1134

砖上圖案为桃心形四花蕾十一卷瓣莲花纹。

25. Floor tile with lotus flower and linked-pearl design

Tang dynasty (618–907)
Clay; H. 35, W. 35, D. 5.5 cm
Collection of the Dunhuang Academy, Z.1197

At the center of this tile is a roundel of linked pearls surrounded by a double-layered, eight-petaled lotus flower. Many small dots are added to enhance the splendor of the design.

25、莲花联珠纹砖

唐（公元618～907年）
粘土，高35×宽35×厚5. 5厘米
敦煌研究院馆藏编号：Z. 1197

砖上圖案为联珠八覆瓣莲花，加上許多小點以增華麗。

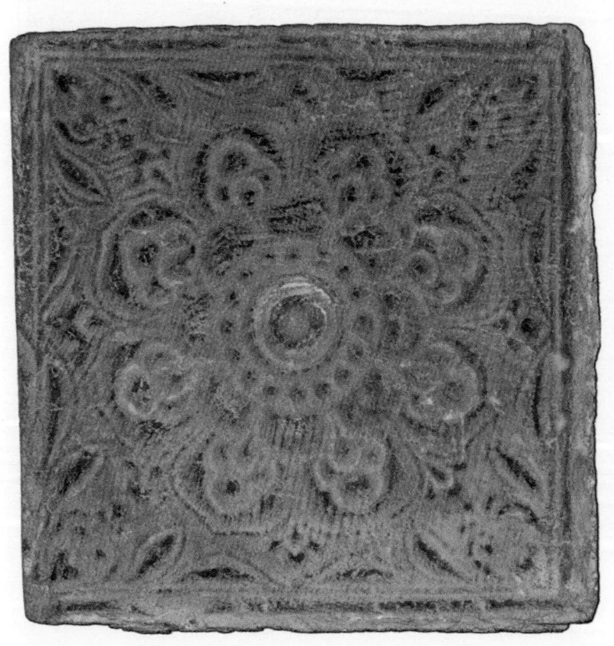

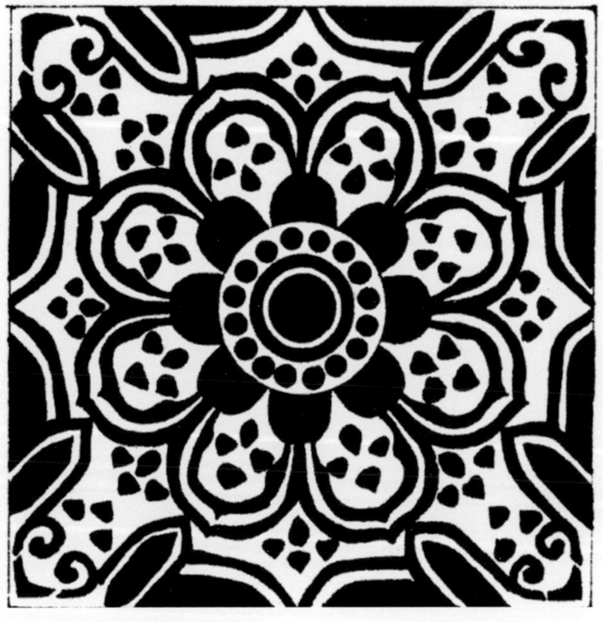

26. Floor tile with *ruyi* and scrolling vines

Tang dynasty (618–907)
Clay; H. 35.5, W. 35, D. 6.5 cm
Collection of the Dunhuang Academy, Z.1363

The design on this tile consists of a small eight-petaled lotus at the core and two surrounding layers of scrolls which take on the shapes of floral plants, clouds, or *ruyi* (an auspicious object).

26、如意卷草纹砖

唐（公元618～907年）
粘土，高35.5×宽35×厚6.5厘米
敦煌研究院馆藏编号：Z.1363

砖上圖案以八瓣小莲花為芯和兩層卷纹构成。卷紋呈花草、云或如意式樣。

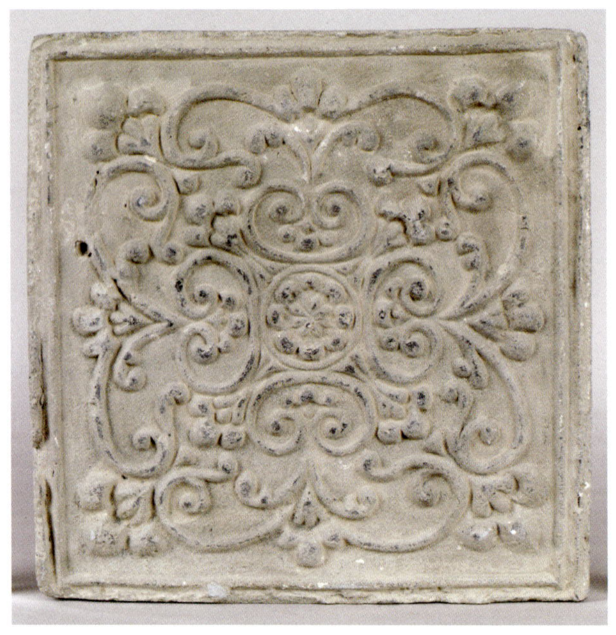

Foreigners in Dunhuang

The garrison town of Dunhuang, originally founded by the Han Chinese in 111 BCE, became a major commercial hub on the Silk Road. It was a launching point for caravans setting out for the West. And it was a place of safety and respite for caravans carrying foreigners and foreign goods that had traveled across the desert headed for the major cities of China. No doubt the devout Buddhists who arrived here gave thanks or prayed for safe passage at the local temples and shrines.

Over its long history, the town was fought over and periodically occupied by non-Han powers: the Xiongnu and the Turkic Tuoba during the Northern Dynasties; the Tibetans for a brief period in the Tang dynasty; the Uighurs followed by the Tangut Xixia (Western Xia dynasty) in the eleventh century; the Mongols during the Yuan dynasty; and the Tibetans again in the sixteenth and seventeenth centuries. Different religions flourished in this area as a result of foreign occupation and Silk Road commerce. In addition to Buddhism, which had spread into China over the Silk Road, and the indigenous practice of Daoism and Confucian ancestor worship, evidence of Nestorian Christians, Zoroastrianism, and Manichaeism could also be found in the Mogao Grottoes.

A large quantity of fragmentary texts in non-Han languages, as well as a number of Persian and Xixa coins, were found in the caves of the Northern Area of the Grottoes. The carved wood mortuary figure of a Westerner (cat. no. 27) attests not only to the multi-ethnic nature of the local community but also to the use of some of the caves in this section of the site for funerals and burials.

敦煌之胡人

公元前111年敦煌便已成为驻军之镇，以后逐渐成为丝绸之路贸易往来的重要枢纽。这里是西出国门的关隘，也是在沙漠中长途跋涉的胡商安全歇脚的城镇。无疑，此处的佛窟寺庙给东西往来的商贾行人，提供了一个祈祷佛陀保佑和感恩的场所。

在其漫长的历史岁月中，不断的战乱，这里也在不同时期被不同的族群所统占，如北朝时的匈奴，拓跋；唐代短暂的为藏族统占；11世纪时为西夏和回鹘所占；元代为蒙古族所占，然后在16和17世纪再次为藏族所占。因此不同的宗教信仰在此共存。除了佛教以外，还有道教，儒家的祖先崇拜，景教，基督教，祆教和摩尼教等。

在北区考古发掘中发现的相当多的文献残篇，都是非汉文的，并且发现了波斯和西夏的钱币。木雕胡俑（参见图录27）也在此区发现，证实这些洞窟也作为埋葬之用。

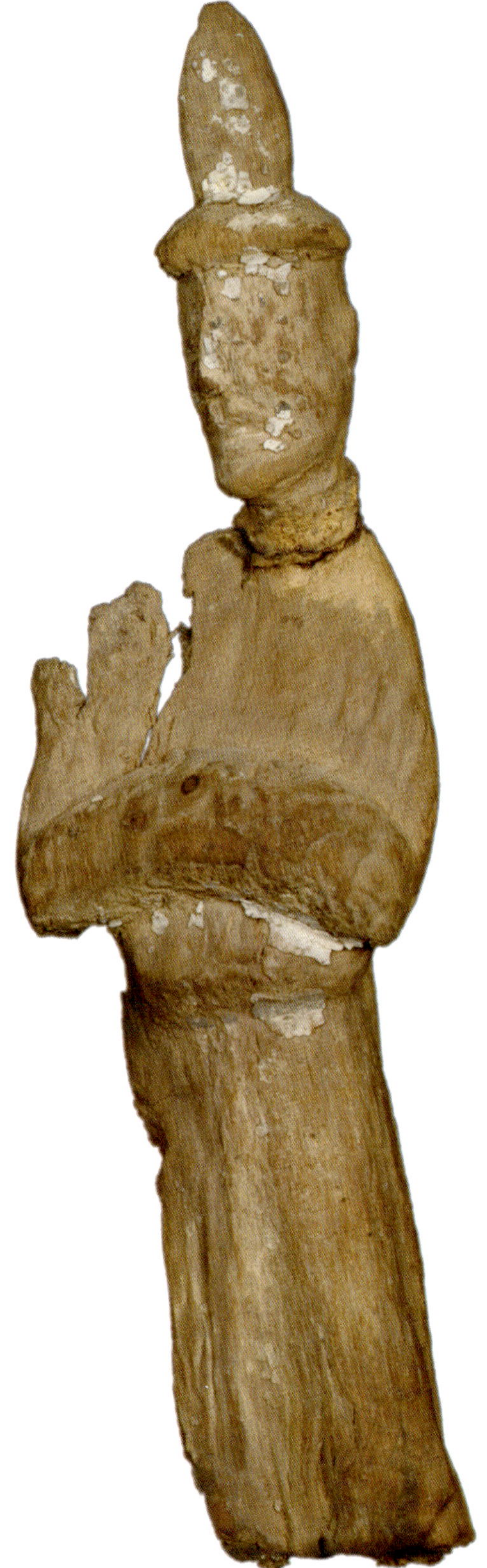

27. Mortuary figure of male Westerner

Tang dynasty (618–907)

Wood and pigments; H. 14.8 cm

Collection of the Dunhuang Academy, B86:11

This mortuary figure wears a pointed hat and has deep-set eyes, a chiseled nose, a wide mouth, and a protruding chin. His folded hands are hidden in his sleeves and held in front of the chest. Both feet and part of the right shoulder have been damaged. Most of the original pigments have come off, leaving only a minute amount of white pigment in places.

27、男胡俑

唐（公元618～907年）

木，彩绘，残高14.8厘米

敦煌研究院馆藏编号：B86:11

此俑高鼻深目、大嘴、下颌突出，头戴尖帽，双手藏于袖内，并拱于胸前，右肩部稍残，足已毁。原有彩绘多已脱落，尚残留少许白色。

28. Persian coin

Sassanian, reign of Peroz I (457–484)
Silver; Width 3.1 cm, Thickness 0.1 cm, Weight 3.88 g
Collection of the Dunhuang Academy, B222:1

One hallmark of Sassanian coinage is its thinner flan when compared to that of its Greco-Roman counterpart.

This Sassanid Persian coin was issued during the reign of King Peroz I (r. 457–484). The heavily worn obverse shows the bust of the king in profile, facing toward the right inside a dotted-border. Although the image is degraded, it can be discerned that he is wearing a winged crown surmounted by ornaments in the shape of a crescent and disk. The illegible inscription around him is in Pahlavi, an ancient Iranian language.

The state religion of the Sassanid dynasty was Zoroastrianism, and the king was considered guardian of the sacred fire. Thus, fire imagery appears on the coin's reverse. Inside the dotted border is a pillar-like fire altar with two attendants dressed in kingly garb by its side. Flanking the flame are a crescent and a five-pointed star. The Pahlavi inscriptions beside the attendants are now mostly obliterated, making them illegible.

28、波斯银币

波斯，萨珊朝卑路斯王时期（公元457～484年）
银，直径3.1厘米、厚0.1厘米、重3.88克
敦煌研究院馆藏编号：B222:1

波斯錢币其中一個特點是比希臘羅馬的薄。這銀幣屬萨珊朝卑路斯王一世时期，正面磨损严重，边缘有一圈联珠纹，中间为國王半身像，脸向右，王冠虽残，但尚可辨其翼冠顶有新月托球狀飾物，後有飄帶；肖像周圍有模糊难認的钵罗婆文字（古伊朗文）。

薩珊王朝信奉袄教（拜火教），國王是聖火守護人，所以錢幣背面中央有祭坛，火焰兩側为新月與星，祭坛两侧各立一侍者穿王者服，兩人外側均有铭文，因磨损过甚无法辨认；边缘也有一圈联珠纹。

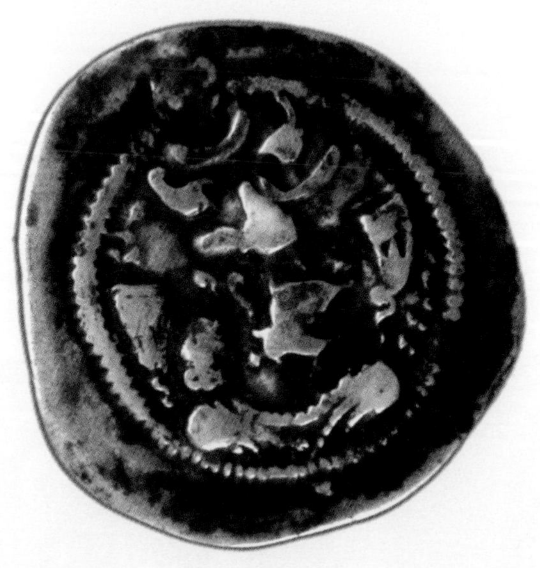

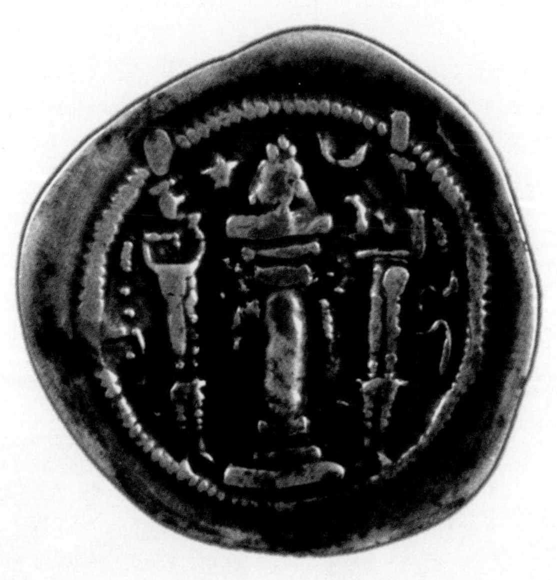

Replicas of Dunhuang Art
敦煌艺术复制展品说明

29. *Deer King Jataka*

Mogao Cave 257, Northern Wei dynasty (386–534)
Replica in mineral pigments on paper
by Chang Shuhong, 1955
60 x 588 cm

In Dunhuang, the use of narrative paintings with multiple scenes distributed in a horizontal band was first adopted in this cave.

According to the tale, the nine-colored (so-called to denote rarity) Deer King, named Ruru, rescues a drowning man; however, the man later forgets what is right and leads hunters to the deer's hideout to profit from the great reward offered by the local king, who wants the deer for its precious horns and beautiful skin. The Deer King fearlessly addresses the king, telling him of the rescued man's betrayal. Greatly moved, the king issues an order prohibiting the capture of the Deer King. Because of his betrayal, the rescued man in one version of the tale is made to suffer from sores on his whole body.

The episodes proceed from two sides towards the center, where the climax of the story is depicted: the conversation between the king and the deer revealing the treacherous deed of the man (see illus. 29-2). This arrangement shows that a story is not necessarily depicted in a chronological sequence.

This painting tells another story to the right of the Deer King Jataka. It is the story of Sumati, a distraught bride who invokes the Buddha to appear before her non-believer father-in-law and wedding guests (see illus., p. 53).

29. 九色鹿本生故事

莫高窟第257 窟，北魏（公元439～534年）
临摹者：常书鸿，1955
纸本，高60厘米、宽588厘米

这幅是敦煌最早期的横条连环故事画，讲述了九色鹿王救起溺水之人， 但溺水人见利忘义，到宫廷告密，并带领国王前往猎取鹿角及皮毛，鹿王毫无惧色，向国王诉述溺水人忘恩负义的劣迹。国王深受感动，下令全国禁捕，而溺水人则因违背誓言而周身生疮受苦。九色鹿故事有趣动人，壁画从两头开始，至中间成爲高潮：鹿王面对国王控诉溺人成为故事的结局。这种布局帮助故事画的剧情发展不一定单向顺序。

29-1

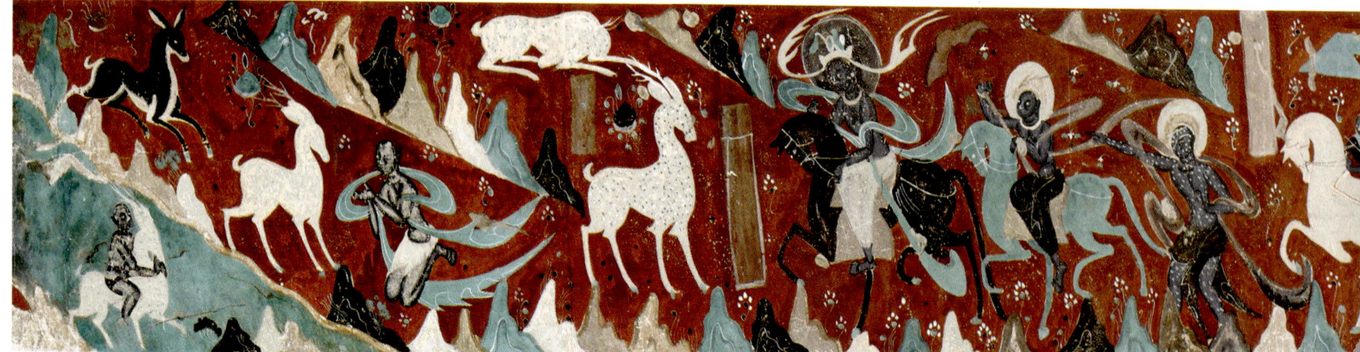

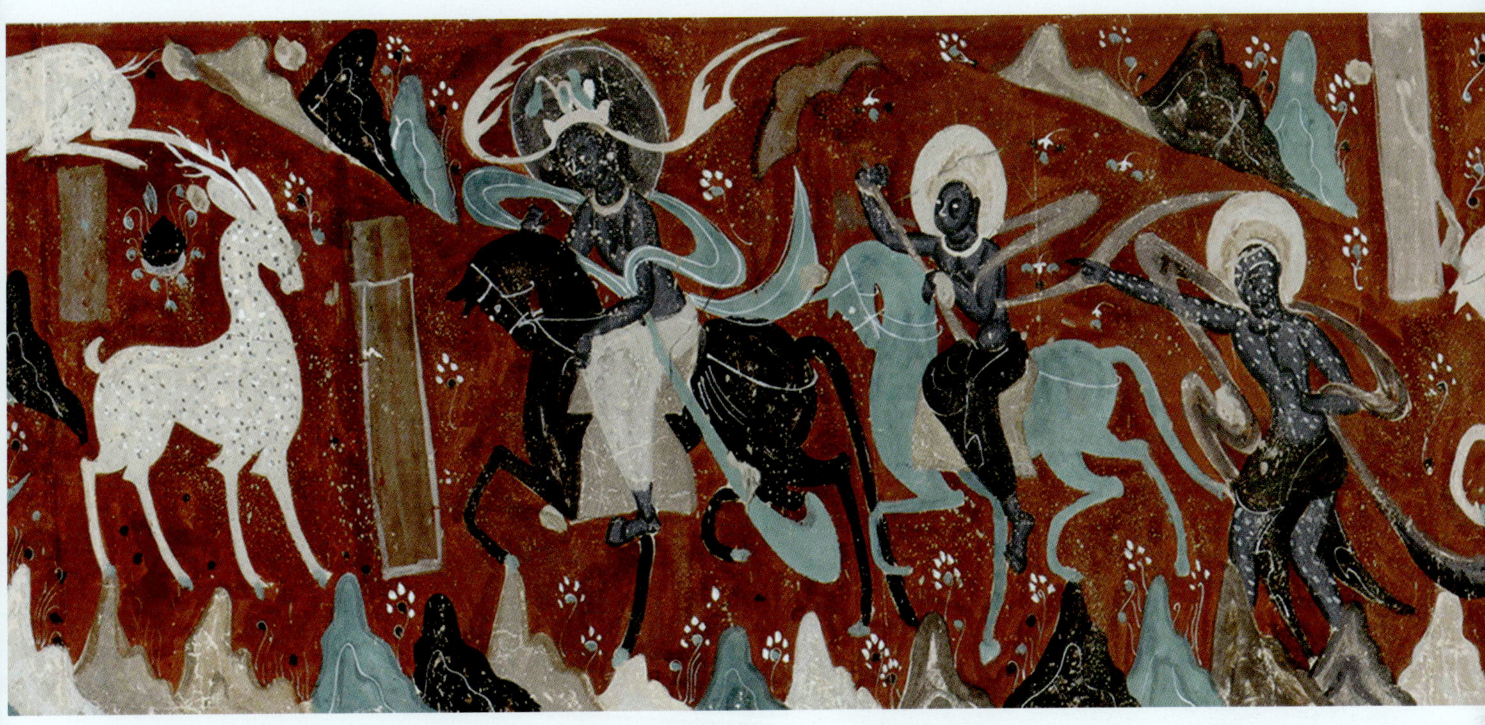

29-2 The king and the Deer-King, detail of *Deer King Jataka*. 国王 与鹿王，九色鹿本生图局部

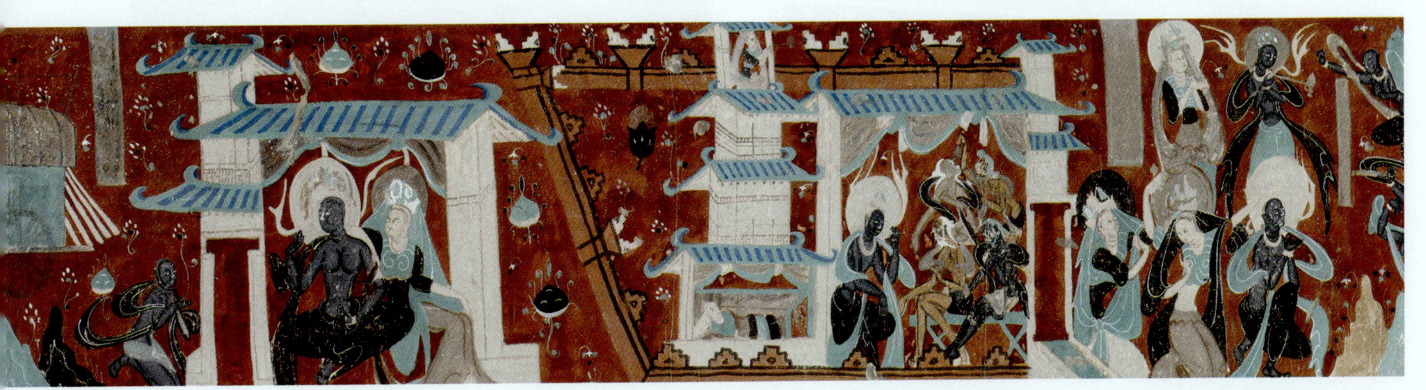

30. Central pillar

Mogao Cave 432, Western Wei dynasty (535–556)

Replica in paint and fiberglass by Du Yongwei and Zhang Li, 2008

H. 365, W. 222, D. 215 cm

This type of central pillar is set up in the main chamber of a cave to be used as an altar for the Buddha, a focus for the prayers of worshippers. There are niches in each of the four sides of the pillar.

Inside the front niche is a Buddha with a flame-shaped mandorla at his back and with adoring bodhisattvas and *apsaras* painted on either side. Two slim bodhisattvas modeled in clay stand outside the niche, smiling calmly as they flank the Buddha. The pillars and arch framing the niche are decorated with lotus flowers and dragon heads. Tiny clay figures are pasted on the curved spandrel between the canopy and arch. Half kneeling, they are dressed in loose robes and either press their palms together or offer lotus buds held in one hand. The remaining three sides of the pillar each have two niches, one above the other. Each niche houses a meditating Buddha with two or four bodhisattvas in Chinese attire, different from those in the front niche which have bared upper torsos.

30．中心柱

莫高窟第432窟，西魏（公元535～556年）

临摹者：杜永卫、张力等，2008

绘彩玻璃钢，高365厘米、纵222厘米、横215厘米、

中心柱是建于洞窟内作爲信众绕佛诵经用的佛坛，柱子四面开龛。

正面佛像有火焰纹背光，两侧画供养菩萨及飞天，龛外两侧塑斜侍菩萨，身材修长，面带微笑。龛柱和龛梁装饰莲花、龙头。龛楣上方遍贴半立体菩萨，穿大袖长袍，胡跪合掌或持莲蕾。

柱子其他三面各开上下龛，均有一佛二或四菩萨。佛像两侧的菩萨着中原汉式衣冠，与正面佛龛菩萨西域式袒胸、露臂、赤足各有不同。

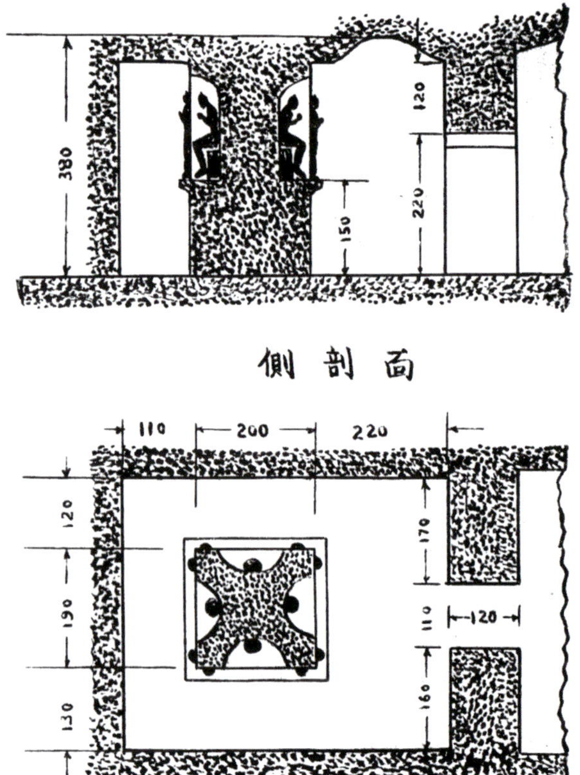

30-1 Floor plan and section drawing of Cave 432. 第432窟平面图

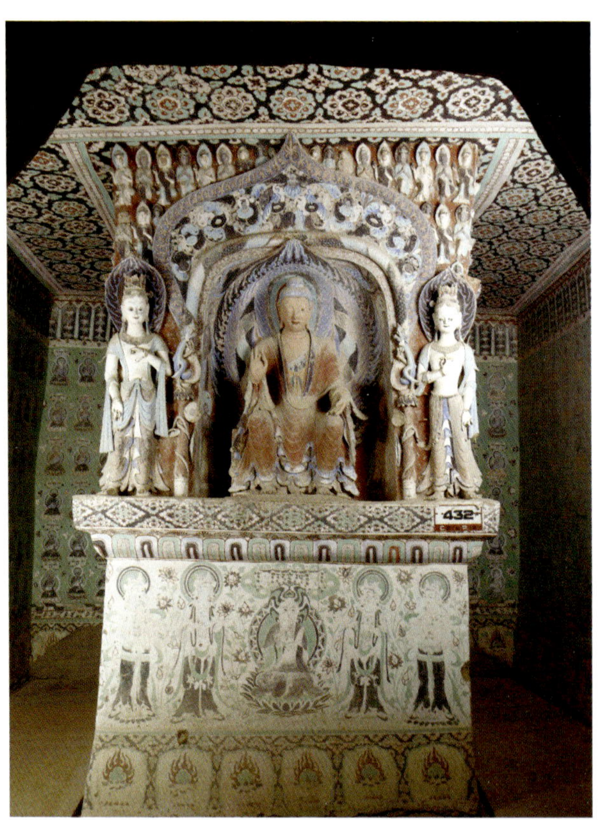

30-2 Central pillar inside Cave 432. 第432窟中心柱

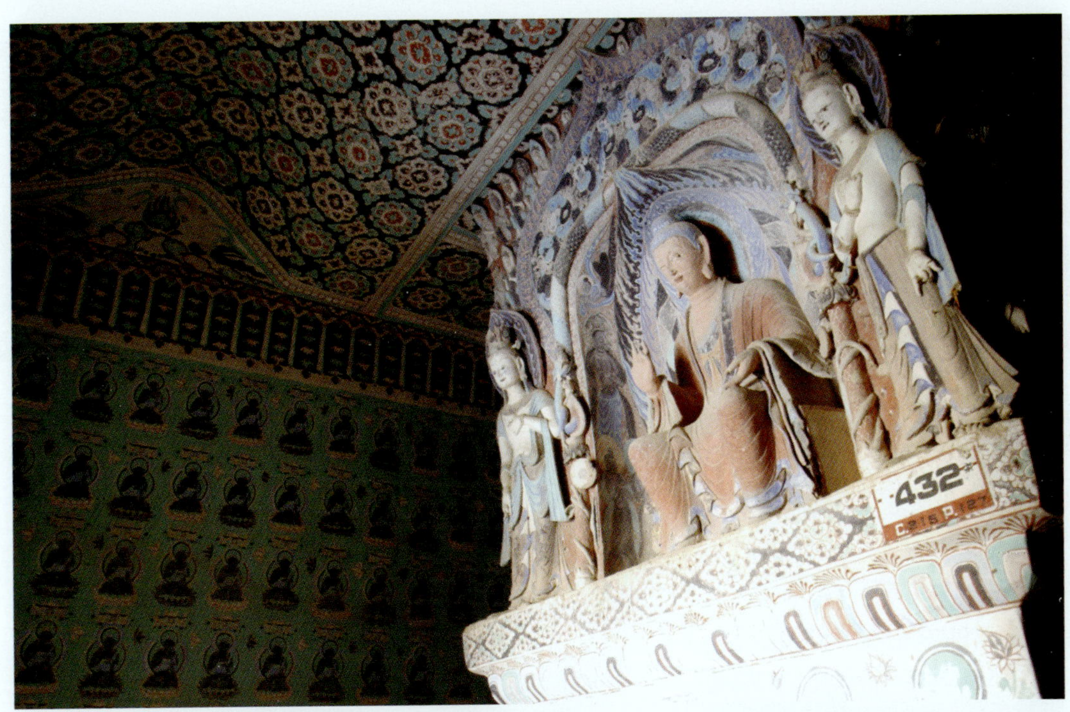

30-3 View of the central pillar's front face and adjoining ceiling area in Cave 432. 第432窟中心柱正面与窟顶

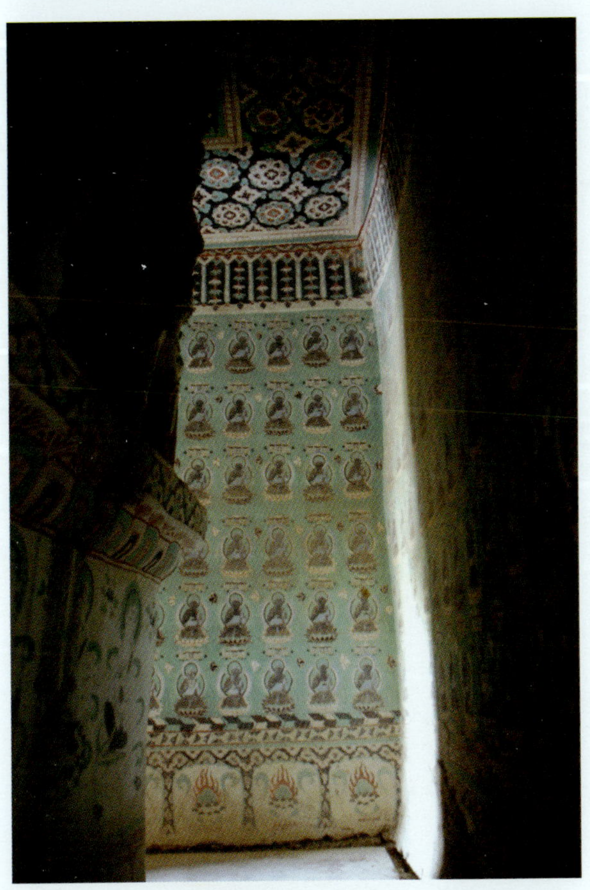

30-4 Rear of Cave 432 along the passage behind the pillar.
第32窟中心柱背面

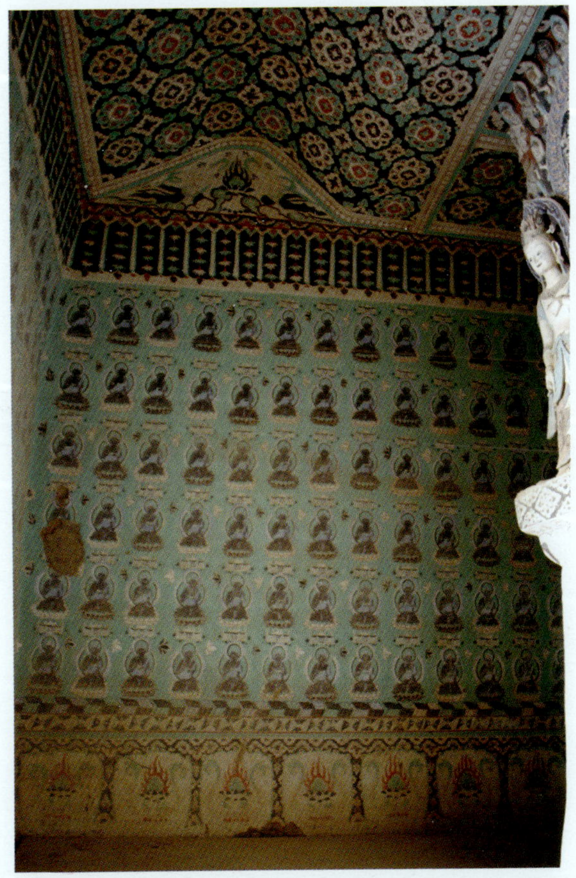

30-5 Painting of the Thousand Buddhas on a wall in Cave 432.
第432窟壁画千佛图

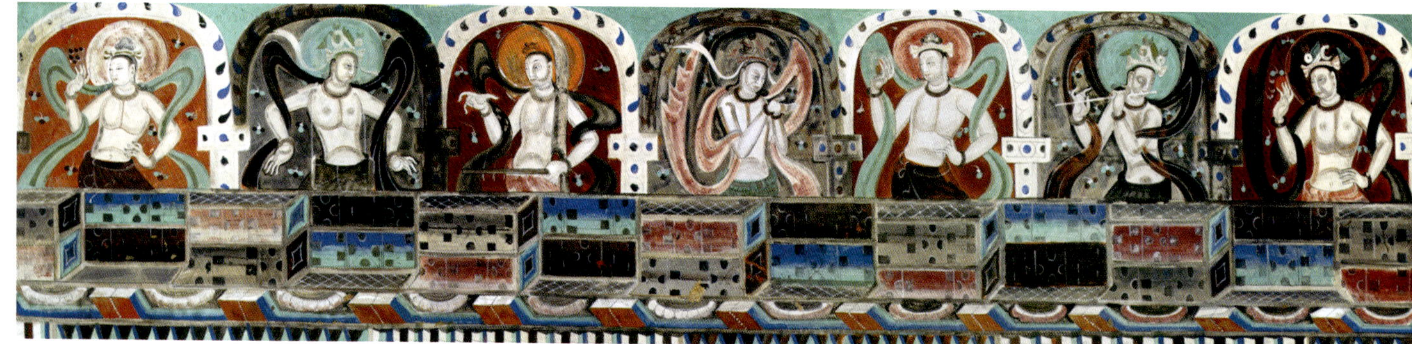

31. ***Celestial Music***

Mogao Cave 288, Western Wei dynasty (535–556)
Replica in mineral pigments on paper
by Shi Weixiang, 1974
52 x 522 cm

A celestial music performance refers to the music and dance of deities as an offering to the Buddha. Such scenes are usually depicted in the upper areas of a cave, symbolically denoting its performance in heaven. The lively yet elegant movements of the figures are deeply imbued with the style of Indian and Central Asian dance.

In this painting, the celestial beings hold offerings or such musical instruments as the lute, waist drum, and harp; some dance empty-handedly. They are lively figures, colorfully and boldly depicted.

31．天宫伎乐图

莫高窟第288窟，西魏（公元535～556年）
临摹者：史苇湘，1974
纸本，52×522厘米

天宫伎乐是指天神以音乐舞蹈供佛，一般画在洞窟的上部表示在天宫中。他們的动作幅度大、体态美妙，有濃厚印度、中亞风格。图中天神或持供品；或持琵琶、腰鼓、箜篌等乐器；或空手而舞。多姿多彩、刚劲生動。

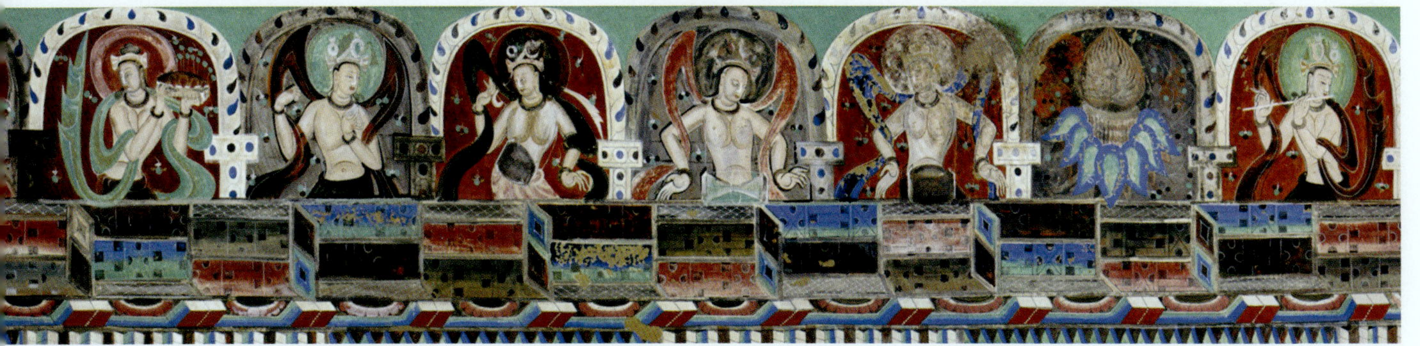

31-1

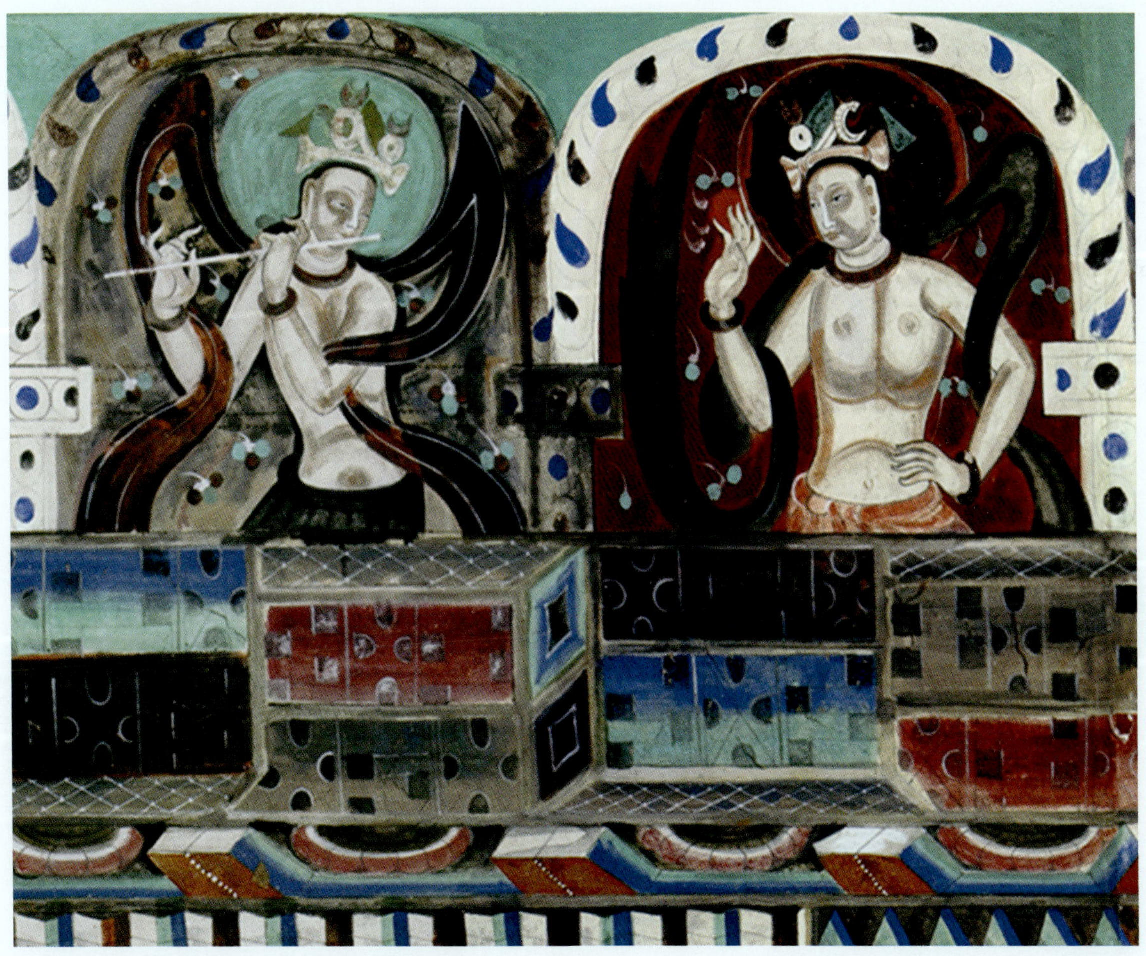

31-2 Detail of *Celestial Music*. 天宫伎乐图局部

32. Mogao Cave 45

High Tang period (705–781)*

H. 503, W. 471, D. 439 cm

Dating from the Golden Age of Dunhuang, Cave 45 is one of China's outstanding cave shrines. It consists of an assembly hall with a single main niche. The ceiling is in the shape of a truncated pyramid. A decorated coffer inset at the crown of the ceiling is called the *zaojing*.

After the localization of Buddhism, as well as Buddhist art, at Dunhuang, the cave shrines assimilated without interruption the structures of imperial architecture, techniques of sculpture, and compositions of murals in the metropolitan style of Tang dynasty China. This cave is a shining example of such integration.

32. 莫高第45窟

盛唐（公元705～780年）*

高503厘米、寬471厘米、深439厘米

第45窟建於莫高窟全盛期，屬殿堂式建筑，有一主龕，窟顶是覆斗形，正中方形裝飾叫藻井。随着佛教及佛教艺术的本土化，不断融入了庙堂式建筑结构、塑像造型和壁画构图等唐代中原風格，该窟是一個傑出的例證。

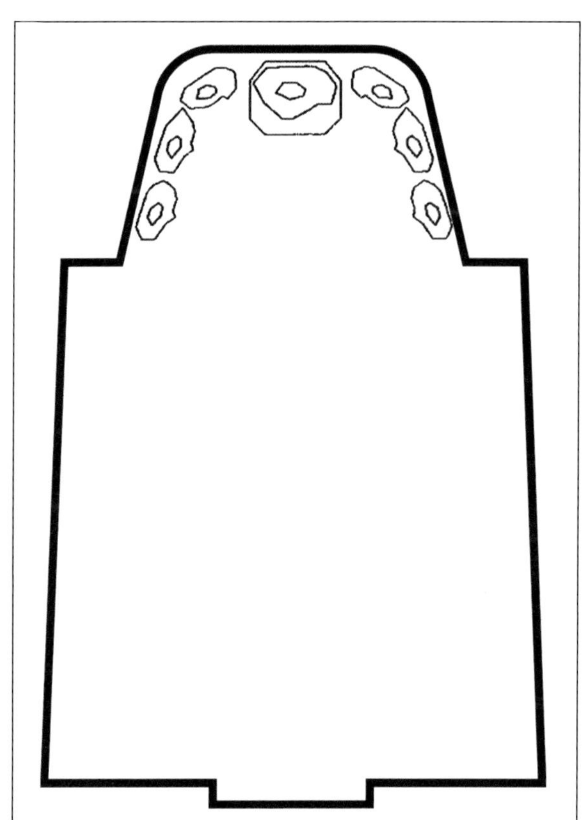

32-1 Floor plan of Cave 45 (assembly hall type).
第45窟（殿堂式）

* The Dunhuang Academy uses the following periodization of the Tang dynasty in their Chinese publications: early Tang (618–704); high Tang (705–780); middle Tang (781–847); and late Tang (848–906). It varies slightly from the one used on their English website and by Western scholars: (618–705); (705–781); (781–848); (848–907). 敦煌研究院在他们的中国出版物中把唐代分成以下几个时期：初唐（618-704）；盛唐（705-780）；中唐（781-847）；晚唐（848-906）。这和敦煌研究院英文网站上所使用的时期及西方学者的观点略有不同：（618-705）；（705-781）；（781-848）；（848-907）。

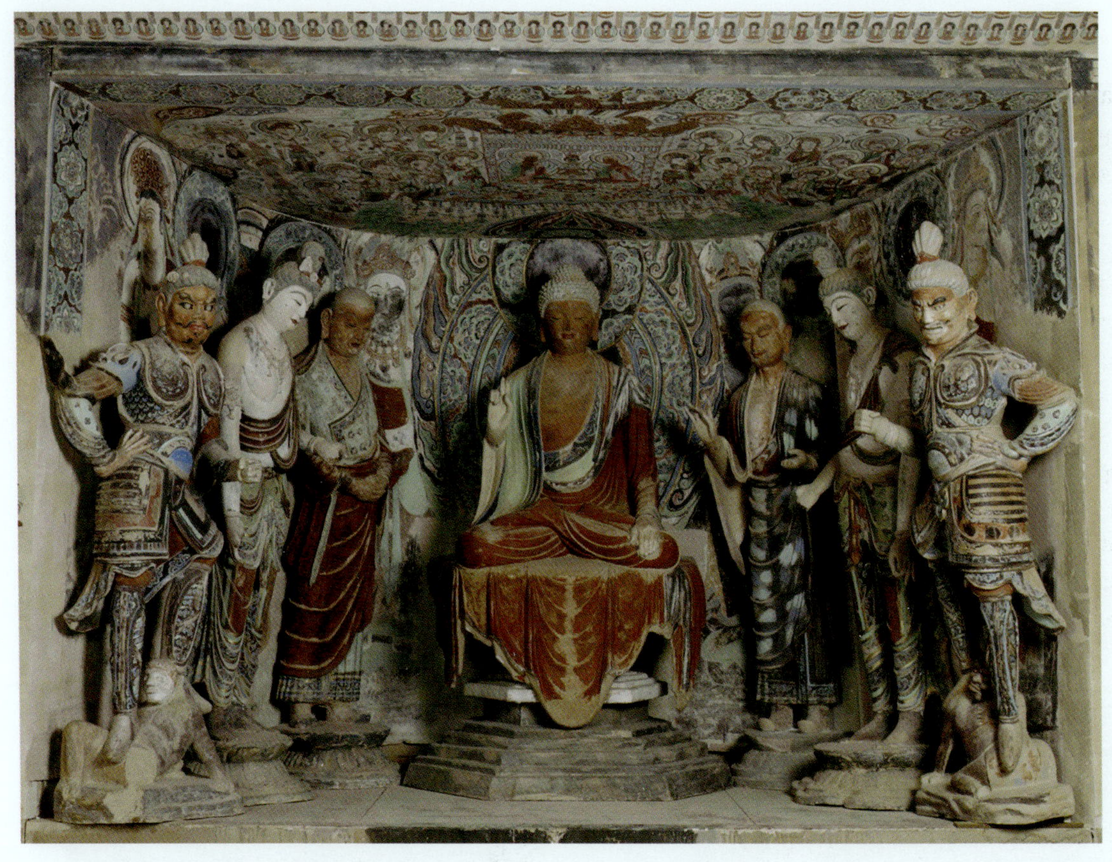

32-2 Buddhist septad in the niche along the west wall of the cave.
西壁佛龛及彩塑

Buddhist septad in the main niche
Mogao Cave 45, High Tang period (705–781)
Replica in paint and fiberglass by Zhang Li and Li Lin, 2004

The Buddha sits in the lotus position, serenely and compassionately looking at the devotees. It's said that this figure is based on the appearance of an emperor: healthy, sturdy, and imposing. Beside him are his two disciples, displaying a contrast between the clever, handsome, and calm face of the younger Ananda and the weather-beaten face and protruding ribs of the older ascetic Mahakashyapa.

The statues of the flanking bodhisattvas, although they are male, are famous for their beautiful and feminized appearance. They are portrayed in a delicate mood, plump but not obese, with arched eyebrows and a double chin. They stand with their elegant bodies in a sinuous S-shaped curve. On their *dhoti* (a long skirt wrapped around the waist) are rosettes edged with gilded lines. The outermost figures of the niche are two *devarajas* (heavenly kings) dressed in military costumes, looking like generals but for their tightly clenched fists and wrathful appearance.

Generally the sculpture of Dunhuang in this period became more delicate, secularized, and humanized. The figures lost their divine nature in order to be closer to the people.

主龛塑像
莫高窟第45窟，盛唐（公元705～780年）
临摹者：张力、李林等，2004
彩绘玻璃钢

佛坐在正中（这姿势叫跏趺坐），柔和悲悯垂视衆生，据说这健硕而又有气势的塑像是依据帝王之相而作。旁边立两弟子：年少英俊、神态安详的阿难与饱历风霜、衰老嶙峋的迦叶，两者形成强烈的对比。两旁菩萨造型圆润丰肥，虽是男性，但蛾眉重颌，身体婀娜，站立成“S”形，裙（裹腰布）上团花有金色钩边，具有女性化的特征。最外面是两天王，将军打扮，可是紧握拳头，相貌凶恶。

敦煌佛像早期一般较注重气质超脱，此时造像则比较精致、趋向世俗审美标准，也更人性化、更接近民众。

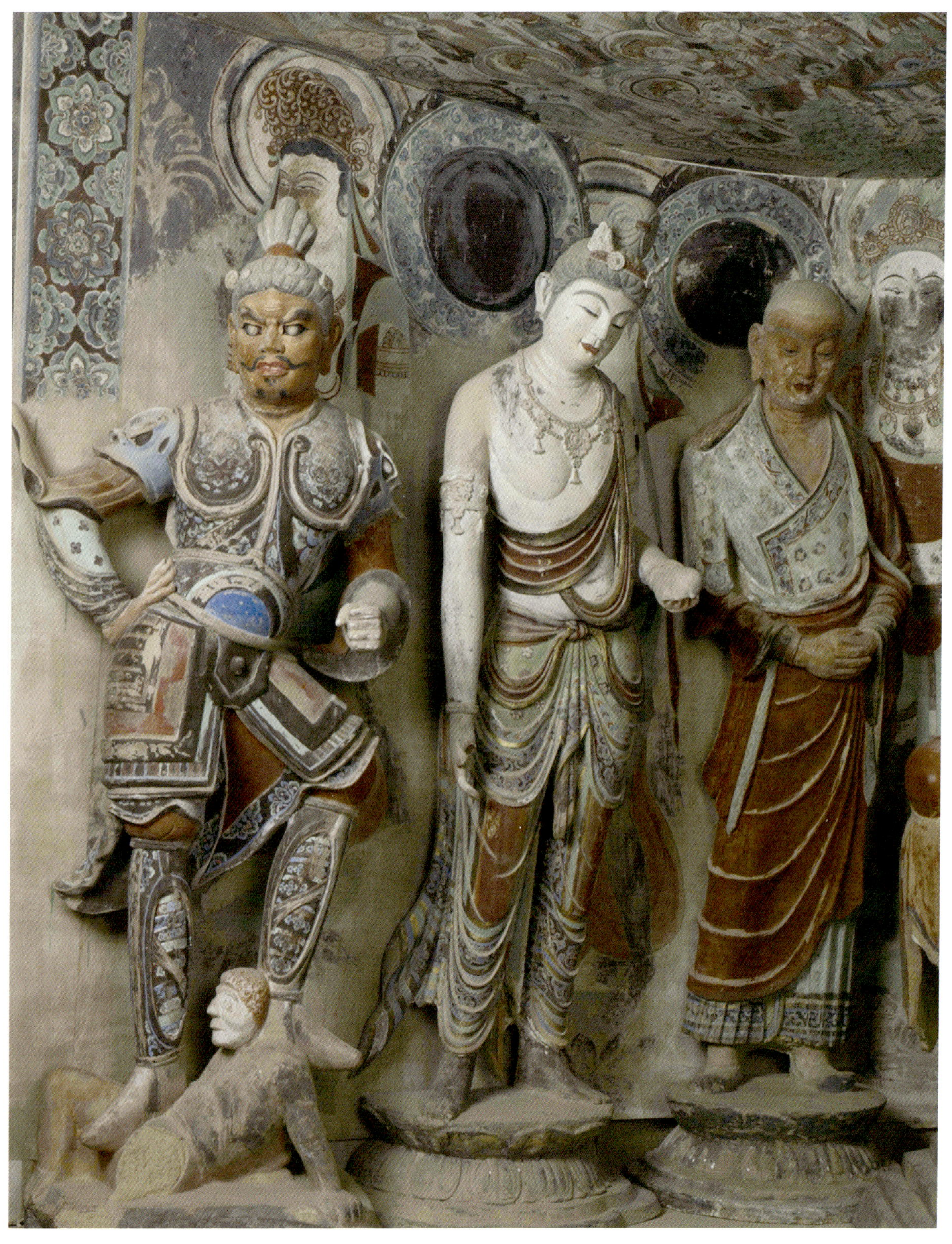

32-3 Ananda, bodhisattva, and *devaraja* on the south side of the niche. 西壁龛内南侧的阿难、菩萨、天王像

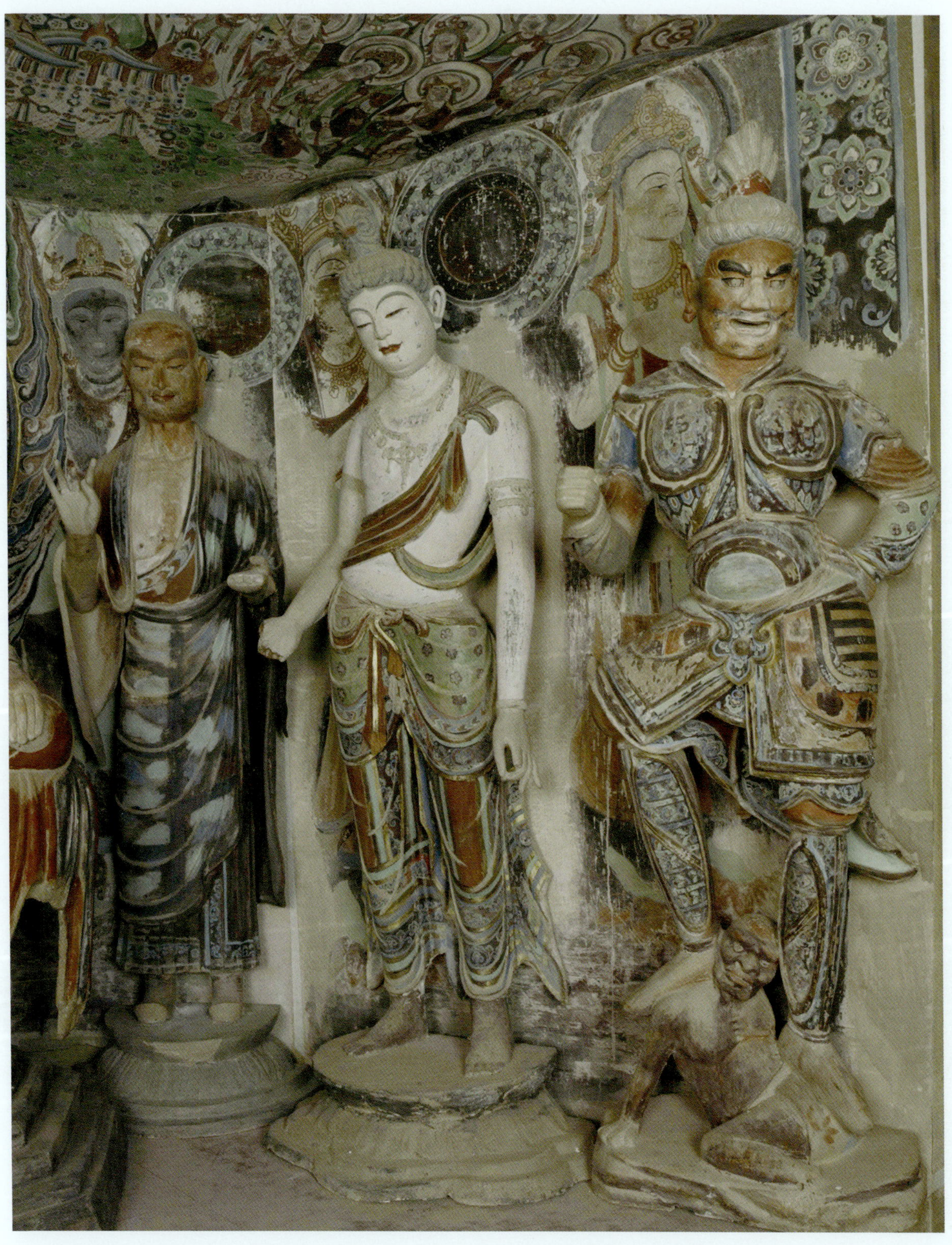

32-4 Kashyapa, bodhisattva, and *devaraja* on the north side of the niche. 西壁龛内北侧的迦叶、菩萨、天王像

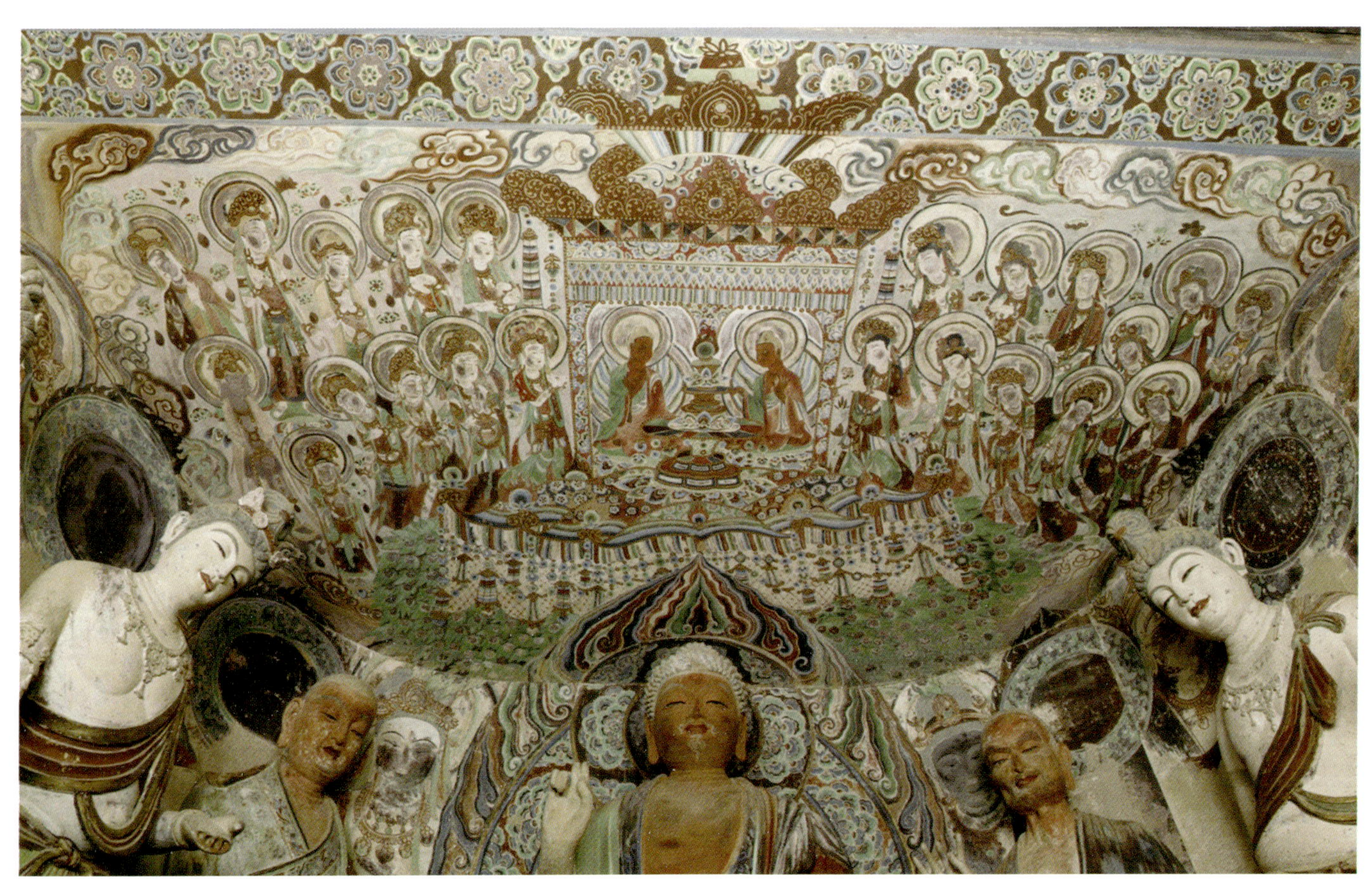

32-5 View of niche ceiling with depiction of Shakyamuni delivering a sermon seated next to Prabhutaratna in the Many Treasures Stupa.
佛龛窟西壁龛顶释迦多宝说法图

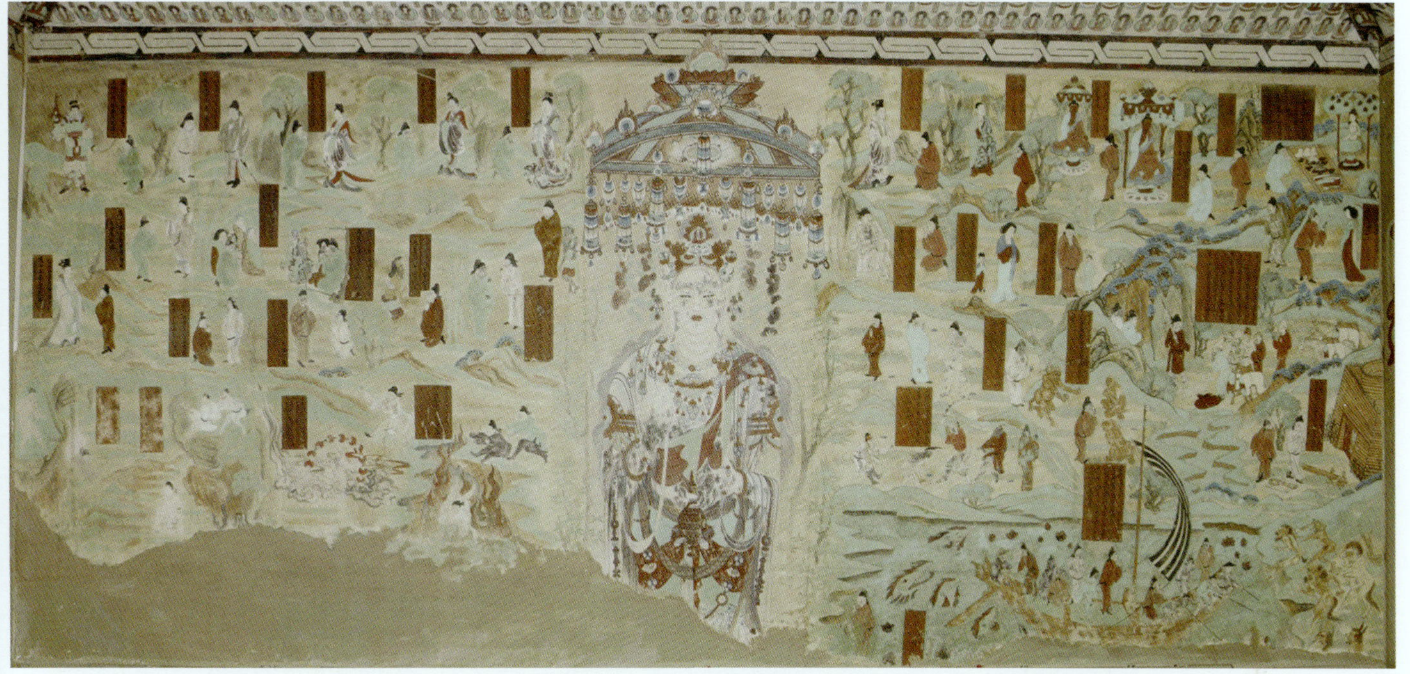

32-6 *Avalokiteshvara Narrative* from the south wall of Cave 45. 南壁的观音经变图

Avalokiteshvara Narrative (Guanyin jingbian)
Mogao Cave 45, High Tang period (705–781)
Replica in mineral pigments on paper by Zhao Junrong and Wang Hong'en, 2004
290 x 472 cm

At the center of the mural on the south wall of the cave is the large image of a standing Avalokiteshvara, or Guanyin, depicted as a handsome man according to Tang dynasty standards: strong and healthy, with green eyebrows and red lips.

The whole mural is skillfully arranged and painted. According to the *Lotus Sutra*, Guanyin appears in 33 (that is, many) manifestations to rescue people who call on him while encountering peril, such as when someone is being robbed, about to be jailed, or about to be killed. Religious themes in depictions of this period tend toward the pragmatic.

The Silk Road was always full of peril for caravans, as they might be attacked by bandits or might suffer from starvation or lack of water. One scene in the mural depicts six Central Asian merchants who join their palms and pray for Guanyin to come to their rescue (illus. 32-7). Their goods are scattered around and two frightened donkeys stand in front of the knife-wielding robbers—a depiction of an actual hardship encountered at that time by caravans going through this road.

This mural, which shows prisons, shipwrecks at sea, beheaded prisoners, women worshiping and praying for babies, etc., is rich with information about life in Tang dynasty society.

观音经变图
莫高窟第45窟，盛唐（公元705～780年）
临摹者：赵俊荣，王宏恩，2004
纸本，290×472厘米

佛窟南壁的壁画正中是高大的观音立像，菩萨壮硕英朗、翠眉红唇，是唐朝的俊男标准。整个画面安排巧妙，《妙法莲华经》说：观音有求必应，常以三十三（代表很多）种化身救渡危难衆生，人无论遇盗、被囚、被追杀，只要呼其名号，即得解脱。此时对宗教的描绘趋于实用。

丝路上充满危机，随时遭贼劫、飢渴之苦。画面中描绘有六位胡（中亚）商遇到抢匪，商人合十称念观音名号，货物散落地上，身后的两头毛驴目露惊恐，表现了穿越丝绸之路的艰辛跋涉。其他画面描绘古代监狱、航海遇难、囚犯被砍头、妇女求子等，皆展现了唐代社会生活，资料丰富。

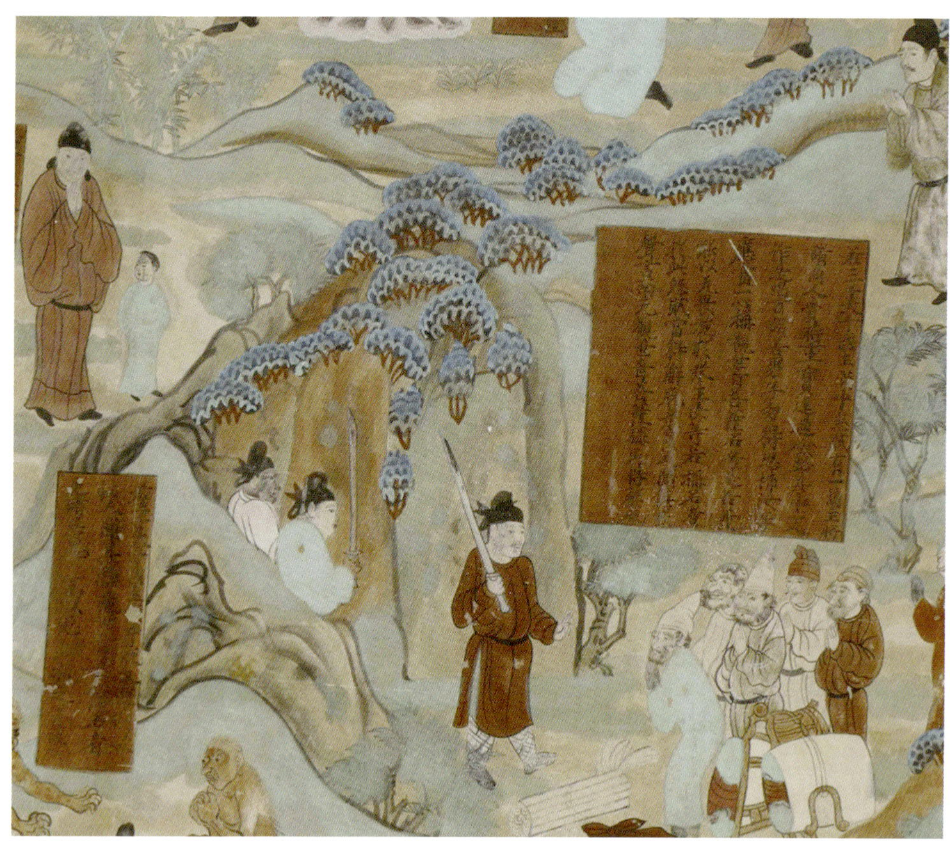

32-7 Foreign merchants being robbed, detail from the west side of the *Avalokiteshvara Narrative*.
南壁西侧的胡商遇盗图

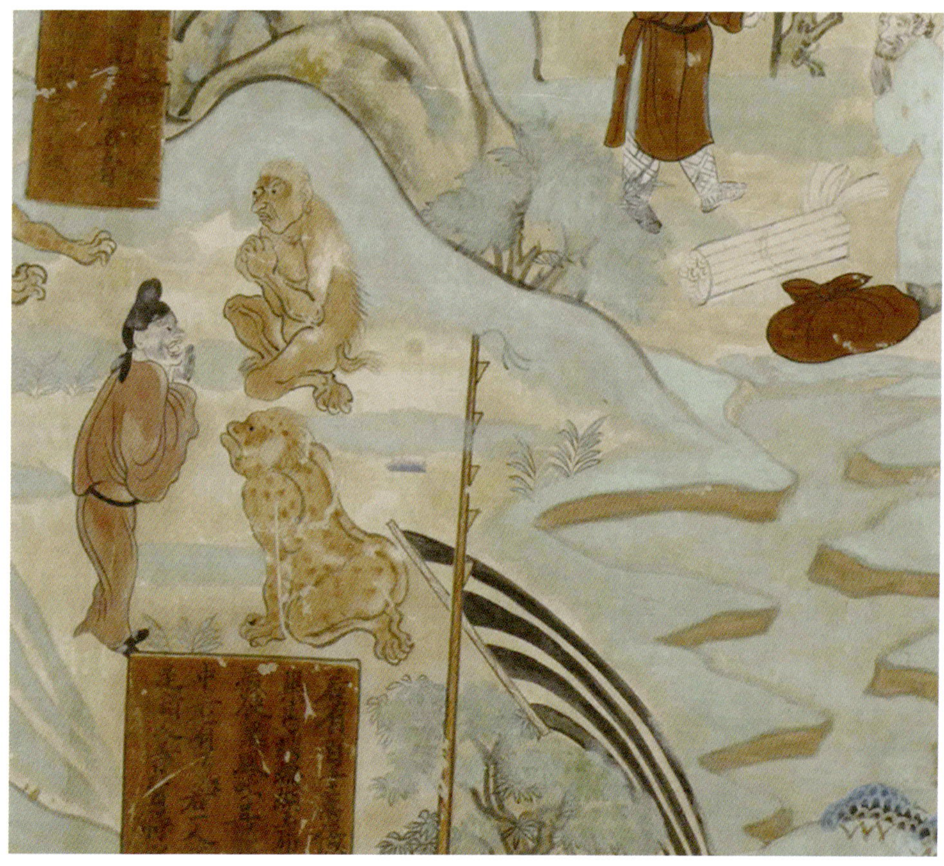

32-8 Traveler assailed by demons, detail from the west side of the *Avalokiteshvara Narrative*.
南壁西侧的旅行者遇鬼图

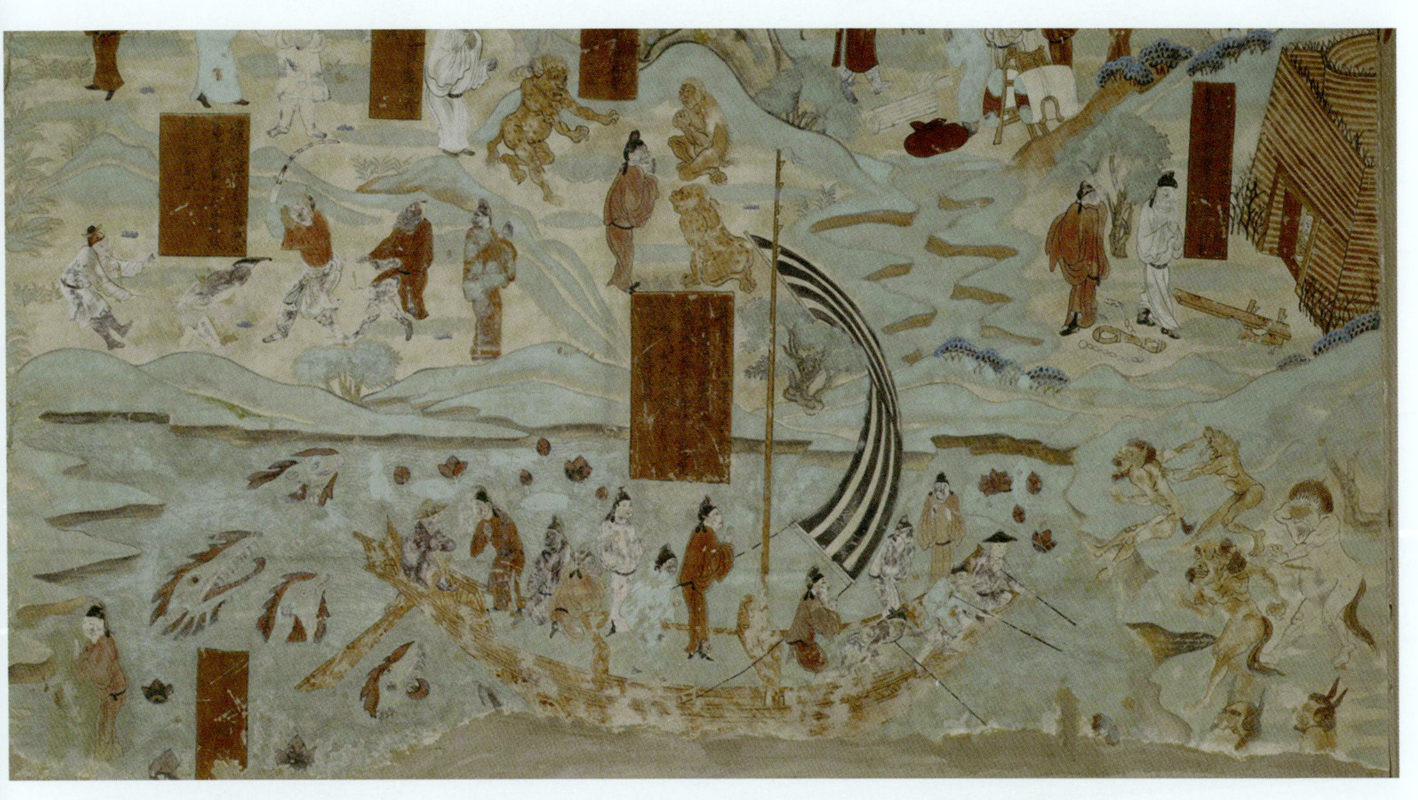

32-9 Avalokiteshvara saving those at peril in the sea, detail from the west side of the *Avalokiteshvara Narrative*.
南壁西侧的观音救海难图

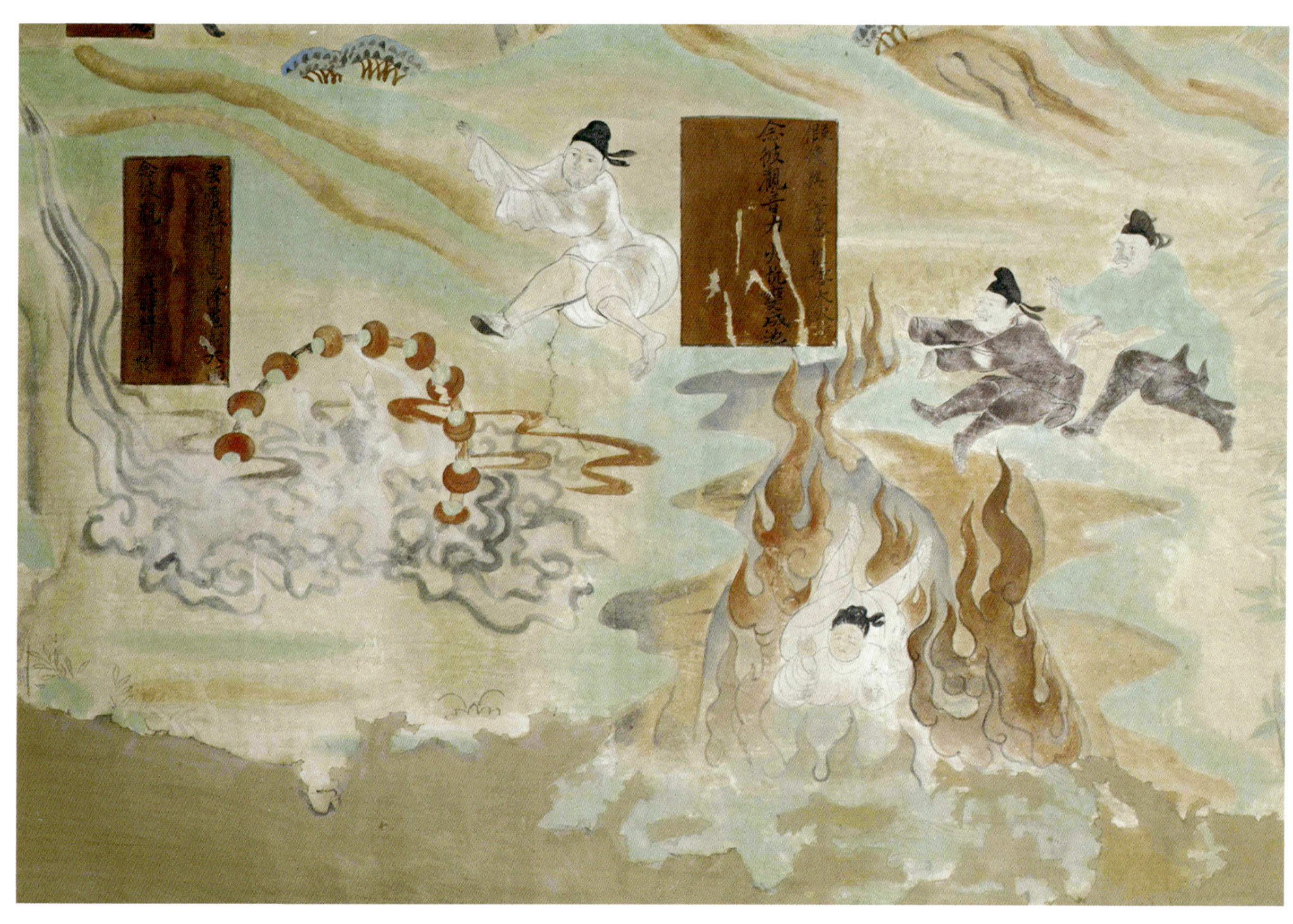

32-10 Scenes of peril, detail from the east side of *Avalokiteshvara Narrative*. 南壁东侧的观音救难图

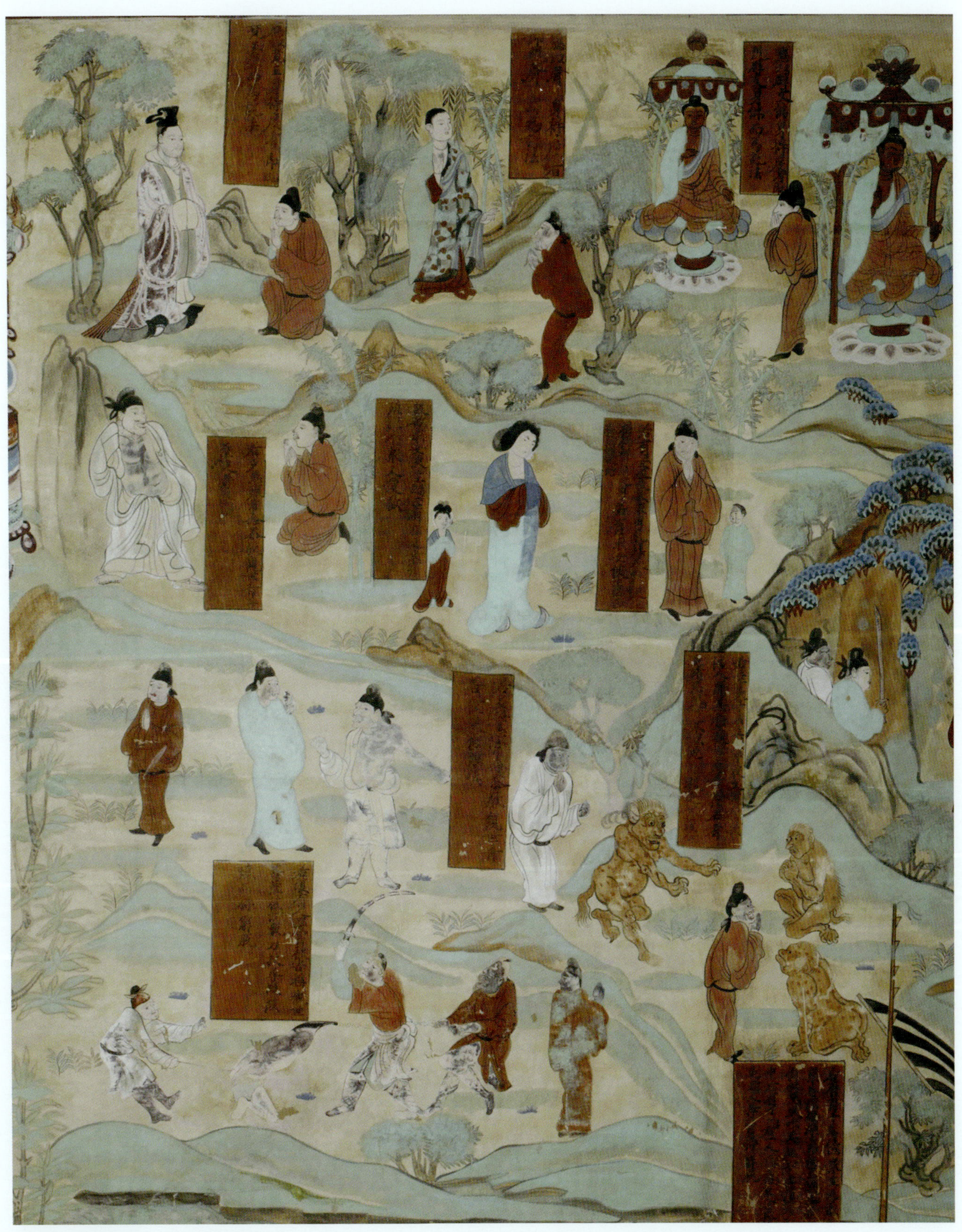

32-11 Avalokiteshvara manifesting himself to save those in peril, detail from east side of *Avalokiteshvara Narrative*.
南壁东侧的观音救难、现身说法图

Sukhavati (Amitabha's Pure Land)
Mogao Cave 45, High Tang period (705–781)
Replica in mineral pigments on paper by Wu Rongjian, Ma Yuhua, and Shen Shuping, 2004
290 x 472 cm

The preaching Buddha in the center of this painting on the north wall of the cave is Amitabha, depicted with all the auspicious and distinctive signs of a Buddha (illus. 32-12). In this grand paradise, there are huge buildings, luxuriant plants, lotus ponds, and entertainment, including dancers performing vigorously. It reveals the ideal world in which devotees hope to be reborn.

On the vertical margins at both sides of the paradise image are illustrations providing further explanation of ways to reach paradise. On one side is the story of Prince Ajatashatru (read in scenes from the bottom up), who usurps the throne and puts his father in prison. His mother, Queen Vaidehi, smuggles food to the poor king but was found out by the son. She is imprisoned and suffers deep agony (illus. 32-13). Therefore, she calls on the Buddha and asks whether there is a paradise for her to be reborn into, since she feels hopeless in this world. Buddha tells her about Amitabha's Pure Land and teaches her how to be reborn there.

The other side of the paradise image depicts the thirteen ways of Vaidehi's practice (read from the top down), including visualizing the sun, water, and earth (see p. 45, fig. 9).

Buildings and landscape are used to separate the scenes, which look orderly without the rigidity of frames and borders. The painting techniques from the prominent "Blue and Green Landscape" school in the Tang can be seen here.

This mural contains more than a hundred people in various styles of clothing according to their rank and occupation, providing precious historical information on costumes.

极乐世界（弥陀净土）
莫高窟第45窟，盛唐（公元705～780年）
临摹者：吴荣鉴、马玉华、沈淑萍，2004
纸本，290×472厘米

佛窟北壁的壁画是极乐世界，或弥陀净土图。画中央是阿弥陀佛瑞相庄严在说法。这幅宏伟的净土图中，有高阁崇楼、奇花异卉、莲池，还有歌舞表演，其中舞者的动作尤见生动活泼。

净土图的两边有条幅（长条连环图），一边的情节自下往上，讲述太子阿阇世（意即未生怨）篡位，囚禁其父王，断其粮水，母韦提希夫人偷送饮食，被发现后亦遭囚禁；夫人悲痛绝望，欲离此罪恶世界、投生善地，求佛开示，佛告以阿弥陀佛净土，并教导往生之法。另一边条幅自上往下，则讲述求生净土的十六种观法（途径），包括以日、水、地等为观想对象的修行方法。故事情节之间以山水或建筑分隔，次序分明，也没有死板的框条。此外，画面上还可找到已失传的著名唐代"碧绿山水"画法。全画有一百多个人物，衣着多式多样，因社会地位、职业而异，提供了非常宝贵的服装史料。

32-12 *Sukhavati* (*Amitabha's Pure Land*), painting on the north wall of Cave 45. 北壁的观无量寿经变图

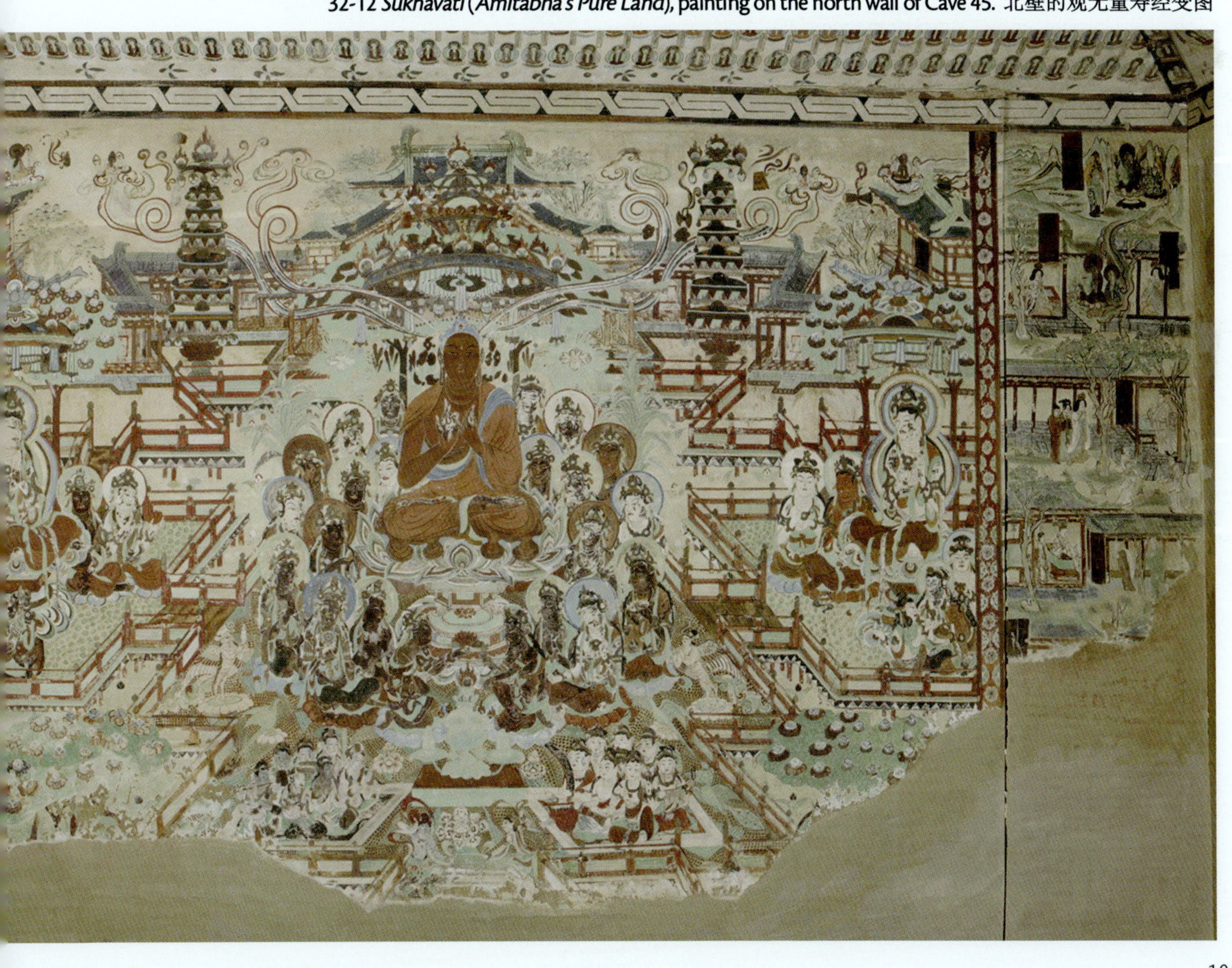

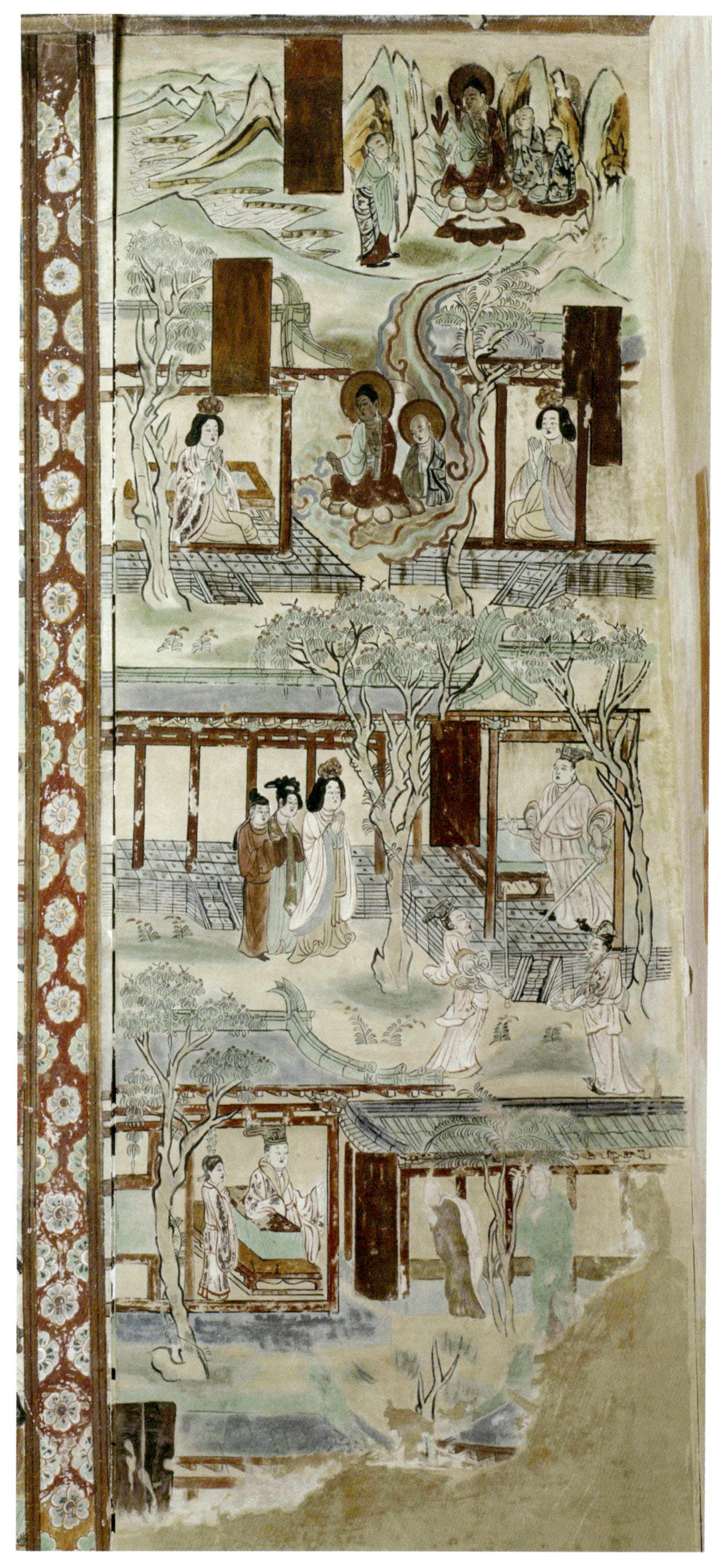

32-13 Queen Vaidehi imprisoned and suffering agony, narrative panel from *Sukhavati* (*Amitabha's Pure Land*) on the north wall. 北壁东侧的未生怨图

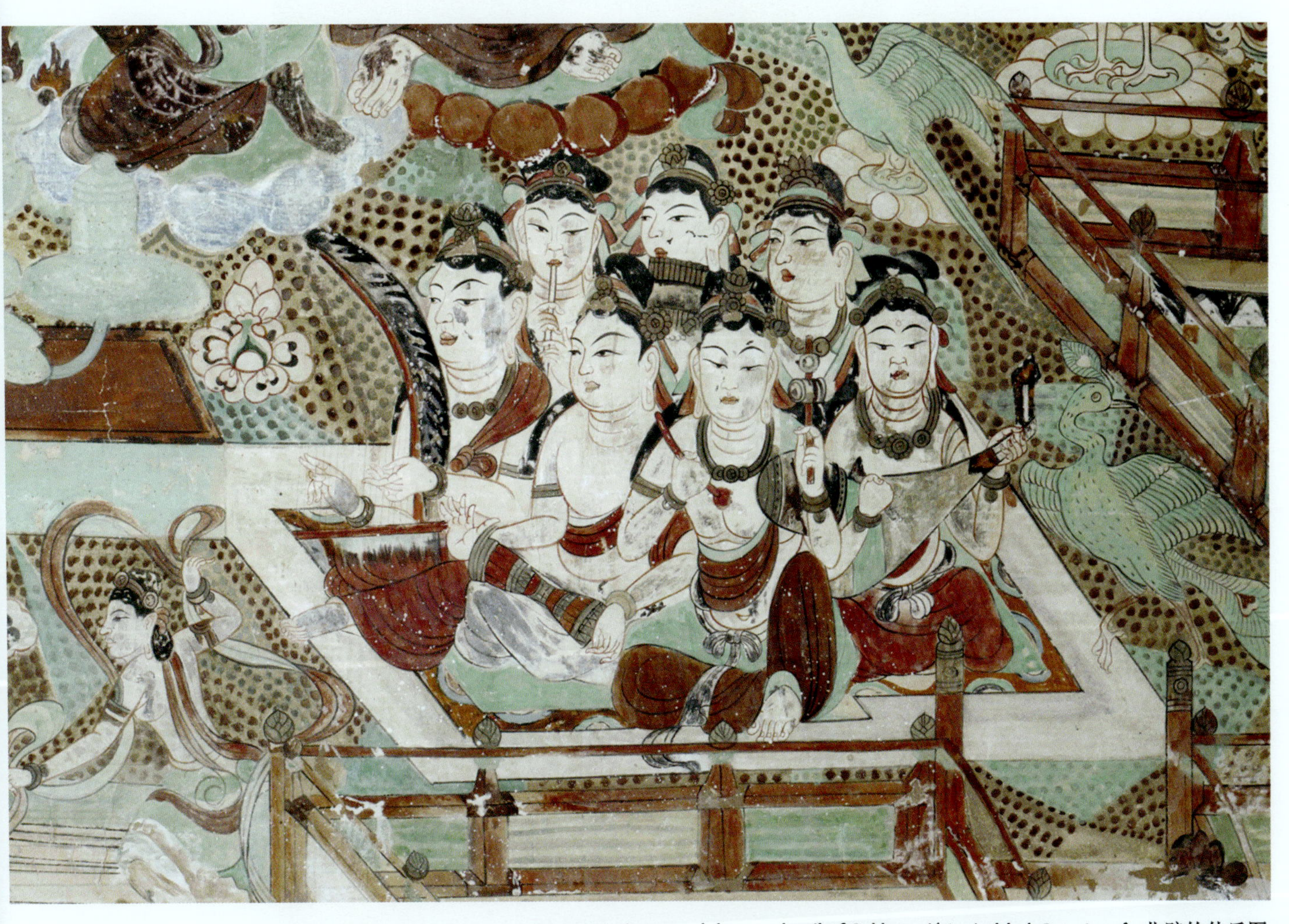

32-14 Musicans and dancer, detail of *Sukhavati* (*Amitabha's Pure Land*). 北壁的伎乐图

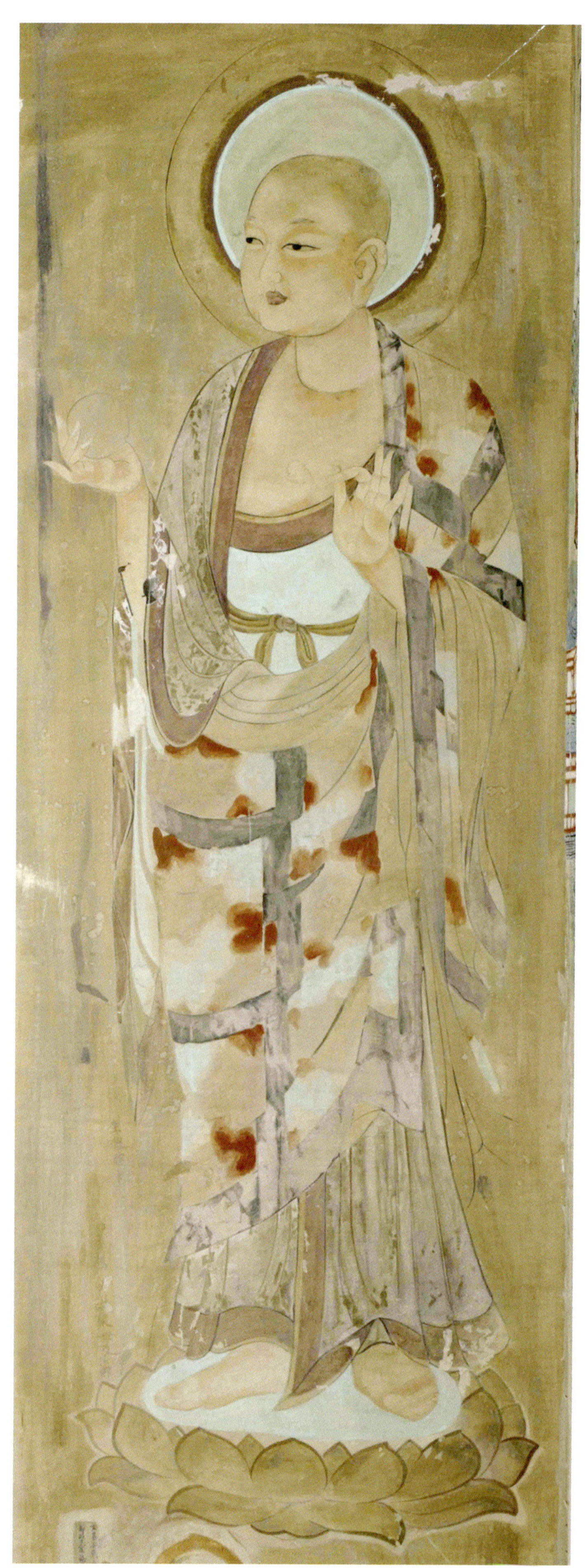

32-15 Life-size image of the bodhisattva Ksitigarbha, a mid-Tang painting on the south side of the west wall, to the right of the niche in Cave 45. Replica in mineral pigments on paper by Hou Liming.
莫高窟第45窟西壁南侧的中唐地藏菩萨像，纸本，侯黎明临摹

Ceiling and *zaojing*

The ceiling together with the *zaojing* in Cave 45 is shaped like a square canopy symbolizing heaven and imparting a splendid and dignified aura. This design imparts a more spacious feel to the cave and disperses the stress that the ceiling places on the walls. It is also characteristic of Chinese cave shrines. The *zaojing* of this cave has a floral medallion in the center enclosed by layers of square and diamond shapes in various designs. A design of valances decorates the outermost border. The four slopes of the ceiling around the *zaojing* are covered with the Thousand Buddha motif.

窟頂與藻井

從覆斗形的窟頂與藻井整體看來，像是佛菩薩頂上的華蓋，象徵至高無上，也營造了宏偉莊嚴的氣氛。在建築上，這種窟顶既可增加洞窟空间感，又能分散窟顶对四壁的压力，這种設計成了中國洞窟寺的特徵。该窟的藻井在中心繪團花，四角畫垂幔，四披是千佛圖案。

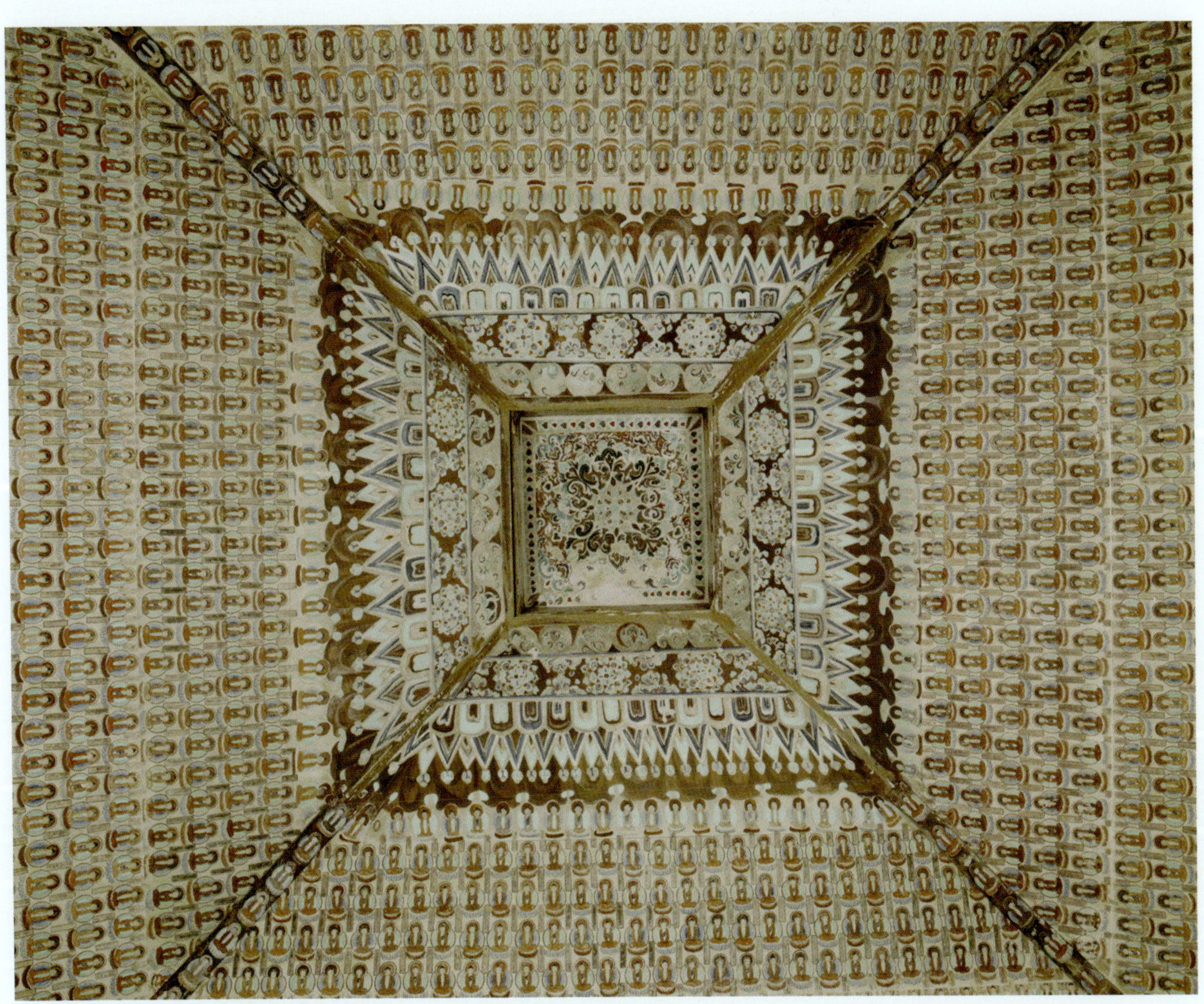

32-16 Painting of the *zaojing* and Thousand Buddha pattern on the ceiling of Cave 45. Replica in mineral pigments on paper by Lou Jie. 莫高窟第45窟窟顶的藻井及千佛，1998年娄婕临摹

APPENDICES
附录

Lou Jie 娄婕
Liang Xushu 梁旭澍
J. May Lee Barrett 鐘美梨
Clarissa von Spee 史明理

Appendix 1

Principal Cave Types at Dunhuang
敦煌佛窟的主要窟形

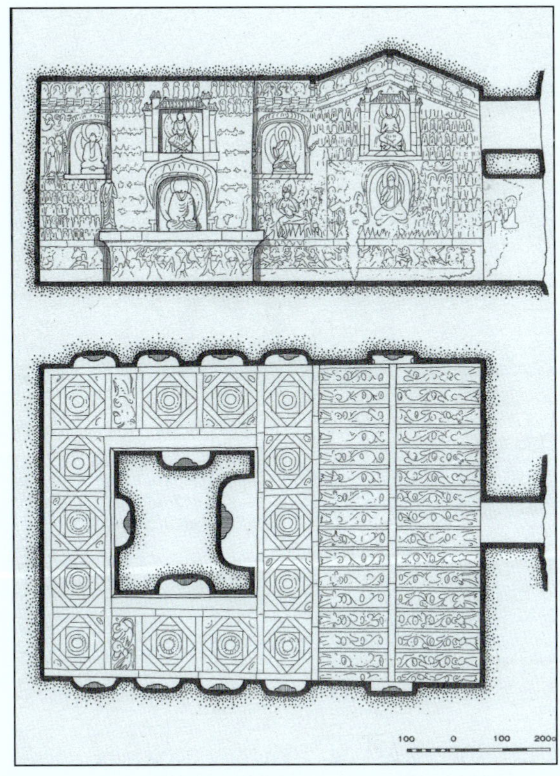

Fig. 1.

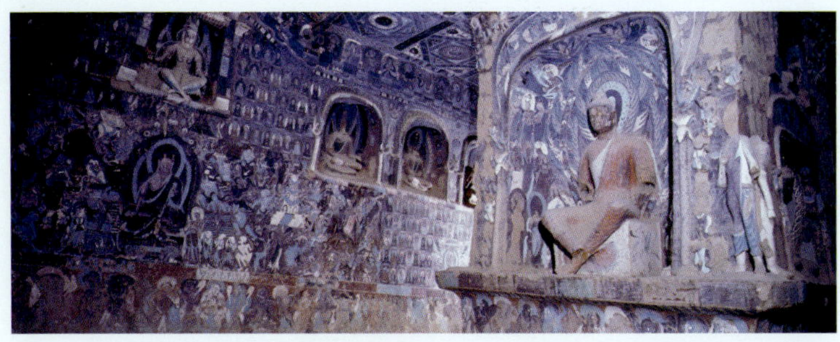

Fig. 2.

1. Central Stupa-Pillar Cave 中心塔柱式

Fig. 1. Plan and elevation of Mogao Cave 254. Northern Wei dynasty (386–534). 莫高窟北魏第254窟实测图

Fig. 2. View of central stupa-pillar in Mogao Cave 254. Northern Wei dynasty (386–534). 莫高窟北魏第254窟中心塔柱

2. Meditation Cave 禅窟

Fig. 3. Plan and elevation of Mogao Cave 285. Western Wei dynasty (535–556). 莫高窟西魏第285窟实测图

Fig. 4. Rear wall of Mogao Cave 285. Western Wei dynasty (535–556). 莫高窟西魏第285窟后壁

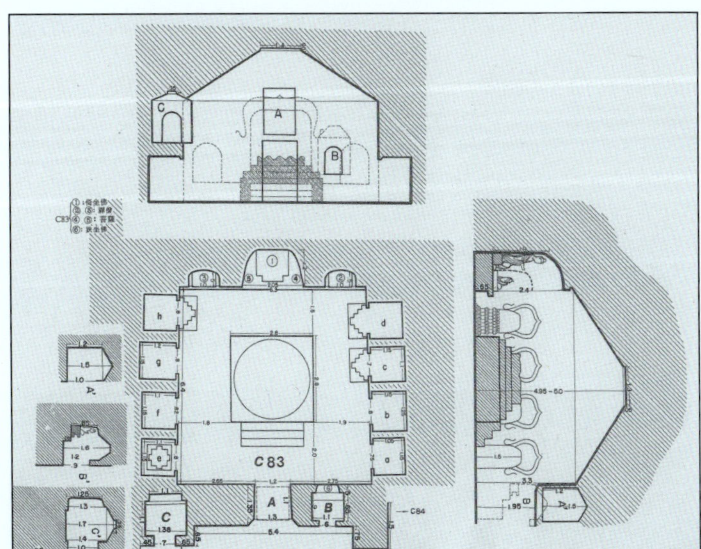

Fig. 3.

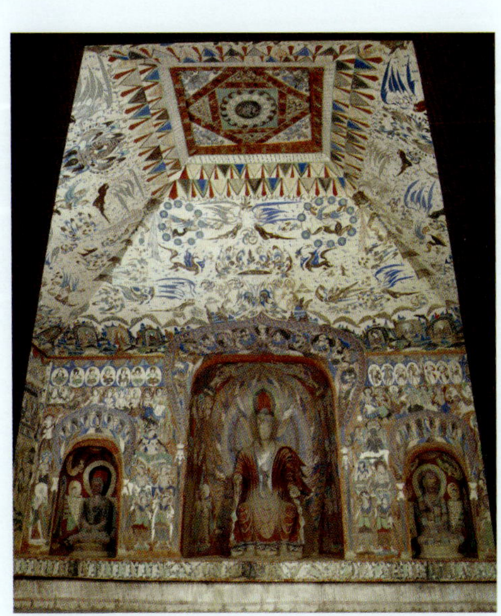

Fig. 4.

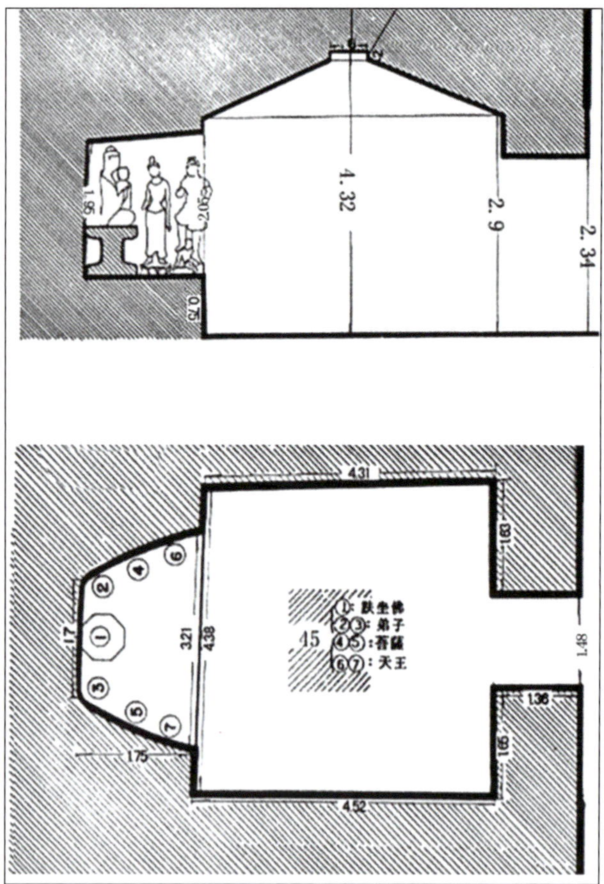
Fig. 5.

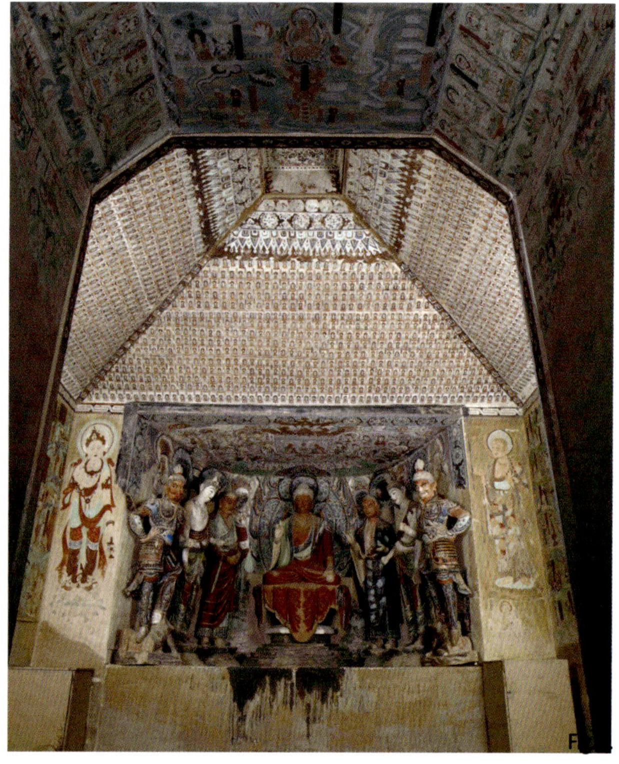

3. **Assembly Hall** 殿堂式

Fig. 5. Plan and elevation of the replica of Mogao Cave 45. High Tang period (705–781). 莫高窟盛唐第45窟复制窟型图

Fig. 6. View of rear wall of Mogao Cave 45. High Tang period (705–781). 莫高窟盛唐第45窟内景

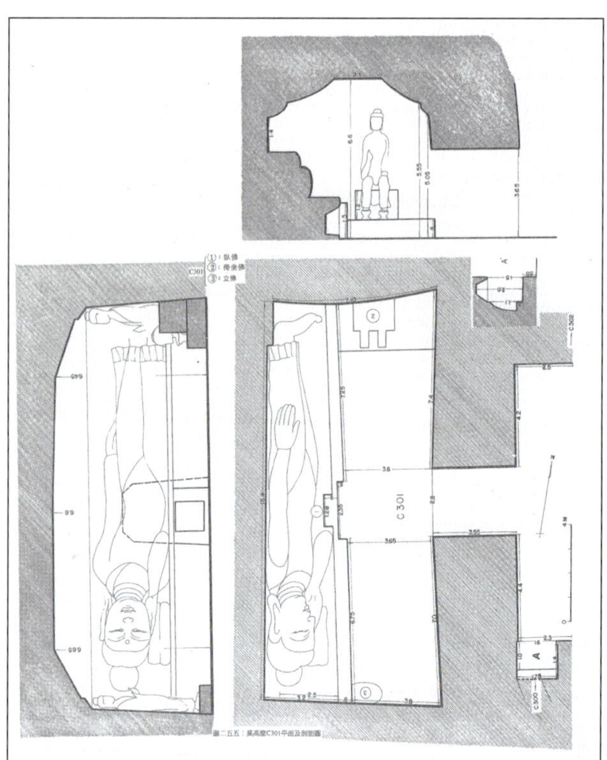

4. **Nirvana Cave** 涅磐窟

Fig. 7. Plan and cross-sections of Mogao Cave 158. Mid-Tang period (781–848). 莫高窟中唐第158窟平面及剖面图

Fig. 8. View of the recumbent Buddha in the *parinirvana* scene along the west wall of Mogao Cave 158. Mid-Tang period (781–848). 莫高窟中唐第158窟西壁佛台的涅般佛像

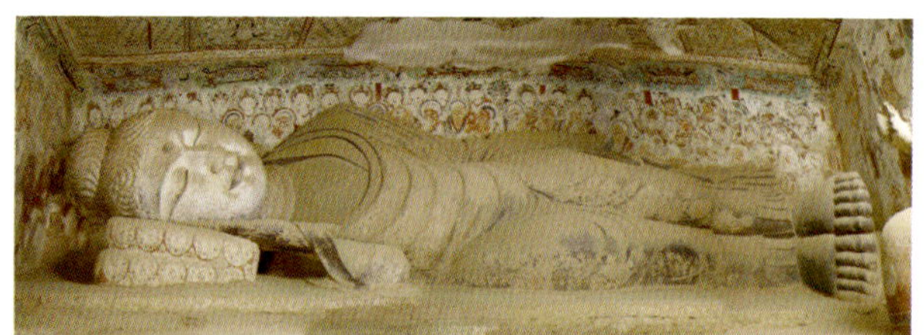

Fig. 7. Fig. 8.

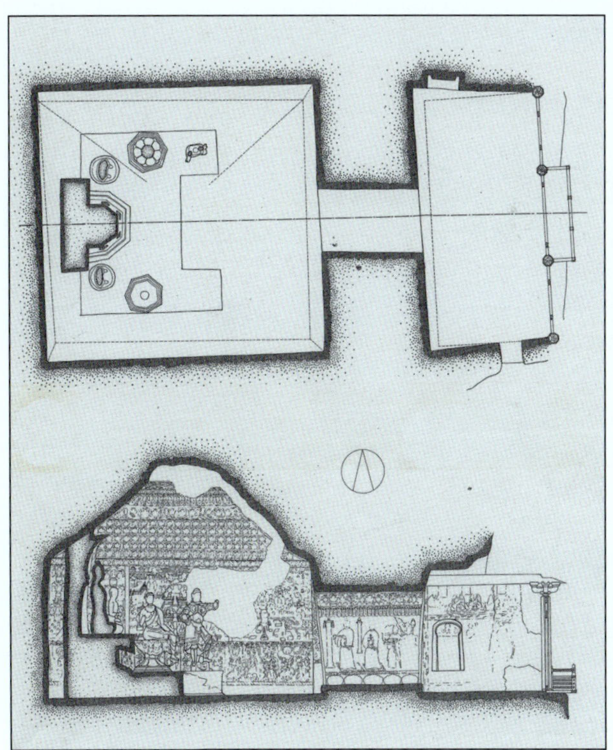

Fig. 9.

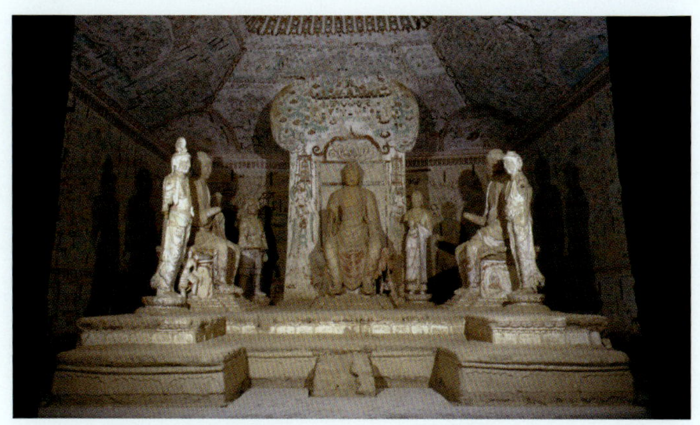

Fig. 10.

5. Screened Altar Cave 背屏窟

Fig. 9. Plan and cross-sections of Mogao Cave 196. Late Tang period (848–907). 莫高窟晚唐第196窟平面及剖面图

Fig. 10. Inside view of Mogao Cave 55. Song dynasty (920–1279); rebuilt in Western Xia dynasty (1038–1227). 莫高窟宋代修建及西夏重修的第55窟背屏式窟内景

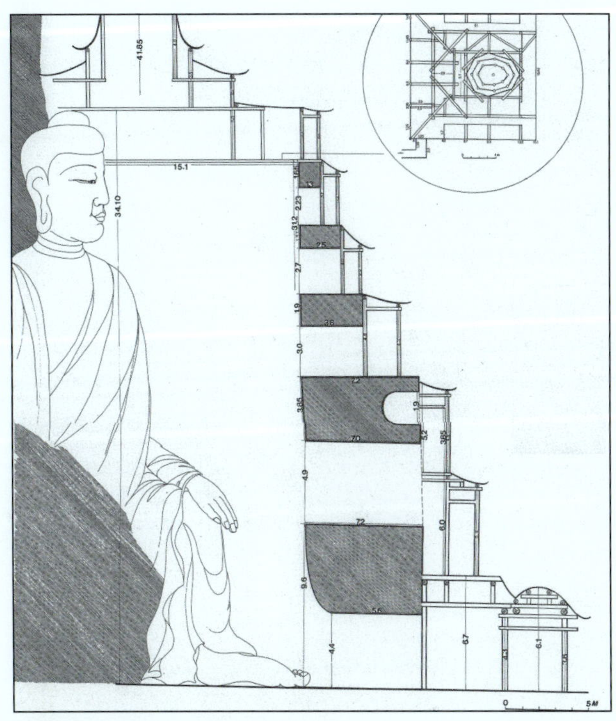

Fig. 11.

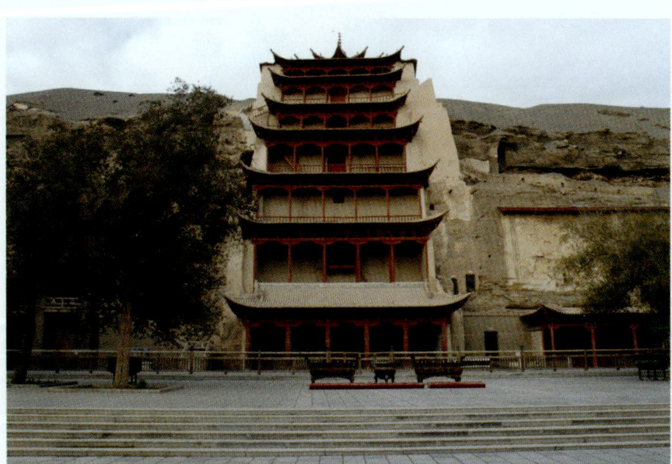

Fig. 12.

6. Cave of Large Images 大像窟

Fig. 11. Elevation of Mogao Cave 96. Early Tang period (618–705). 莫高窟初唐第96窟平面及剖面图

Fig. 12. Exterior view of Mogao Cave 96. Early Tang period (618–705). 莫高窟初唐第96窟外景

Appendix 2

Paintings from the Library Cave
藏经洞佛画举例

1. The Library Cave and the Dispersal of Silk Road Treasures

History of the Cave

Invaluable cultural treasures—manuscripts, printed texts, paintings, textiles, and other artifacts—had been hidden away at the Mogao cave shrine complex until modern times in what is now referred to as the Library Cave (*cangjingdong*), also known as Cave 17. Discovered in 1900 by a Chinese Daoist priest, this cave was a small chamber originally built as a memorial chapel to Hong Bian (d. ca. 862), the chief of monks in Hexi. It had become a storehouse sometime in the tenth century for the Three Realms Monastery, located at the cave site, and was walled up to safeguard its contents in the early eleventh century.[1]

Some items were removed from the cave in the first few years after the discovery, but over the course of a decade beginning in 1907, tens of thousands more—almost eighty percent of its contents—were taken out of the country by the foreign explorers Aurel Stein, Paul Pelliot, Otani Kazui,[2] and Sergei Oldenburg and are now held in such institutions as the British Museum (see below), the National Museum in Delhi, the Bibliothèque nationale de France, the Musée Guimet, the Tokyo National Museum, and the Institute of Oriental Manuscripts in St. Petersburg, Russia, among others.[3]

In the midst of this exodus of cultural treasures, more than 8,000 manuscripts were recovered by order of the Ministry of Education at the urging of the antiquarian Luo Zhenyu (1866–1940) and others. Representing just a small part of the total Library Cave trove, these manuscripts were brought back to Beijing in 1910 and now form the core of the Dunhuang collection at the National Library of China in Beijing. A good portion of Otani's Central Asian collection never left China and is now housed in the Lüshan Museum; more than 600 Dunhuang scrolls were eventually transferred from the Lüshan Museum to the National Library. The large number of Tibetan manuscripts which had been left behind by the foreign explorers is now divided between the Dunhuang Museum, the Dunhuang Academy, and a few provincial museums in Gansu.

Manuscripts and paintings which had trickled out of Dunhuang in the early years after the discovery of the Library Cave ended up in private collections in China and abroad. Although some of these works have over time come to reside in various museums and scholarly institutions, many remain in private hands.

Paintings on Silk and Paper

Hundreds of paintings on silk, hemp, and paper, predominantly of religious subjects, were found in the Library Cave. Most of the best paintings are now in the collections of the British Museum and the Musée Guimet in Paris. Small holdings in other museums, such as the Freer Gallery of Art in Washington, D.C.,[4] and the Zhenjiang Museum in Jiangsu (see below, sec. 3),

---

1. It is argued by Rong Xinjiang that the cave was sealed soon after the latest reliably dated document, that is, not long after 1002. A brief history of the dispersal of the contents of the Library Cave and theories about its closing are given in Rong Xinjiang, "The Nature of the Dunhuang Library Cave and the Reasons for its Sealing," trans. by Valerie Hansen, *Cahiers d'Extrême-Asie* 11 (1999–2000): 247–75, available online at http://www.persee.fr/web/revues/home/prescript/article/asie_0766-1177_1999_num_11_1_1155.

2. Otani organized three exploratory trips to Central Asia, but did not go to Dunhuang himself. His Dunhuang team included Zuicho Tachibana and Koichiro Yoshikawa.

3. The various archaeological expeditions to Dunhuang and the surrounding region are described in the various "Collections" pages of the International Dunhuang Project website, http://idp.bl.uk/. Information is also given about current collections, large and small, of Dunhuang and other Central Asian materials acquired through the expeditions and other sources.

4. The Freer Gallery has one manuscript and two paintings from Dunhuang. See the Freer Gallery website for the Northern Song painting *Guanyin of the Water Moon* (ink and color on silk, 106.8 x 58.9 cm), dated to 968, http://www.asia.si.edu/collections/singleObject.cfm?ObjectNumber=F1930.36.

were made through purchases or donations. Paintings from the Library Cave date no earlier than the seventh century in the Tang dynasty and range into the late tenth century in the Northern Song dynasty.[5] These finds have, in particular, contributed greatly to our knowledge of Tang dynasty painting, a knowledge which before the twentieth century had been mostly based on literary descriptions and surviving copies made by later generations. It was a period celebrated for the accomplishments of named artists working at the Tang capital Chang'an. Something of their painting style can be seen in the works from the Library Cave as well as in the murals at Dunhuang. At the same time, the influence of Indian, Tibetan, and Uighur painting styles carried along the Silk Road is evident.

The Library Cave Today

A lifelike sculptural portrait of Hong Bian has been restored and returned to its original position in this chamber.[6] The figure sits on a meditation platform in front of a mural depicting two attendants and trees from which hang his travel bag and water flask. The story of the Library Cave's discovery from the Chinese perspective is told in a museum located opposite the cave. It is housed in the former residence of Wang Yuanlu, the Daoist priest who had made the discovery and subsequently sold off a large portion of the contents.

International collaboration has made more and more of this dispersed material accessible to students and scholars. The ongoing International Dunhuang Project,[7] in which the Dunhuang Academy participates, has been cataloguing, conserving, and digitizing the fragile and widely dispersed material from the Library Cave, other Dunhuang sources, and other Central Asian sites on the Silk Road. Formed in 1994, the IDP's directorate was established at the British Library and has centers in China, Russia, Japan, Germany, France, and Korea. The digitization of the British Museum's Dunhuang collection is discussed below.

---

5. This range was determined from the material removed by Aurel Stein and Paul Pelliot. See Roderick Whitfield and Anne Farrer, *Caves of the Thousand Buddhas: Chinese Art from the Silk Route* (New York: George Braziller, 1990), p. 20.

6. See the Dunhuang Academy website, "Mogao Cave 17 (late Tang, 848–907)," fig. 1, http://enweb.dha.ac.cn/000C/index.htm (accessed November 16, 2012).

7. The IDP website contains frequent updates on the progress of the project and provides links to the websites of collaborating institutions, http://idp.bl.uk/.

2. A Silk Painting from Cave 17 near Dunhuang and a brief introduction to the Stein collection at the British Museum

Buddha Preaching the Law (*Shuxia shuofa tu*) is among the earliest Buddhist silk paintings in the British Museum (fig. 1). The scroll's blues and greens and warm shades of red have stayed brilliant for over a millennium. Backed by the jeweled trunks and foliage of a bodhi tree, the Buddha is accompanied by four seated bodhisattvas and six monk disciples. The presence of this tree and the six monks suggest that this is Shakyamuni, the historic Buddha, who attained enlightenment beneath the bodhi tree. Vertical cartouches and a monumental stele depicted below the Buddha are left blank for dedicatory inscriptions. A female donor figure is seated on the bottom left, and the headdress of a male donor is still visible on the right. On the basis of the female's high-waisted dress, which is similar to the attire of court ladies in wall paintings of eighth-century imperial tombs, this painting dates to the early Tang dynasty.[8] The painting was found in a secret library (also called Cave 17) hidden among the Caves of the Thousand Buddhas, situated about 25 kilometers southeast of Dunhuang in Gansu province.[9]

This cave was sealed in the eleventh century and remained unnoticed until 1900, when the local caretaker of the complex, the Daoist priest Wang Yuanlu, discovered a crack in the wall of a corridor leading to a larger cave. A dry desert climate served to preserve well over 40,000 manuscript scrolls, artists' sketches, silk paintings, and textiles dating from the fifth to the early eleventh centuries. The cave's manuscripts present a wide range of religious and administrative documents in Chinese, Tibetan, Sanskrit, Tocharian, Uighur, Sogdian, and Khotanese. The latest securely dated document refers to the year 1002, providing a *terminus ante quem* for the dating of the discovered material.[10] The exact circumstances surrounding the sealing of the cell remain unknown, but some event must have prompted this action. In fact, since the early eleventh century, Muslims from Kashgar had been threatening to attack Khotan, an important center for trade situated on the southern Silk Road to the west of Dunhuang. The cell's sealing therefore may have been a measure of protection against advancing Muslims. Belief in *mofa*, or the "Latter Days of the Buddhist Law," as predicted in the sacred texts provides another possible explanation for the cave's closure.

The first Westerners on the scene to view the cave's contents were the Hungarian archaeologist Aurel Stein (1862–1943) and the French explorer Paul Pelliot (1878–1945). Stein had undertaken three expeditions to Central Asia in the years 1900 to 1903, 1906 to 1909, and 1913 to 1916.[11] Having heard rumors about Wang's discovery, Stein passed through Dunhuang on his second southern Silk Road expedition in 1907. He negotiated with Wang Yuanlu and persuaded the monk to allow him to view the cave's manuscripts and paintings. Eventually, Stein removed part of the contents, leaving in return a small compensation to help Wang Yuanlu restore the caves. Stein's acquisitions were shipped to London where the material came to be divided between three institutions. The paintings and textiles were classed as "objects"; one portion was sent to the National Museum in Delhi in 1919, while the other part remained in the British Museum. The written documents, which were classed as "manuscripts," became part of the British Library's collection when the institute moved out of the British Museum into a separate building in 1973. Remaining in the collection of the British Museum are about 320 paintings and banners on silk, over 30 woodblock prints, stencils, and sketches on paper, and about 200 textiles. Today, contents of Cave 17 can be found in various museums, libraries, and holdings around the world: in China, the UK, France, India, Japan, Korea, Russia, and the United States.[12]

---

8. For a discussion of the Buddhist silk paintings in the Stein collection at the British Museum, see Whitfield and Farrer, *Caves of the Thousand Buddhas*, and Roderick Whitfield, *The Art of Central Asia: The Stein Collection in the British Museum* (Tokyo: Kodansha, 1982–85), vols.1–3.

9. On the Caves of Dunhuang, see Fan Jinshi, *The Caves of Dunhuang*, trans. by Susan Whitfield (Hong Kong: The Dunhuang Academy together with London Editions, 2010).

10. See Sarah Fraser, *Performing the Visual: The Practice of Buddhist Wall Painting in China and Central Asia, 618–960* (Stanford, Calif.: Stanford University Press, 2004), p. 5.

11. On Aurel Stein, see Susan Whitfield, *Aurel Stein on the Silk Road* (London: British Museum Press, 2004); on the Stein collections in the UK, see Helen Wang and John Perkins, eds., *Handbook to the Stein Collections in the UK*, British Museum, Occasional Paper, no. 129, rev. ed. (London: The Trustees of the British Museum, 2008), http://www.britishmuseum.org/pdf/Stein%20Handbook%20final%283%29.pdf.

12. See the website of the International Dunhuang Project (IDP) based at the British Library in London, http://idp.bl.uk/, where IDP is described as "an international collaboration to make information and images of all manuscripts, paintings, textiles and artefacts from Dunhuang and archaeological sites of the Eastern Silk Road freely available on the Internet and to encourage their use through educational and research programmes."

Since the beginning of the twentieth century there has been continuous international research on Dunhuang, its paintings, and related material. The British Museum displayed paintings from Dunhuang for the first time in 1910,[13] while publications of the paintings in the British Museum have appeared since the 1920s.[14] Research projects, publications, and exhibitions on the Museum's so-called Stein collection were often undertaken with considerable international collaboration.[15]

Due to the material's fragile and light sensitive nature, the British Museum's Stein collection can only be temporarily displayed. Since 2000, however, the collection has been made more accessible to scholars as well as to the general public through ongoing digitization in close cooperation with the International Dunhuang Project based at the British Library.[16] First, the 323 silk paintings, prints, drawings, sketches, and textiles were digitized. Then a large group of archaeological material from the Silk Road which Stein brought back from his three expeditions to Central Asia—three-dimensional objects made of wood, ceramic, stucco, glass, metal, and textile fibers—was added to the museum's online database. Finally, other archaeological material in the British Museum collected from the Silk Road by Rudolph Hoernle (1841–1918), Clarmont Percival Skrine (1888–1974), and Joseph Needham (1900–1995) was digitized. As a result, about 1,600 three-dimensional objects have been digitized in addition to the first group of paintings and textiles. Professionally photographed images, well-researched and mostly bilingual entries in English and Chinese, and references to further studies all reflect the high standards of the British Museum's online database and make its Stein collection accessible for study worldwide.[17]

—*Clarissa von Spee*

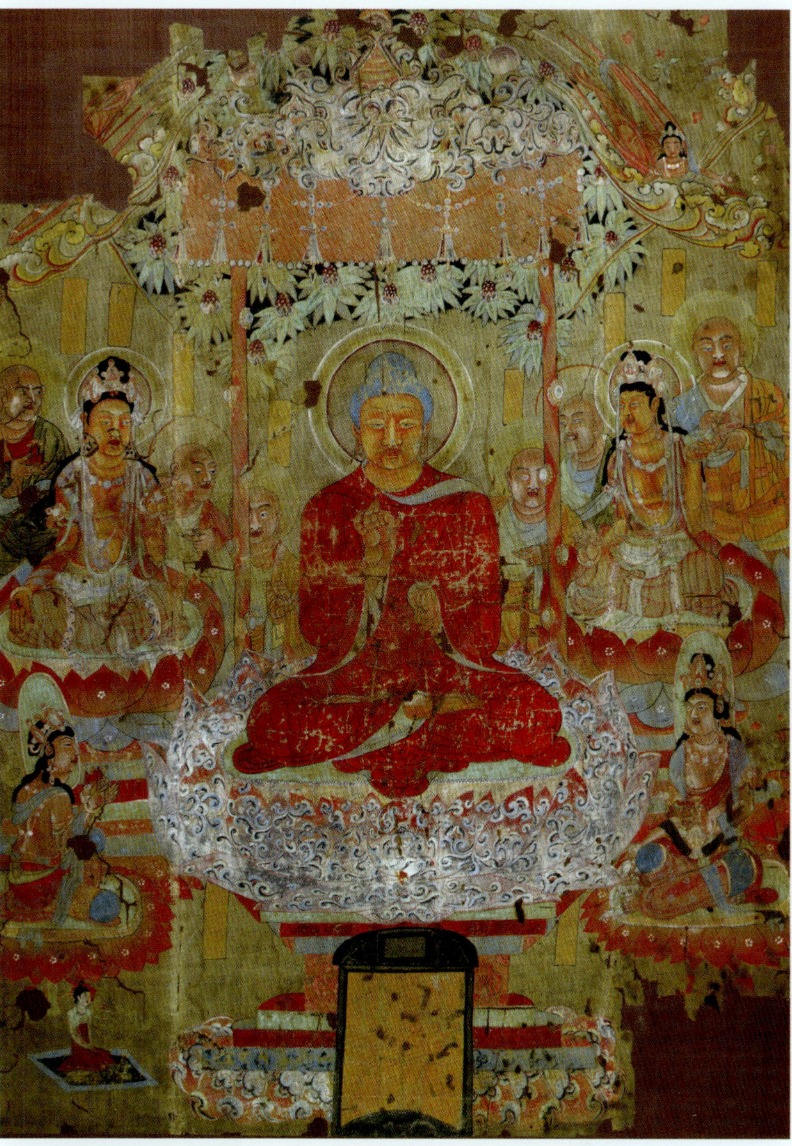

Fig. 1. *Buddha Preaching the Law.* Tang dynasty, ca. 701–750. Ink and color on silk; 139 X 102 cm. The British Museum, 1919,0101,0.6. Photo © The Trustees of the British Museum

13. See British Museum, *Guide to an Exhibition of Chinese and Japanese Paintings (fourth to nineteenth century, A.D.)* (London, 1910). Another exhibition of Dunhuang material was held in 1914 in the newly opened King Edward VII Gallery (today, The Joseph E. Hotung Gallery); see British Museum, *Guide to an exhibition of paintings, manuscripts and other archaeological objects collected by Sir Aurel Stein, KCIE, in Chinese Turkestan* (London, 1914).

14. See Arthur Waley, *An Introduction to the Study of Chinese Painting* (London: Ernest Benn Ltd., 1923), and Arthur Waley, *A Catalogue of Paintings recovered from Tun-Huang by Sir Aurel Stein* (London: British Museum, 1931).

15. See, for example, Zhao Feng et al., *Textiles from Dunhuang in UK Collections* (Shanghai: Donghua University Press, 2007).

16. See Carol Michaelson, "A History of the Stein and Central Asian Digitisation Project at the British Museum," http://www.britishmuseum.org/pdf/18_Michaelson.pdf. The digitization was made possible with major support from the Mellon Foundation.

17. See the British Museum online database collection http://www.britishmuseum.org/research/search_the_collection_database.aspx. Coins and potsherds found by Stein still await digitization.

3. Portrait of a Monk from the Zhenjiang Museum

Portraiture is one of the achievements of Tang art, both in painting and in sculpture. The stucco figure of Hong Bian, originally in the Library Cave, and a painting in the British Museum's Dunhuang collection are rare examples of monk portraits.[18]

A ninth-century painting of a monk in the Zhenjiang Museum in Jiangsu likely also came out of the Library Cave (fig. 2). The monk is seated under a jeweled canopy in a dignified and unaffected manner; the brushstrokes are simple and heavy, and the colors—red and yellow in combination with white pigment and ink—are still bright. A pouch hangs from a staff, which stands by his side. There are two lines of script at the bottom right of the painting and faint traces of writing in the damaged section at the bottom left, roughly a quarter of the painting. The flaming halo around his head indicates that he is probably a holy personage. A very similar painting in the collection of the British Museum carries a Tibetan inscription identifying it as a portrait of the Arhat Kalika, one of the Buddha's early disciples, and naming the artist as Do-khon-legs.[19] The Zhenjiang painting could well have been part of a set of Arhat portraits by the same artist.

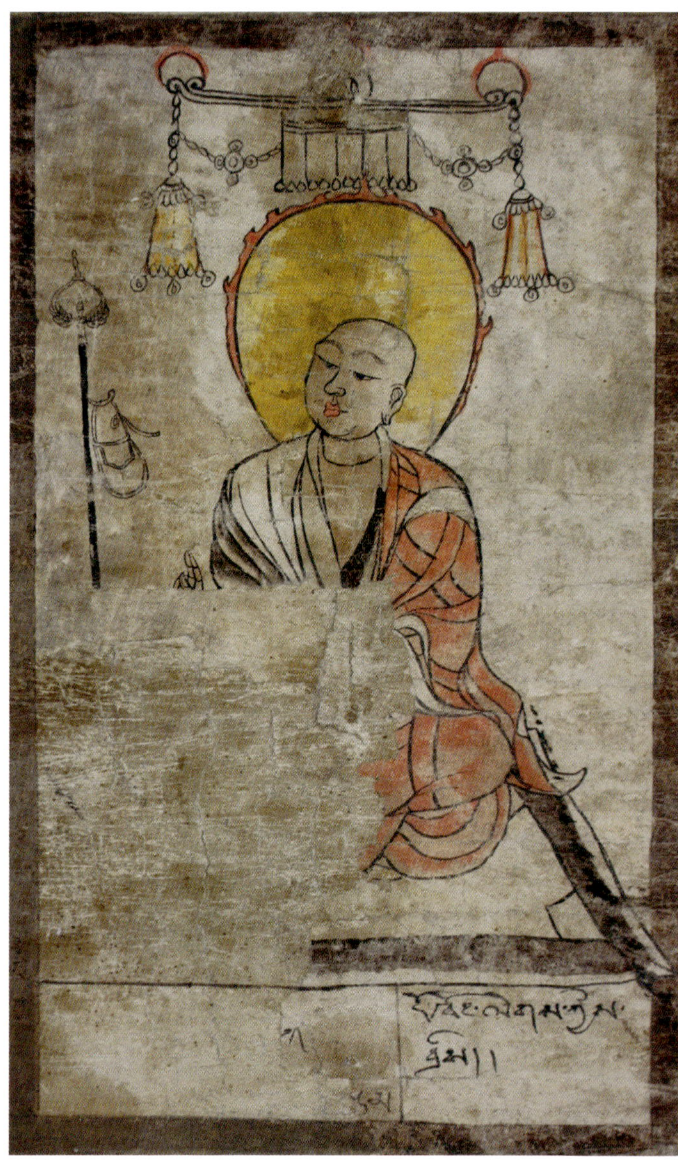

Fig. 2. Anon., Portrait of a Monk. Late Tang dynasty (9th–10th century). Vertical scroll painting; ink and color on paper; 43.5 x 26 cm. Zhenjiang Museum, Jiangsu. Donated by Ms Chen Yinmei, from Liyang, Jiangsu. Photo courtesy of Zhenjiang Museum

18. Whitfield and Farrer, *Caves of the Thousand Buddhas*, p. 76, no. 56.

19. Ibid., p. 76, no. 54.

Appendix 3

Dunhuang Artisans and Patrons
敦煌的画师工匠和供养人

Construction of a Buddhist cave shrine at Dunhuang involved a series of steps: preparing the cliff face, excavating the cave, making paintings and sculpture, and building the decorative eaves and temple halls. Specialized artisans were needed for each step in the building of such caves.

一个洞窟从始建到完成，大体经过整修崖面、凿窟、绘制壁画塑像、修造并装饰窟檐或殿堂等一系列的营造程序。这些都需要有特殊的画师和工匠来完成。

Sources of Dunhuang's painters and artisans
敦煌石窟的画师与工匠的来源

Textual research and analysis of art styles of different periods show that the painters and artisans at the Dunhuang caves came from many different places. They were mainly composed of the following types:

1. Painters coming from the Western Regions (Central Asia west of Yumen) along with the transmission of Buddhism.
2. Artisans coming with ousted officials or powerful families, part of the migration from the China's Central Plains to the frontiers.
3. Artisans coming with officials appointed by Chinese emperors.
4. Painters coming from the Central Plains.
5. Ethnic minority painters from bordering areas like Tibet or Mongolia, bringing with them new art styles and techniques during the Tibetan Occupation, the Western Xia dynasty, and the Yuan dynasty.

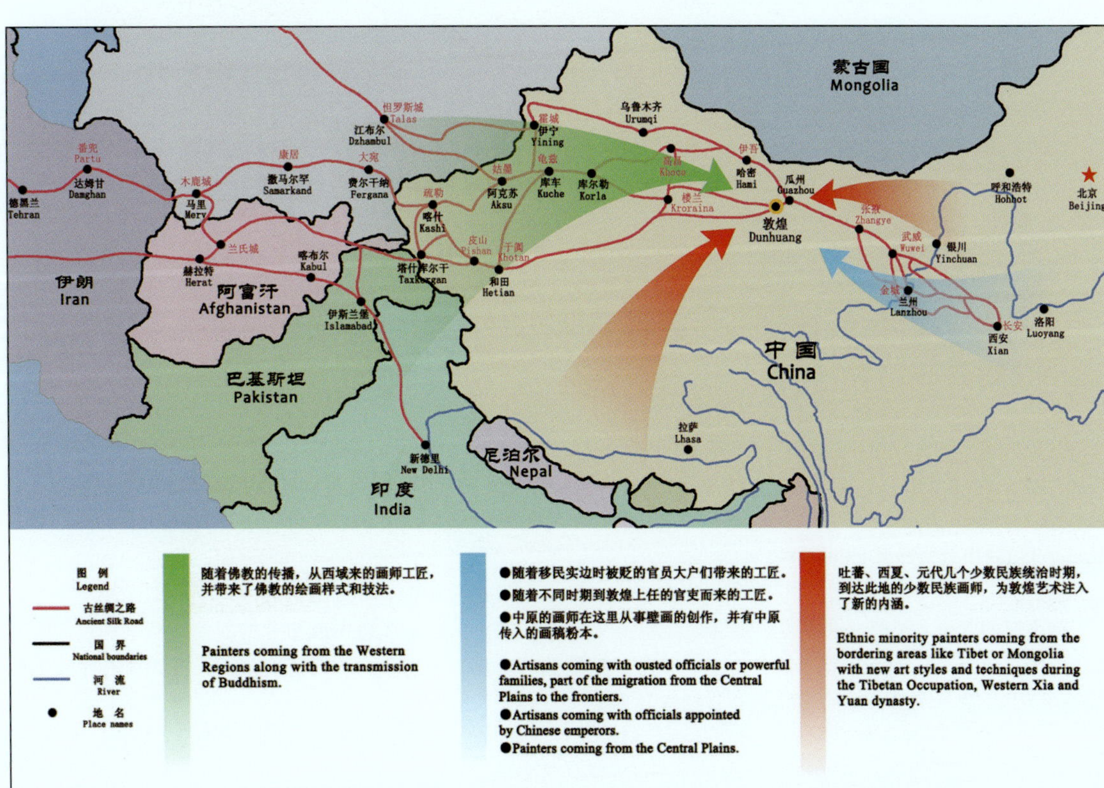

Fig. 1. Origins of the Dunhuang Artisans.
敦煌画师与工匠的来源

从文献和各时代的艺术风格上分析，敦煌石窟的画师和工匠组成，主要有以下几个方面：

1、 随着佛教的传播，从西域来的画师工匠，并带来了佛教的绘画样式和技法。

2、 随着移民实边时被贬的官员大户们带来的工匠。

3、 随着不同时期到敦煌上任的官吏而来的工匠。

4、 中原的画师在这里从事壁画的创作，并有中原传入的画稿粉本。

5、 吐蕃、西夏、元代几个少数民族统治时期，到达此地的少数民族画师，为敦煌艺术注入了新的内涵。

Division of labor among the artisans at Mogao
莫高窟工匠的分工

Patrons and donors hired specialized, highly accomplished artisans to construct the Mogao Grottoes. The artisans were divided into *lianggong* (excellent workmen), who hollowed out the caves from the cliff face, and *qiaojiang* (skilled artisans), who created the paintings and sculptures.

Therefore, construction of caves involved detailed division of labor from the very beginning. They include the following:

1. Chiselers who carved the cave into the cliff.
2. Stonecutters who handled stone materials and stone tools and also excavated caves.
3. Bricklayers who built wooden or earthen structures.
4. Carpenters who built structures and also made and repaired wooden tools.
5. Sculptors who modeled and colored the clay figures.
6. Painters who made the paintings.

Within these groups, artisans were ranked according to their technical ability as follows:

1. The ***duliao*** (*dushi*, *dujiang*), which refers to the highly skilled artisans who could develop and oversee the plan for a project as well as execute the technical work.
2. The ***boshi***, which refers to senior artisans who had mastered technologies and could undertake difficult technical work; they could also independently implement a technical undertaking in the field. There were *boshi* in all kinds of trades.
3. The ***shi*** (master), who were mainly highly-ranked painters and sculptors. Technically, they should at least be *boshi*. Any *boshi* among the painters and sculptors who could teach disciples could be addressed as *shi* or master.
4. The ***jiang***, which refers to those able to undertake general technical work. They accounted for the majority of the artisans.
5. The ***sheng***, which refers to the level at which painters could paint under the guidance of masters or independently.

In the late Tang, Five Dynasties, Song, and perhaps some earlier periods, imperial and local "Painting Studios" and similar civil guilds were founded in which a group of highly skilled Buddhist art experts made a living by creating Buddhist paintings on silk or paper and in caves. Most painters from local painting studios or guilds were hired to paint the caves at Dunhuang.

莫高窟的营造者主要是由窟主、施主、工匠三方面组成的。工匠是在窟主或施主的雇佣下从事洞窟的营造活动，依其分工，分为劈岩凿窟的“良工”和绘制塑画的“巧匠”两部分。洞窟营造工程一开始就有比较细致的职业分工。参与洞窟营造的工匠主要有如下几类：

1、打窟人：即在莫高窟崖壁上凿岩镌窟之工匠；
2、石匠：从事石窟开凿、建筑石料加工、石质工具的制造和修理等之工匠；
3、泥匠：从事土木建筑之工匠；
4、木匠：从事土木建筑及木质器具制造、加工、修理之工匠；
5、塑匠：从事泥塑赋彩之工匠；
6、画匠：从事绘画之工匠。

古代各个行业的工匠们，按其技术可分为都料、博士、师、匠、工等级别。

1、都料（都师、都匠）：都料是具备高级技艺的师傅，作为都料，要能够从事本行业工程规划和组织实施， 并负责行内事务。
2、博士：博士这一级别的工匠在各行各业都有，他们应是具备过硬的专业本领、可以从事高难度技术劳动、 能独立承担本行业所有技术施工任务的高级工匠。
3、师（先生）：敦煌工匠中的"师"或"先生"，主要是从事画、塑行业的。从技术上讲，称师与先生者最少应是 博士级、或者说，博士级画、塑工匠能教带徒工者，即可称师或先生。
4、匠：在工匠阶层中能被称作匠者，当为独立从事本行业一般技术性劳动者。这是工匠队伍中的多数，是主体力量。
5、生：生级别的画工既能在匠师们的带领下从事绘画劳动，亦能独立从事绘画劳动。

在敦煌晚唐五代宋或者说更早一些时期就有"画院"、"画行"或其他的民间组织，有相当一批佛画专家和高手，以为人们画供养画如绢画、纸本画、麻布画和洞窟壁画而得以糊口生计。

Patrons of the Dunhuang caves
敦煌石窟的供养人

Construction of caves required a lot of manpower and financial resources. The people usually associated with commissioning cave construction at Dunhuang are as follows:

1. Powerful or noble families—they were the only group who could sponsor an entire cave or build a large cave.
2. Frontier generals and soldiers.
3. Temple monks and nuns as well as lay persons.
4. Commoners—devout believers, community members, merchants, artisans, and the like—who due to their lower social position and financial limitations would usually come together to build a cave.
5. Elite members of ethnic minorities, such as the king of Khotan and Uighur princesses.

石窟的营建要耗费大量的人力与财力。敦煌石窟的开凿大致有以下几方面的人士：

1、豪门贵族：凡是独资造窟并造大窟者，非他们莫属。
2、戍边将士：节度使、军将、校尉、押衙等。
3、寺院僧侣：僧统、寺主、法师、比丘、比丘尼等宗教职业者，以及信教的居士。
4、庶民百姓：信徒、社人、奴婢、工匠等。庶民百姓力单势薄，采取共同兴建石窟的办法。
5、少数民族：如于阗国王、回鹘公主等。

APPENDIX 4

Creating the Buddhist Caves at Dunhuang
敦煌佛窟的制作

Steps in creating the paintings at the Mogao Grottoes
莫高窟壁画的绘制步骤

The wall paintings at the Mogao Grottoes were made in the following steps:
莫高窟各时期的壁画壁面制作方法基本一致。

1. Making the plaster ground 地仗制作

The Mogao Grottoes were carved into loosely-structured sandstone aggregate that is vulnerable to collapse. Extremely rough, the surface of the exposed cliff wall was not suitable for painting on directly and had to be thickly covered with a plaster ground before painting. The surface was prepared with the following:

a. Coarse mud layer: made from local sandy earth mixed with straw and water. This layer was often several inches thick.
b. Fine mud layer: made from local washed clay mixed with fibers and water.
c. Powder layer: The fine mud layer was covered with a thin, smooth layer of powdered kaolin (a fine white clay used in manufacture of porcelain), lime, or gypsum mixed with water.

莫高窟等敦煌石窟开凿在酒泉系砾岩上，此种地层结构粗糙又易风化疏松，岩壁极不平整，无法直接绘制壁画，要在将要绘画的砂砾岩壁面上制作“壁画地仗”。然后按照以下的步骤来完成。

一、粗草泥层：用取自洞窟附近的粉质沙土，掺加麦秸草调和制成泥，压抹在洞窟的砾石岩面上。
二、细泥层：用莫高窟窟前宕泉河河床的澄板土，在其中掺加麻筋，调制成泥，涂抹在粗草泥层之上。
三、白粉层：最后在细泥层上涂刷一层非常薄的高岭土、石灰或石膏之类的粉层即可绘制壁画。

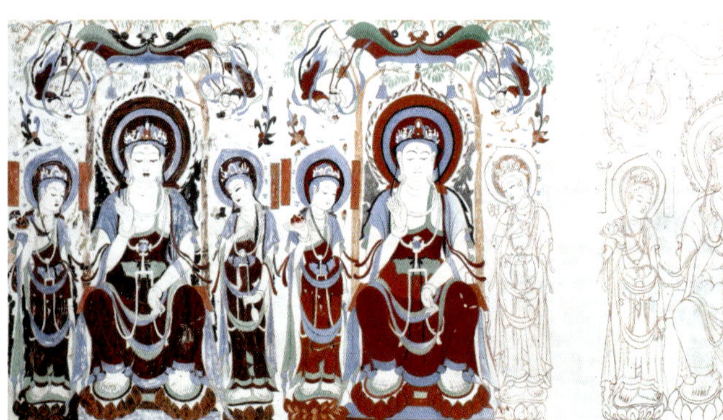
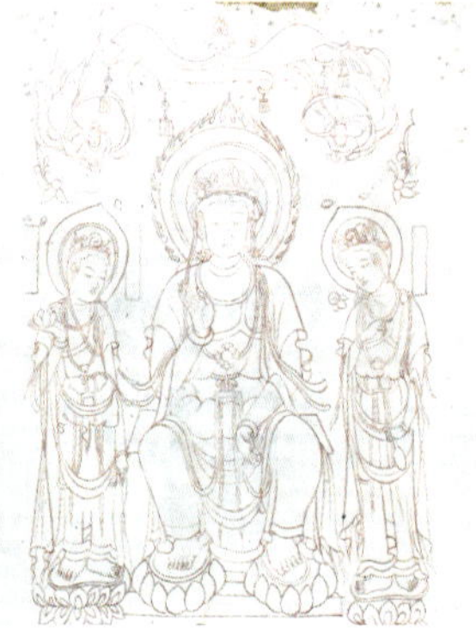
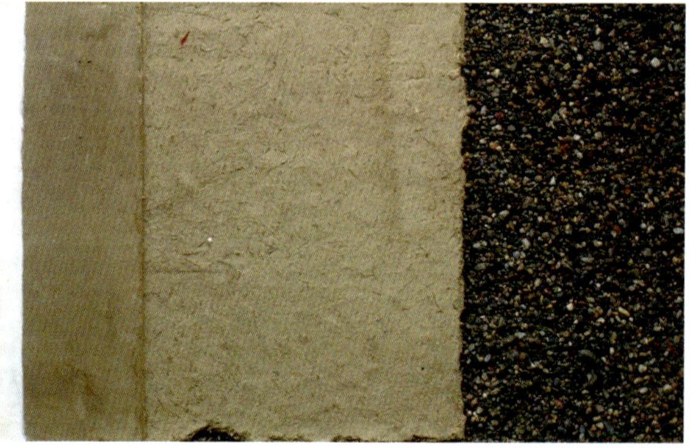

Fig. 1. Steps in the creation of a mural at Dunhuang. 敦煌壁画的制作步骤

2. Making an overall design of the cave murals

The first step was to make a general plan and draft of the contents and themes to be painted on the different walls and of the special religious wishes of the donors and patrons. This is seen, for example, in the original planning drawings discovered for the paintings in Mogao Cave 148.

绘制洞窟壁画的第一道工序是根据窟主和施主们特定的宗教意愿，依据佛经，对整个窟内各壁所要绘画内容和题材进行总体规划，设计画稿。

3. Making the paintings 绘画

a. Preparatory Drawings 起稿

1) Freehand sketch. The artisans divided the walls into large areas and then drew the line skillfully on the wall without a preliminary sketch. It was usually drawn with a brush using earthen red pigment.

直接起稿一按内容对整窟墙体进行大块面的整体划分之后，用娴熟的绘画技巧，徒手直接在墙面上绘制。一般是用毛笔蘸淡土红颜色直接在墙壁上勾画的。

2) Drawing from a draft. The artisans created a grid on the wall surfaces and then redrew the draft picture onto the wall to scale.

按比例划分墙面起稿一根据事先画好的构图小稿，按比例放大。

b. Pounces 粉本刺孔

In ancient Dunhuang, besides preparatory and planning drawings, pounces (special stencils with perforations along the inked lines) were used to transfer the drawing in chalk to the cave walls. The technique was useful for repeating identical figures such as in the Thousand Buddha design. While preparatory and planning drawings had to be made before painting any cave, pounces were used much less frequently because the painters were so good at freehand sketching. This explains why only a few pounces were discovered among the Dunhuang manuscripts and historical artifacts.

粉本刺孔：古人於墨稿上加描粉笔，用时扑入缣素，依粉痕落墨故名之也。但敦煌的画师显然技艺娴熟，可以自由信手勾绘起草，所以在敦煌文献中很少见到刺孔粉本。

c. Color application 着色

The finished draft was marked with color labels by masters and then filled in with color by students. Generally the master indicated the color choice by writing a color label directly on the cave wall in running or cursive hand, sometimes using part of the character and sometimes the whole word. These labels are now visible in some cave murals where the original colors have degraded. However, there were also many wall paintings that were painted without color labels because the painters had perfect mastery of the required skills.

画稿完成之后，师傅写上色标，由弟子工匠涂色完成。“色标”就是色彩分布的代号。敦煌壁画中已发现用行草书法写上的布色符号有“夕”（绿）、“工”（红）、“”青、“廿”黄等，各取字形中的局部为代号；或者有“紫”、“青”、“朱”、“禄”（绿）等，各用全字。当然在敦煌壁画中大量的壁画并不标示色标，而是直接上色。这是由于画工画匠们具有娴熟的绘画技法，驾轻就熟。

d. Line drawing 勾线

The final step was to touch up the lines that formed the shapes.
壁画绘制最后一道工序是描线成形，也称之为“定形线”。

Pigments most used in the murals of the Mogao Grottoes in different times
莫高窟壁画中历代主要使用的颜料

Mineral pigments were made from naturally-occurring minerals. A series of steps such as selecting of materials, filtering, smashing, removing the iron, grinding, and classifying are involved to produce different colors of different grades. These colors are pure, deep, bright, and elegant, possessing excellent qualities such as weather resistance, acid and alkali corrosion resistance, and lightfastness. The brightness remains unchanged even after being buried underground for years, presenting a better effect than artificially synthesized pigments.

Animal glues are the binding medium of mineral pigments. They cause the particles of mineral pigments to adhere and allow the overlapping of different colored pigments, producing a color effect unique to mineral pigments and adding a gorgeous multicolored allure to the pictures.

天然矿物色以天然矿石为原料，它经过选料、粉碎，除铁，研漂分级等程序，制造出适用于绘画所需深浅不同的各种颜色。其色彩纯正浑厚、艳而不俗，具有耐候性、耐光性、不怕酸碱腐蚀等特性，即使没于土内多年也不会影响其色泽的艳丽, 具有化工合成颜料难以达到的表现效果。

动物胶是矿物色的黏结剂，巧妙地将矿物色的各颗粒粘接，不同颜色的颜料叠加，产生了矿物色特有的发色效果，使画面呈现了斑斓多变的色彩魅力。

Steps in sculpture-making at the Mogao Grottoes
莫高窟塑像的步骤

The brittle stone of the local region was unsuitable for carving figures. Sculpture could not be carved into the living rock, nor could more suitable rock be transported to Dunhuang. Therefore, the sculpture had to be fashioned from clay and its surface prepared for painting. Most of the clay figures were made by the following process:

1. The armature is built with round logs and poles.
2. The figure’s shape is developed using bundles of reeds. This helps to decrease the amount of mud required and reduces the weight put on the armature. A wooden wedge attached to the armature through a hole in the wall behind the sculpture fixes it in place.
3. The padded figure is covered with plaster mud. A mixture of local washed clay with fine sand and added fiber was suited to the shaping of the sculpture. The mud can be fine or coarse depending on the percentage and kind of fiber used. A coarse mud made by mixing the clay with straw is used for the general shape of the statue. A fine mud is made with thirty-percent fine sand and seventy-percent clay mixed with cotton or the like. It is used to shape the face, clothing folds, and accessories.
4. Tools are used to model and refine the surface.
5. Clay molds were extensively used in ancient times to make reliefs on the central pillars or side walls and for the accessories of free-standing sculpture. In addition, prefabrication of parts of the statues (e.g. the heads of small statues, the fingers and toes of large statues) was also used, which not only saved time and labor, but also took into account the vulnerability of the accessories, fingers and toes, so that they could be replaced if damaged.

敦煌的砂砾岩不便雕塑，也没有合适的岩石能够运到敦煌。因此敦煌的塑像是用草木为构架，敷以当地河床的澄板土塑造后敷以彩绘而成。

1. 用圆木搭制的骨架。
2. 用芨芨草或芦苇捆扎出人物的大体结构，既省泥，又可减轻圆木立柱的负重。骨架上还有横向的木桩楔入背后壁上凿出的孔里，把塑像固定起来。
3. 制泥：当地河床沉淀在表层的泥土，叫澄板土，质细而无胶性，用其塑制塑像。制泥时需要加入适量的细砂和纤维。加细砂的比例不等。根据加入纤维的不同，大体分为粗泥和细泥。粗泥用澄板土加麦秸，塑作人物大样。细泥用澄板土七成、细砂三成，加水合成稠泥后，再加麻筋或棉花，以塑造人物表层及五官、衣褶、佩饰等细部。
4. 塑造。
5. 古代匠师们还广泛使用了泥范（即泥制的模具）来制作中心柱或窟壁上的浮雕和圆雕人物身上的瓔珞、串珠、花冠等装饰。此外，还采用预制局部（如小型塑像的头部及大型塑像的手指、脚趾等）的方法，即节省工时，又考虑到了细部装饰及指、趾容易损坏的情况。

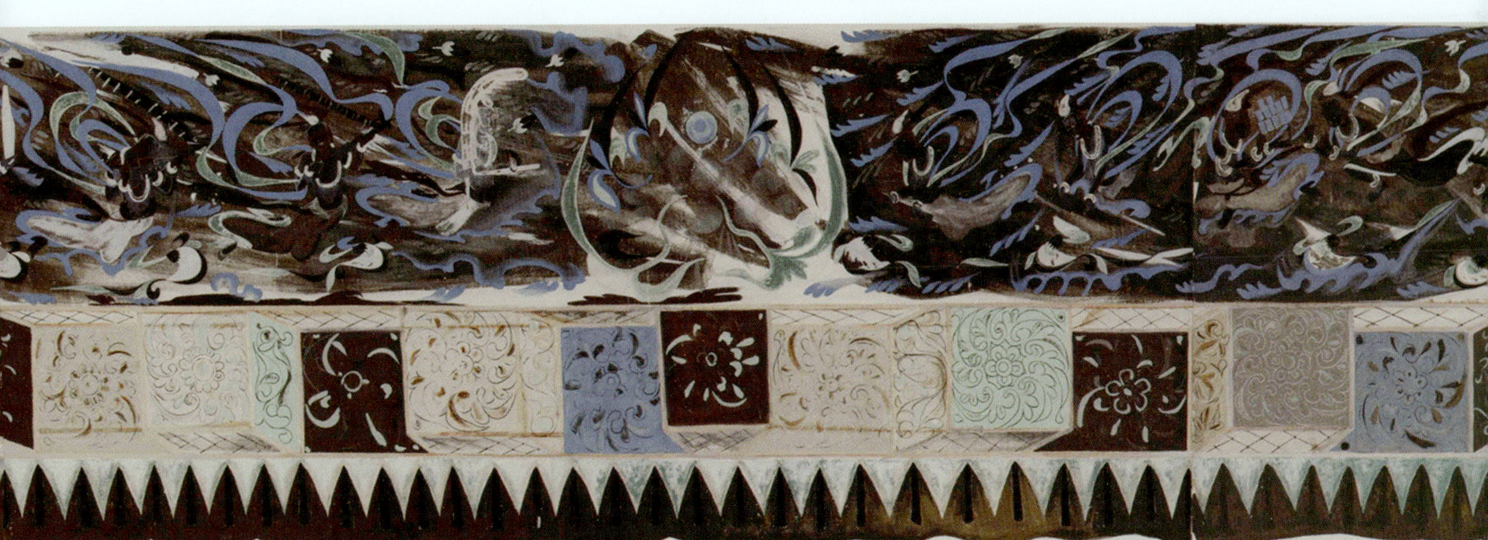

Depiction of flying *apsaras* from Cave 420, Mogao Grottoes. Sui dynasty (581–618). Replica by Li Qiqiong and Huo Xiliang.
莫高窟隋第420窟伎乐飞天，李其琼 、霍熙亮临摹

APPENDIX 5

Table of Sanskrit and Chinese Terms

梵汉文对照词汇选

Buddhist names and terms in this publication	Sanskrit with diacritical marks	Chinese terms
Abhidharmapitaka	*Abhidharma Piṭaka*	*lunzang* 论藏
abhaya mudra	*abhaya mudrā*	*shiwuweiyin* 施无畏印
Ajatashatru	Ajātaśatru	*Asheshi* 阿阇世
Amitabha	Amitābha	Amituo fo 阿弥陀佛
Amitabha Sutra	*Amitābha Sūtra*	*Amituo jing* 阿弥陀经
Amitayuh Sutra	*Amitāyuḥ Sūtra*	*Wuliangshou jing* 无量寿经
Amitayurdhyana Sutra	*Amitāyurdhyāna Sūtra*	*Guan wuliangshou jing* 观无量寿经
Amitayus	Amitāyus	Wuliangshou 无量寿
amrita	*amṛta*	*amiliduo / ganlu* 阿密哩多 / 甘露
Ananda	Ānanda	Anan 阿难
apsara	*apsarāḥ*	*feitian, feixian, tianren* 飞天、飞仙、天人
arhat	*arhat*	*luohan* 罗汉
avadana	*avadāna*	*yinyuan* 因缘
Avalokiteshvara	Avalokiteśvara	Guanyin pusa 观音菩萨
Bhaisajyaguru	Bhaiṣajyaguru	Yaoshi fo 药师佛
bhumisparsha	*bhūmisparśa mudrā*	*chudiyin* 触地印
bhutata-thata	*bhūtata-thatā*	*yiru* 一如
Bimbisara	Bimbisāra	Pinposuoluo 频婆娑罗
bodhi	*bodhi*	*puti* 菩提
chaitya	*caitya*	*zhiti* 支提
chintamani	*cintāmaṇi*	*ruyizhu* 如意珠
devaraja	*devarāja*	*tianwang* 天王
dharani	*dhāraṇī*	*tuoluoni / zhouwen* 陀罗尼 / 咒文
Dharma	*dharma*	*fa* 法
Dharmakaya	*dharmakāya*	*fashen* 法身
Dharmaksema	Dharmakṣema	Tanwuchen 昙无谶
Dharmaraksa	Dharmarakṣa	Zhu fahu 竺法护
dhoti	*dhotī*	*qun* 裙
Diamond Sutra	*Vajracchedikā Prajñāpāramitā Sūtra*	*Jingang jing* 金刚经
dvarapala	*dvārapāla*	*chenmen* 晨门
jataka	*jātaka*	*bensheng* 本生
Kalika	Kālika	Jialijia 迦力迦
kalpa	*kalpa*	*jiebo* 劫波
kasaya	kāṣāya	*jiasha* 袈裟
Kashyapa	Kāśyapā	Jiaye 迦叶
Ksitigarbha	Kṣitigarbha	Dizang pusa 地藏菩萨
kundika	*kuṇḍikā*	*jingping* 净瓶
Lankavatara Sutra	*Laṅkāvatāra Sūtra*	*Lengjia jing* 楞伽经
Lotus Sutra	*Saddharma Puṇḍarīka Sūtra*	*Fahua jing* 法华经

Mahabhaisajya	Mahābhaiṣajya	Dayao 大药
Mahabhaisajya Upayakaushalya Sutra	*Mahābhaiṣajya Upāyakauśalya Sūtra*	*Foshuo dayao shanqiao fangbian jing* 佛说大药善巧方便经
Mahakashyapa, see Kashyapa		
Mahaparinirvana Sutra	*Mahāparinirvāṇa Sūtra*	*Daban niepan jing* 大般涅槃经
Mahasthamaprapta	Mahāsthāmaprāpta	Dashizhi pusa 大势至菩萨
Mahayana	Mahāyāna	*dasheng* 大乘
Maitreya	Maitreya	Mile fo / Mile pusa 弥勒佛 / 弥勒菩萨
Maitreya Sutra	*Maitreya Sūtra*	*Mile jing* 弥勒经
mala	*mālā*	*nianzhu* 念珠
Manjushri	Mañjuśrī	Wenshu 文殊
mantra	*māntra*	*zhou* 咒
Medicine Buddha	Bhaiṣajyaguru	Yaoshi fo 药师佛
Medicine Buddha Sutra	*Bhaiṣajyaguru Vaidūryaprabharāja Sūtra*	*Yaoshi jing* 药师经
Mulasarvastivada-vinaya	*Mūlasarvāstivāda-vinaya*	*Genbenshuo yiqie youbu pi'naiye zashi* 根本说一切有部毗奈耶杂事
Nirmanakaya	*nirmāṇakāya*	*yingshen* 应身
nirvana	*nirvāṇa*	*niepan* 涅盘 / 涅槃
padmasana	*padmāsana*	*lianhuazuo* 莲花坐
parinirvana	*parinirvāṇa*	*banniepan* 般涅盘
Prabhutaratna	Prabhūtaratna	Duobao 多宝
pradaksina	*pradakṣiṇa*	*yourao* 右绕
Saddharmapundarika, see *Lotus Sutra*		
Sakyapa (Tibetan, *Saskya*)		*Sajiapai* 萨迦派
Samantabhadra	Samantabhadra	Puxian pusa 普贤菩萨
Samboghakaya	*sambhogakāya*	*baoshen* 报身
samsara	*saṃsāra*	*shengsi* 生死
Shakyamuni	Śākyamuni	Shijiamouni 释迦牟尼
Shravasti	Śrāvastī	Sheweicheng 舍卫城
stupa	*stūpa*	*dubo (ta)* 堵波(即塔)
Sukhavati	Sukhāvatī	Jileshijie 极乐世界
Sukhavativyuha Sutra	*Sukhāvatīvyūha Sūtra*	*Wuliangshou jing* 无量寿经
Sumati	Sumati	Xumoti 须摩提
Sutrapitaka	*Sūtra Piṭaka*	*jingzang* 经藏
Tathagata	Tathāgata	Rulai 如来
trikala	*trikāla*	*sanshi* 三世
Tripitaka	*Tripiṭaka*	*sanzang* 三藏
Upasika	*upāsikā*	*youpoyi* 优婆夷
Vaidehi	Vaidehī	Weitixi 韦提希
Vairochana	Vairocana	Lushene 卢舍那佛
vajra	*vajra*	*jingang* 金刚
vajrapani	*vajrapaṇi*	*jingang lishi* 金刚力士
vara, see *varada* mudra		
varada mudra	*varada mudrā*	*shiyuanyin* 施願印 / 施愿印
vihara	*vihāra*	*piheluo* 毗诃罗
Vinayapitaka	*Vinaya Piṭaka*	*lüzang* 律藏
yasti	*yaṣṭi*	*chagan* 刹竿

Selected Bibliography
参考书目选

Abe, Stanley K. "Art and Practice in a Fifth-Century Chinese Buddhist Cave Temple." *Ars Orientalis* 20 (1990):1–31.

———. "Mogao Cave 254: A Case Study in Early Chinese Buddhist Art." PhD diss., University of California at Berkeley, 1989.

Akiyama, Terukazu, and Saburo Matsubara. *Arts of China: Buddhist Cave Temples, New Researches.* Trans. Alexander C. Soper. Tokyo, Japan & Palo Alto, CA: Kodansha International, 1969.

Barrie, Thomas. *The Sacred in-Between: The Mediating Roles of Architecture.* London: Routledge, 2010.

Beningson, Susan L. "Shaping Sacred Space: Studies in the Ritual Architecture and Artistic Program of Early Buddhist Cave Temples and their Relation to Tombs in Fifth Century China." PhD diss., Columbia University, 2009. UMI 3386118.

Behrendt, Kurt A. *The Art of Gandhara in the Metropolitan Museum of Art.* New Haven and London: Yale University Press, 2007.

British Museum. *Guide to an Exhibition of Chinese and Japanese Paintings (fourth to nineteenth century, A.D.).* London, 1910.

———. *Guide to an exhibition of paintings, manuscripts and other archaeological objects collected by Sir Aurel Stein, KCIE, in Chinese Turkestan.* London, 1914.

Dunhuang: A Centennial Commemoration of the Discovery of the Cave Library. Beijing: Morning Glory Publishers, 2000.

Dunhuang wenwu yanjiusuo 敦煌文物研究所 (Dunhuang Research Institute), comp. *Dunhuang Mogaoku* 敦煌莫高窟 [Dunhuang Mogao caves]. Zhongguo shiku 中国石窟 [Chinese cave temples], 5 vols. Beijing: Wenwu chubanshe, 1981– .

Fan Jinshi. *The Caves of Dunhuang.* Trans. Susan Whitfield. Hong Kong: Dunhuang Academy together with London Editions, 2010.

Fraser, Sarah. *Performing the Visual: The Practice of Buddhist Wall Painting in China and Central Asia, 618–960.* Stanford, Calif.: Stanford University Press, 2004.

Frédéric, Louis. *Buddhism: Flammarion Iconographic Guide.* Paris: Flammarion, 1995.

Gansu sheng wenwu gongzuodui 甘肃省文物工作队 (Gansu Cultural Relics Work Group) and Binglingsi wenwu baoguan suo 炳灵寺文物保管所 (Bingling Temple Cultural Relics Preservation Institute), comp. *Yongjing Binglingsi* 永靖炳灵寺 / *The Binglingsi Grottoes.* Beijing: Wenwu chubanshe, 1989.

Ghose, Rajeswari. *In the Footsteps of the Buddha: An Iconic Journey from India to China.* With the collaboration of Puay-peng Ho and Yeung Chun-tong. Hong Kong: University Museum and Art Gallery, The University of Hong Kong, 1998.

Inagaki, Hisao, trans. *The Three Pure Land Sutras.* In collaboration with Harold Stewart. Berkeley, CA: Numata Center for Buddhist Translation and Research, 2003.

Ho, Puay-Peng. "The Symbolism of the Central Pillars in Cave-Temples of Northwest China." In *Sacred Architecture in the Traditions of India, China, Judaism, and Islam*, edited by Emily B. Lyle. Cosmos: The Yearbook of the Traditional Cosmology Society 8, pp. 59–70. Edinburgh, Scotland: Edinburgh University Press, 1992.

Ji Xianlin 季羡林, *Ji Xianlin wenji* 季羡林文集 [Collected writings of Ji Wenlin]. Vol. 6, *Zhongguo wenhua yu dongfang wenhua* 中国文化与东方文化 [Chinese culture and Eastern culture]. Nanchang: Jiangxi jiaoyu chubanshe, 1996.

Juliano, Annette L. *Buddhist Sculpture from China: Selections from the Xi'an Beilin Museum, Fifth through Ninth Centuries.* New York: China Institute Gallery, 2007.

———. Review of *Shaping the Lotus Sutra: Buddhist Visual Culture in Medieval China*, by Eugene Y. Wang. *Harvard Journal of Asiatic Studies* 66, no. 2 (December 2006): 568–69.

Juliano, Annette L., and Judith A. Lerner. *Monks and Merchants: Silk Road Treasures from Northwest China.* New York: Harry N. Abrams, Inc., with the Asia Society, 2010.

Kezier shiku 克孜尔石窟 [Kizil Cave Temples]. Zhongguo shiku 中国石窟 [Chinese Cave Temples]. 3 vols. Beijing: Wenwu chubanse, 1989.

Lee, Sonya S. *Surviving Nirvana: Death of the Buddha in Chinese Visual Culture.* Hong Kong: Hong University Press, 2010.

Lewis, Mark Edward. *China Between Empires, The Northern and Southern Dynasties.* London and Cambridge, MA: The Belknap Press of Harvard University Press, 2009.

Lundquist, John M. *The Temple: Holy Precinct for Sanctuary, Ritual, and Sacrifice.* Paperback edition.

Maitra, K. M., trans. *A Persian Embassy to China: Being an Extract from Zubdatu't Tawarikh of Hafiz Abru.* 1934. Reprint, New York: Paragon Book Reprint Corp., 1970.

Murray, Julia K. "Buddhism and Early Narrative Illustration in China." *Archives of Asian Art* 48 (1995): 17–31.

Ng, Zhiru. *The Making of a Savior Bodhisattva: Dizang in Medieval China.* Honolulu: University of Hawai'i Press, 2007.

Pepper, France. "The Thousand Buddha Motif: A Visual Chant in Cave-Temples Along the Silk Road." *Oriental Art* 44, no. 4 (1998/9): 39–45.

Rong Xinjiang. "The Nature of the Dunhuang Library Cave and the Reasons for its Sealing." Trans. Valerie Hansen. *Cahiers d'Extrême-Asie* 11 (1999–2000): 247–75.

Sadakata, Akira. *Buddhist Cosmology: Philosophy and Origins.* Trans. Gaynor Sekimori. Tokyo: Kosei Publishing Co., 1997.

Soper, Alexander Coburn, "The 'Dome of Heaven' in Asia." *Art Bulletin* 29, no. 4 (December 1947): 225–48.

———. *Literary Evidence for Early Buddhist Art in China.* Ascona, Switzerland: Artibus Asiae Publishers, 1959.

Sullivan, Michael. *The Birth of Landscape Painting in China.* Berkeley and Los Angeles: University of California Press, 1962.

Tanaka, Kenneth K. *The Dawn of Chinese Pure Land Buddhist Doctrine: Ching-ying Hui-yuan's Commentary on the Visualization Sutra.* Albany: State University of New York Press, 1990.

Tianshui Maijishan yishu yanjiusuo 天水麦积山石窟艺朮研究所 (Art and Research Institute of the Maijishan Cave Temples at Tianshui), comp. *Tianshui Maijishan* 天水麦积山 [Maijishan Cave Temples at Tianshui]. Beijing: Wenwu chubanse; Tokyo: Heibonsha, 1998.

Tsiang, Katherine R. *Echoes of the Past: The Buddhist Cave Temples of Xiangtangshan.* Chicago: Smart Art Museum, University of Chicago, 2010.

Waley, Arthur. *A Catalogue of Paintings recovered from Tun-Huang by Sir Aurel Stein.* London: British Museum, 1931.

———. *An Introduction to the Study of Chinese Painting.* London: Ernest Benn Ltd., 1923.

Wang, Eugene Y. "Painted Statue in an Optical Theater: A Fifth Century Chinese Buddhist Cave." *Source: Notes in the History of Art* 30, no. 3 (Spring 2011): 25–32.

———. *Shaping the Lotus Sutra: Buddhist Visual Culture in Medieval China.* Seattle and London: University of Washington Press, 2005.

Wang, Helen, and John Perkins, eds. *Handbook to the Stein Collections in the UK.* British Museum, Occasional Paper, no. 129. Rev. ed. London: The Trustees of the British Museum, 2008.

Watson, Burton, trans. *The Lotus Sutra.* New York: Columbia University Press, 1993.

Watt, James C. Y. et al. *China: Dawn of a Golden Age, 200–750 AD.* New York: Metropolitan Museum of Art; New Haven and London: Yale University Press, 2004.

Whitfield, Roderick. *The Art of Central Asia: The Stein Collection in the British Museum.* 3 vols. Tokyo: Kodansha, 1982–85.

Whitfield, Roderick, and Anne Farrer. *Caves of the Thousand Buddhas: Chinese Art from the Silk Route.* New York: George Braziller, 1990.

Whitfield, Roderick, Susan Whitfield, and Neville Agnew. *Cave Temples of Mogao, Art and History on the Silk Road.* Los Angeles, The Getty Conservation Institute and the J. Paul Getty Museum, 2000.

Whitfield, Susan. *Aurel Stein on the Silk Road.* London: British Museum Press, 2004.

Whitfield, Susan, and Ursula Sims-Williams, eds. *The Silk Road: Trade, Travel, War and Faith.* Chicago: Serindia Publications for The British Library, 2004.

Zhang Baoxi 张 宝玺, ed. *Gansu shiku yishu diaosu bian* 甘肃石窟艺术雕塑编 / *Grotto Art of Gansu Sculpture.* Lanzhou: Gansu meishu chubanshe, 1994.

Zhao Feng et al. *Textiles from Dunhuang in UK Collections.* Shanghai: Donghua University Press, 2007.

Overleaf: Depiction of flying *apsaras* from Cave 420, Mogao Grottoes. Sui dynasty (581–618). Replica by Li Qiqiong and Huo Xiliang. 莫高窟隋第420窟伎乐飞天，李其琼 、霍熙亮临摹

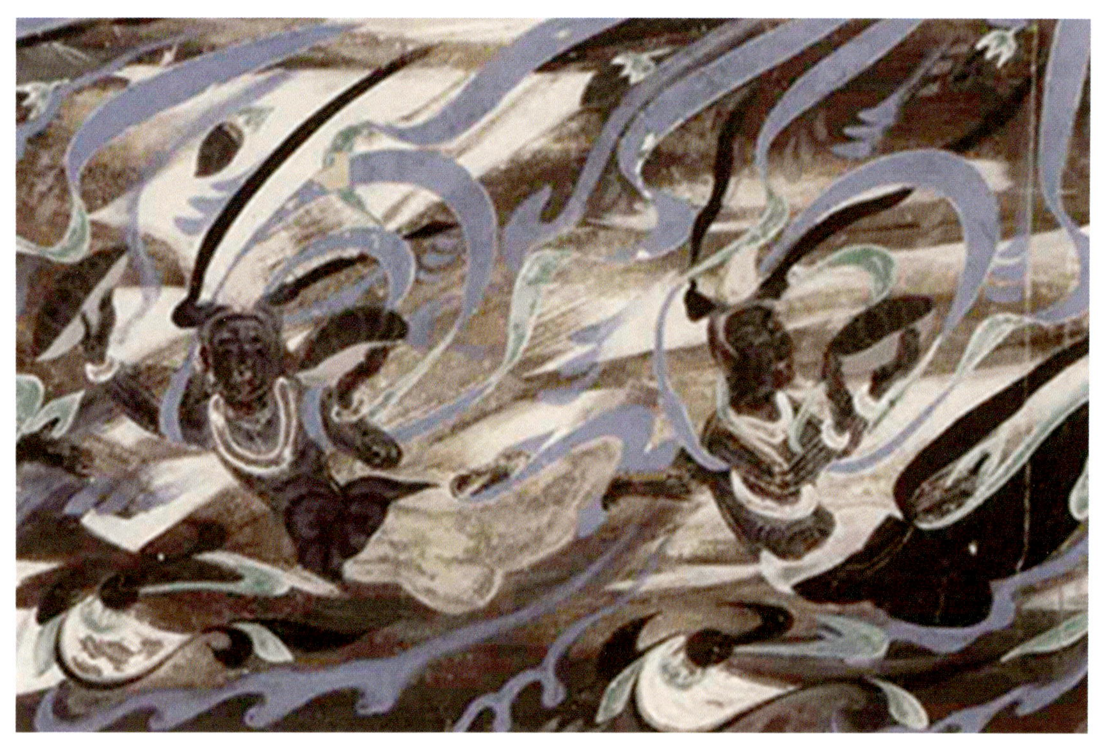

Dunhuang Academy
敦煌研究院

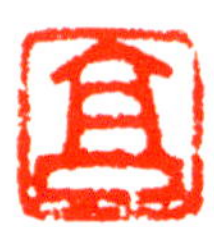

China Institute
华美协进社

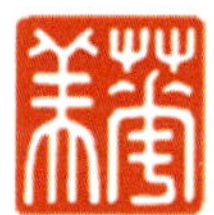